KiNTSugi

the JAPANESE Art of EMBRACING the IMPERFECT and LOVING YOUR FLAWS

TOMÁS NAVARRO

Translated by Jennifer Adcock

Kintsukuroi: El Arte de Curar
Heridas Emocionales

KintSugi

the JAPANESE Art
of EMBRACING the
IMPERFECT and
LOVING YOUR
FLAWS

sounds true
BOULDER, COLORADO

Sounds True
Boulder, CO 80306

This book is not intended as a substitute for the medical recommendations of physicians, mental health professionals, or other healthcare providers. Rather, it is intended to offer information to help the reader cooperate with physicians, mental health professionals, and health providers in a mutual request for optimum well-being. We advise readers to carefully review and understand the ideas presented and to seek the advice of a qualified professional before attempting to use them.

Published 2019

First published in English as *Kintsugi: The Art of Healing Our Emotional Wounds* in Great Britain in 2018 by Yellow Kite, an imprint of Hodder & Stoughton, an Hachette UK company

Cover design by Tara DeAngelis
Book design by Beth Skelley

Printed in Canada

Library of Congress Cataloging-in-Publication Data

Names: Navarro, Tomás, author.
Title: Kintsugi : the Japanese art of embracing the imperfect and loving your flaws /
    Tomás Navarro ; translated by Jennifer Adcock.
Other titles: Kintsukuroi. English
Description: Boulder, CO : Sounds True, 2019. | "First published in English as Kintsugi:
    The Art of Healing Our Emotional Wounds in Great Britain in 2018 by Yellow Kite—Verso.
Identifiers: LCCN 2019001608 (print) | LCCN 2019981407 (ebook) |
    ISBN 9781683643685 (paperback) | ISBN 9781683643692 (ebook)
Subjects: LCSH: Resilience (Personality trait) | Self-actualization (Psychology) | Emotions.
Classification: LCC BF698.35.R47 N32613 2019 (print) | LCC BF698.35.R47 (ebook) |
    DDC 155.2/4—dc23
LC record available at https://lccn.loc.gov/2019001608
LC ebook record available at https://lccn.loc.gov/2019981407

10 9 8 7 6 5 4 3 2 1

To those who try to smile despite
the pain they are feeling

Contents

Introduction

Sokei's Dream

A door ajar revealed the silhouette of Sokei sitting on his heels, preparing around thirty balls of clay. He was a pupil of Chojiro, one of the best ceramicists in Kyoto, and he'd been doing this all morning. Perfectly calm and composed, he picked up each ball of clay to analyze it and put it back on the table. Suddenly, a slight smile came to Sokei's lips. He'd finally found the right one!

Sokei was an intelligently persistent person. Choosing the most suitable ball of clay was important to him because each had a different feel and inspired something unique in the maestro. The difference between the ordinary and the extraordinary was the care that went into each detail, and Sokei was determined to create a unique and extraordinary piece.

With his hands together at his chest, he made a reverence to the chosen ball of clay and moved to gently pick it up, enjoying all the sensations associated with that special moment. He noticed the moist and slightly cool feel of the clay. His soul connected with the soul of the piece, with its history and with the journey it had been through before reaching his hands. Sokei had spent days seeking the best-suited clay. His steps had led him to forests, riverbanks, and even the shore of Lake Biwa. There, he closed his eyes as he sank his hands into the clay to connect better with its essence. In that moment in the workshop, when he closed his eyes, he remembered the hopes and dreams he had poured into his choice, and he felt fortunate and grateful.

He sat in a corner of the workshop, next to the window, in the place where he'd spent so many hours learning. Young people nowadays are in a rush to learn. If they don't learn quickly, they feel disenchanted, unmotivated, and they stop learning. They don't realize that in order to learn and consolidate what has been learned, we need time and a receptive and inquisitive attitude. But Sokei was not a young person like any other; Sokei had the patience of an elderly man but a child's desire to learn. Sokei's mind was racing with thoughts, his eyes were sparkling with hope, and his heart was galloping at the frenetic rhythm of impatience. He knew it was a special moment, but he needed to calm his body, his mind, and his soul.

Chojiro watched him attentively from a corner of the workshop. "Young people are so energetic," he thought. But Sokei was different. He had special sensitivity and extraordinary emotional strength. Chojiro knew that before his eyes was his successor, a young man with the serenity of someone who has lived their entire life, and the energy of someone who has their whole life ahead of them.

Sokei touched the clay with his eyes closed. He centered all his attention on kneading the piece, feeling his fingers converge with the clay, the earth, nature, and art. With the piece in his hands he felt that everything was possible, that any of the millions of forms that lived within it were waiting to connect with the hands of the ceramicist. Sokei connected with each and every one of those possible forms, imagining them and feeling them. Little by little he raised the walls of the bowl, thinking nothing, focusing his mind on the here and now because it's impossible to do two things at once well. He was aware that if he wanted to make something extraordinary, he needed to focus all his attention on this. His level of concentration was such that he lost all notion of time and space. His whole universe was concentrated on his hands. In that precise moment, nothing existed but him and his bowl.

He knew that beauty lies in simplicity, that the extraordinary does not require ornaments or flourishes, that it is simply beautiful and harmonious, and with those ideas in mind he glazed the piece delicately and slowly. The result was an austere bowl. What is essential is beautiful. What is rustic is inspiring. What is authentic is strong. To Sokei, the bowl was a projection of his soul, of his life, of his creativity, and of his liberated mind. The texture of the bowl was a journey through the history of his hands, the spirituality of his life, and his love for nature.

Chojiro prepared the kiln for the crucial part of the process; the most complex, but also the most beautiful. Sokei put the bowl into the kiln. Little by little, the piece changed color under the effect of the temperature. When the piece turned white, he gripped it firmly with iron tongs and lowered it into a receptacle filled with sawdust. The smoke and the flames of the combustion embraced Sokei's bowl, blending into one, building and creating a new entity. The glaze of the piece also wanted to form a part of that essential and transformative dance, offering up a delicate range of colors with whimsical shapes and sheens. Sokei contemplated the entire process with the excitement of someone who is a direct witness of the birth of something beautiful and unique. He could barely contain his emotion.

The time had come to remove the piece. Fire, earth, and air had drawn arbitrary and whimsical shapes, painting lights and shadows on his bowl. After so much time, so much dedication, so much patience, Sokei could at last see the result of all his work and love. The truth is that it was so precious that Sokei could not avoid trembling with emotion. A chill ran down his spine. He felt the cold breath of Buruburu, the ghost of fear, which made him shudder head to toe and from his shoulders to his fingertips, causing the piece to fall to the ground and break into six pieces. Sokei dropped the red-hot tongs to the ground, knelt down next to the piece, and remained still with a perplexed expression on his face. His hands were trembling; his eyes were filled with tears. How ephemeral the life of his creation had been. He felt a hand on his shoulder.

"Don't cry, Sokei," said Chojiro.

"But it's my life. How can you ask me not to cry?" responded Sokei. "You are right to put your whole life and passion into this piece, but ceramics are beautiful and fragile, like life. Ceramics and life can break into a thousand pieces, but that should be no reason to stop living life intensely, working intensely, and keeping alive all our hopes and dreams. Far from avoiding living, we must learn to repair ourselves after adversity. Sokei, pick up the pieces; the time has come to repair your dreams. The broken pieces can be put back together again, and when you do this, don't try to hide your fragility because your apparent fragility has become an evident strength. Dear Sokei, it is time for me to teach you a new technique. I will explain the ancestral art of kintsugi to help you repair your life, your dreams, and your work. Go and find the gold I keep in the box on the top shelf."

Kintsugi ("golden joinery") is the ancient Japanese art of repairing what has been broken. When a ceramic piece breaks, the masters of kintsugi repair it with gold, leaving the reconstruction highly visible because, for them, a reconstructed piece is a symbol of fragility, strength, and beauty. Chojiro was the first known kintsugi master, in the sixteenth century, and Sokei was his first pupil. This story is a re-creation of what might have taken place in Chojiro's workshop.

Ceramics are fragile, strong, and beautiful at the same time, like people. Just like our lives, they can break, but they can also be healed if you know how. In this book I provide the details of a method for repairing your life after it has been broken, to heal your emotional wounds. We will start by understanding the role played by adversity in our lives, how we react to adversity, and what consequences that has for our life and our health. In part 2 of the book I explain what the art of repairing your life consists of with a simple and efficient method that is a product of the most rigorous and valuable contributions of psychology, as well as twenty years of experience working with people who have had to repair their lives, heal their emotional wounds, and embellish their scars. Finally, in part 3, I share different stories that are as true as life itself; each chapter starts with a story, followed by an explanation of the key issues and resources to tackle that situation. You'll see that for each illustrated case I apply the method that we have worked on, providing details on the process in a practical way so that you yourself can apply what you have read if you need to.

Throughout the book I narrate different situations I have come across in my professional practice. All of them are real cases. And unfortunately, they are all too common. I have decided to compile them all and share them with you, so that if you ever find yourself in that position, if you are experiencing that situation, or if you want to help someone who needs to repair their life, here is a guide to help and inspire you.

I have placed the emphasis on explaining the "how to." Yes, the how to. I think there is a lot of literature that tells you what you have to do and what for, and there is even literature that is encouraging and motivational. But in my opinion, we need more books with a how-to approach. We professionals who possess the knowledge as a tool are often afraid to share it. This is not the case for me. I have always believed that psychology needs to be taken out of the consultation room, out of the lecture hall, and placed at the service of people. In my first book, *Emotional Strength*, I suggested a concept, a method, and a how-to approach for readers. In *Kintsugi* I go a step further, including real cases with real solutions laid out as a guide so that the reader can work independently.

The goal of psychology is to make people strong and happy so that they can overcome adversity, and in some cases all we need to know is how to do it. Because we are not always able to access the services of a psychologist, I have gone to great lengths to ensure this book is a resource to help you overcome adversity, a resource that helps you repair your life independently, without compromising on rigor or effectiveness.

In *Kintsugi* I will help you repair different situations with three objectives. In the first place, I want you to see that what you are experiencing is not unusual or rare. Sometimes we stigmatize ourselves, or other people stigmatize us; we feel like freaks; we believe that we are not responsible for what is happening to us and that we do not have the capacity to overcome it. But this is not the case. Throughout my professional experience, I've seen repeated over and over the same problems. I've isolated the common factors, and I have developed, analyzed, and explained them. When we understand things, we can overcome them. When you read this book, you might feel it resonates with the case of someone you know. If that happens, I encourage you to phone them up and tell them that now you understand them better. Share your pain, share their pain, and share your healing as the best example to follow.

My second objective is for you to be able to show the people around you what is happening to you and how you feel. Sometimes we are prejudged offhandedly, and we feel unable to defend ourselves or even to explain what we are going through. But it is precisely when we are struggling that we need greater doses of empathy, understanding, support, and compassion. I have seen many clients, many. I have suffered with them. I have also felt joy for their successes. In this book I explain in a practical and compassionate way some things that you might be feeling or experiencing.

Finally, my third objective is to provide you tools and strategies so that you can overcome adversity and rebuild your life as an authentic kintsugi master. After reading this book you will be stronger and more beautiful because you will overcome adversity, learn from it, and feel capable of coping with what life has presented to you, whether it is challenges, problems, or setbacks.

Much is said about resilience, but I have decided to go beyond that and provide you a method to rebuild your life. I would like you to read *Kintsugi* slowly, taking your time, savoring each and every one of the concepts, the stories, and the resources I share with you. Forget about speed-reading, forget about scanning, forget about reading, and instead have a conversation with me. I am trying to imagine you, I am trying to explain things to you in the first person, and I am trying to talk to you and listen to you. Have a conversation with the book, with me; do it bit by bit, thinking and savoring. Connect with *Kintsugi*, connect with me, and connect with slow reading.

I have written this book a little at a time, often in the mountains, surrounded by marmots and chamois. So I am asking you to also read it a little at a time. You can read it on the subway or at the airport, but I encourage you to find a space where you feel comfortable, enjoying it as much as possible. Find a park or go to the beach or the hills; go for a walk and find the silence you need to have a conversation with me and with yourself.

In this book I encourage you and help you to live intensely, to rebuild yourself, and to repair your life. Citing Chojiro, do not forget that ceramics and life can break into a thousand pieces, but not for that reason should we stop living it intensely, working at it intensely, and depositing in it all our hopes and dreams. Far from avoiding living, we need to learn to repair ourselves after adversity.

Part One

"Dear Sokei, the most important thing in this life is to live."
Chojiro's words resounded in Sokei's head over and over.
"Sokei, live intensely, work each piece with infinite
love, knowing that if life or a piece breaks,
you will be able to repair it again."

Raku-yakī: The Art of the Essential

The most important thing in this life is to live, which is not the same thing as to survive. There is a clear difference between living and surviving. When we live, everything is more intense; colors are brighter, kisses are full of passion, and our bodies are moved with each emotion. Living is reserved only for the brave because it involves making decisions, overcoming complacency, and actively seeking our development and growth. When we live intensely, we run more risks and we become more fragile.

Living calls for large doses of emotional strength, because it requires a strong mind-set that acts as a safeguard from the external pressures we receive. However, we must not forget that we also pressure ourselves without being aware of it. Often, we are our own worst judge. We internalize the expectations of others, and we turn them into pressures that burden our souls and our lives. We become overwhelmed for no reason. We push ourselves to achieve unrealistic goals, dreams that someone one day wanted us to have, fantasies incompatible with our lives, in an entire fantasy movie that we came up with and created in our heads.

Living intensely requires coherence in order to make your own decisions regardless of the expectations that other people might have placed on you. Yes, the kind of coherence that is incompatible with keeping up a facade, a shop window, or an image cobbled together out of scraps of others' desires.

An intense life is an authentic life. Being different is the best thing that has happened to you. Don't try to be like others. Don't abandon or hide your idiosyncrasy to live the life that everyone else lives. We are not here just to pay our bills and relax for one month of the year. You are a compendium of virtues that are waiting to be activated. Discover them, and put them to good use.

Living intensely is essential and necessary, because what is at stake is our happiness and that of our loved ones. But sometimes living is dangerous because people who live intensely can get hurt. We already know that people who do nothing suffer nothing. But avoiding doing things out of fear of getting hurt is not a path to growth. Your body is designed to repair damage, in the same way that your mind and your emotions also are. Yes, our bodies, our minds, and our emotions have what is called the drive to heal, which is in charge of repairing and healing everything that is broken and in pain. If you don't want to suffer, if you don't want to break, then limit yourself to surviving without leaving the house, the place where everything is under control, the place that provides you safety and comfort; but know that your body is capable of repairing the pain, wounds, and suffering.

Don't try to live a pleasant life devoid of suffering because, if you do, you will be resigning yourself to surviving instead of living intensely. Instead, seek an active and full life, knowing that you are stronger than any of the adversities you could ever encounter, aware that you will always be able to heal. You can limit yourself to surviving, to living day by day as a routine, not asking yourself questions, not loving because you are scared of being hurt, not running for fear of getting tired, not jumping for fear of falling, not skinny-dipping in the sea for fear of losing your clothes, not taking the time to lie in the sun in a field and think, not kissing the person you love, not messing up your hair or losing your composure—ultimately, not enriching your days with a double dose of passion and vitality. Or you can start to live.

Don't avoid living out of fear of suffering adversity. Adversity is nothing more than a challenge, so do some training to overcome it.

Prepare yourself for when it appears because, don't forget, the most important thing is to live. Leap, run, let your hair down. Live intensely!

Allow me to start by explaining an important concept, *perspective*. Life is the way it is, but depending on where you focus your attention, you will be able to see some things instead of others.

Let me share an illustrative example. I remember a trip I took years ago from my home in northern Spain to the Dolomites. I took the car with the idea of driving nonstop because I wanted to reach my destination before dark. But on the way, I decided to make a stop in Nice, to go for a dip in the sea, and because of this detour I arrived in the Dolomites after nightfall. I camped in the dark; I couldn't see anything beyond what the headlights revealed, and I went to sleep with the impression that this place had nothing that couldn't be found in any valley of the Pyrenees. But that impression changed the following morning when I woke up. The view when I came out of the tent was stunning and unforgettable. The Dolomites, with their reddish hues, ablaze in the first rays of sun, dominated the entire valley, which was buried in shadow. Thanks to the sunlight, I was able to gain perspective. The view had always been there, but without light I was not aware of it. The fact that I could not see the Dolomites did not mean they were not there, in the same way that not knowing what you are capable of does not mean you do not have plenty of virtues and strengths. So the question is: Are you prepared to light up your life, gain perspective, and adopt a new viewpoint on adversity and your ability to cope with it?

Sokei knew this was not the first piece to ever break. Nor was it likely to be the last. But he did know that it was the most precious, the most adored, the most beloved. Could he continue to love each piece? Sokei was afraid of not being able to stand a new disappointment, a new misfortune, new adversity.

Living with Adversity and Pain

"I think people don't know what life is all about," said my interlocutor suddenly, unprompted, with no preamble. He was an intelligent and skeptical scientist who was challenging me to a deep conversation in the green room of a television studio.

I must admit that my plan was to use those minutes to prepare for the interview I was about to give, but I gladly abandoned my task to talk with him. When I find a brilliant mind, I like to explore it, play together, and have a conversation; I could not afford to miss such a good opportunity for learning.

"People have unrealistic expectations. They think that life has to be wonderful; also, these unreal expectations are irresponsibly promoted by self-help and motivational books," he went on.

Things were getting interesting. He was right—we do constantly get bombarded with messages about floating on cloud nine and living happily ever after, but the reality is that if there is anything we should aspire to, it's to be strong because life brings us constant challenges that we have to face whether we like it or not. Happiness is a transient state and cannot last forever. We believe ourselves to be incomplete, we believe we need something more in order to be happy, we go in pursuit of nirvana thinking that when we reach it we will be happy, and all the while we are unaware that happiness, if it is to be found anywhere, is in the journey. Each mountain we climb, each river we ford, each desert we cross will make us stronger, and knowing ourselves to be stronger, we will feel safer, better prepared, and, for a while, happier.

Often, the only choice we have is to be strong. Each and every one of the billions of inhabitants on planet Earth, at some point or another, will have to stand face-to-face with adversity, pain, suffering, sadness, or any other challenge in the shape of a problem or calamity. That is inevitable. And since we will have to face adversity, we'd better make sure it finds us well prepared. Adversity is an inevitable part of life and, far from trying to deny it or run from it, we have to look it square in the eye and deal with it, manage it, or overcome it. In this book, I am not going to teach you to be happy, but to be strong, to live with adversity and handle the challenges and problems of daily life and their consequences.

Not long ago, I met someone who had just lost her mother in a car accident. She was in pieces, just broken. Her gaze was vacant, she was incapable of holding a conversation, her eyes were red from crying, and her hands would not stop shaking. She was in a very bad state. She felt lonely and helpless, she didn't know what to do, and she had even spent a few days just wandering around the house with no clear occupation. My dear friend was faced with the hardest thing she could have imagined, the hardest thing she had ever experienced. To make matters worse, she had to face it with a huge handicap: at the age of twenty-nine, she had never had to overcome any adversity. Her mother and father had made sure to clear the rocks from her path, paint a radiant sun in her life, keep away the clouds that threatened with any storm, and provide her a placid, comfortable, and sheltered life. From a place of love, her parents thought that was best for her, without realizing that in reality they were only damaging her because by not giving her the chance to learn to face adversity, they had not allowed her to put into practice the necessary abilities to overcome it.

Life is dynamic and unstable. Change is a part of life, the world, and our existence. What worked yesterday, today no longer does.

The picture that life painted for us as little children has nothing to do with what we will come across as we grow up. Life cannot be predicted or controlled, and any such attempts are based on self-delusion, on building imagined realities that crumble away as time goes by, leaving tremendous existential crises in their wake.

Throughout our lives we will experience problems and crises, there is no question about that, but the good news is that we can learn to manage and overcome them. A failing grade, a broken arm, or an unhappy love affair are situations that can be worked on and learned from. A crisis, a problem, or any adversity is nothing more than a difficulty that must be overcome. That is what we must believe, and that is what we must teach our children.

We live with adversity day by day. In the same way that we learn to run and jump, read and write, eat and dress, we should learn to identify and manage adversity because the way in which we deal with it conditions our chances of success. Learning to manage adversity is an emotional strength so important that, in my opinion, it should be taught as part of the school curriculum, along with other emotional strengths. We are not taught that life can bring us challenges and problems, or that proper management is what our happiness and our mental and physical health depend on. Instead, we are made to believe that life has to be a bed of roses, when in reality that idea is completely irrational and biased.

Life is a constant state of flux, a continuous challenge that we cannot and should not try to avoid. A path with ups and downs, it's demanding, uncertain, and sometimes random, and it will put us face-to-face with beauty and pain, with success and frustration, with love and disappointment. Life is as beautiful as it is challenging; it will reward us and it will test us. Adversity is simply a problem, a frustration, or a challenge that needs to be managed. But are you prepared to live with adversity?

Why Do We Feel Pain?

To stay alive. Pain is necessary to be able to live; it has a clear adaptive function. All living creatures need to be capable of reacting to harmful stimuli, dangers, and threats. Pain is an essential mechanism of adaptation that alerts us sooner rather than later of the presence of something that might hurt, attack, or wound us, whether it is at the physical or emotional level.

So when we ignore the emotional pain inflicted on us by a toxic partner, for example, we are ignoring the warning signs that our body is sending us. Do not ignore pain, especially emotional, because it is telling you that you have to make some changes and decisions and take action.

We Don't All Suffer in the Same Way

It was December 26, 2015, and we were on our way home after spending Christmas away. We opened the gate to the yard and parked the car. In that moment I saw my dog, Duna, appear, a thirteen-year-old boxer. Immediately after came Vilu, my daughter's two-year-old border collie, but I didn't see Idefix, my partner's four-year-old Westie. We unpacked the car and went into the house. "Darling, open up for Idefix, he must be on the porch," I said to my wife. "Has he not come in?" she replied.

Idefix had not come in. He was lying lifeless in the corner where he usually napped in the sun, having apparently had a heart attack. All I remember from that moment on is a lot of sadness and crying. But were we all equally affected in my family by the death of Idefix?

Was it more painful for my wife or for my daughter? Can pain be quantified? Is it possible to say who suffered the most? Was it the one who cried the hardest or who cried the longest? Without a doubt, the death of Idefix had a deep impact on us all, and the three of us suffered, but not all of us did so in the same way. It is difficult to categorize the impact that adversity has on a person and compare it with that on another person because there is a subjective component that determines the value we give to adversity and the impact we believe it will have on our lives. Perhaps that's where the key resides, in the word *believe*.

And now I ask myself this: Will Duna's death be more painful to me? Or is it possible that I'm better prepared to face it? Duna is an old dog by now—she's practically a hundred in dog years. With Duna we have traveled all over Europe. She is in photos with the Little Mermaid in Copenhagen, the Atomium in Brussels, and the Eiffel Tower in Paris. She has gone up the Pyrenees, the Alps, and countless European mountain ranges; she has bathed in Norwegian fjords and in all the lakes we have traveled past, from Bergen to Cádiz. She has traveled by boat, train, bus, and even by cable car. She has made friends all over and stolen the hearts of many people with her sweet goofiness. Duna has lived intensely a few years longer than we would normally expect of a boxer. To this day she enjoys running through tunnels, exploring trails, and swimming in the first river or lake she goes past. Duna runs by my side, practically touching me. She is blind and deaf, but she won't miss any opportunity to go out to the mountains and run and jump around.

Will the foreseeable death of Duna be more painful than the unexpected death of Idefix? Well, I don't know. I cannot predict it; I cannot even imagine it. And my wife, will she find the death of Idefix more painful than the death of Duna? In any case, what does "more painful" mean? How to quantify pain? Is there a scale we can measure it on? Pain is subjective, and how we experience it can vary enormously. It is possible that one person, in the same situation, might feel varying intensities of pain. Think about it. Try and remember that toothache you had. Find in your memory a tummy ache, a headache, or some period cramps. Now try to analyze if your head always aches with the same intensity, if each month your ovaries hurt in the same way, if each tummy ache or toothache is the same as the previous one. You'll see that depending on different factors, the intensity of the pain might vary. So if for one person the same pain might manifest in different ways at different times, imagine the variations for different people. Until now, no one has found a trustworthy and universal measure to quantify pain, so, in the meantime, all we can do is guide ourselves by the subjective assessments of pain, knowing that these can be affected by our mood, our fatigue, or our ability to cope.

The Physiology of Pain

Pain starts with the activation of special receptors called *nociceptors*, specialized in the detection of pain. These are distributed throughout the body and are capable of differentiating between innocuous and harmful stimuli. When they are activated, they send signals to the brain through the spinal cord and cause the reflex of avoidance, which allows us to remove the body part that is being injured from the source of pain. After the signals reach the brain, the experience of pain is activated as a completely subjective sensory experience that is difficult to quantify but that tends to bring with it emotional states such as sadness or anxiety.

But don't forget that the brain is a kind of center for tangible reality, and virtual reality, in such a way that, on occasion, we can feel pain even when no physical element is activating the pain nociceptors. Pain is a highly complex, adaptive, physiological process that nature and evolution have designed and perfected to allow us to stay alive. But sometimes, despite the efficiency of the design, we might suffer for things that have never happened and never will.

Pain Is One Thing, and the Expression of Suffering Is Another

Sometimes we mistake one of these concepts for the other. Allow me to explain with a real example I once experienced. I was teaching a class on communication when something interesting happened. Suddenly, in the middle of the class, someone stood up and started walking in circles and speaking loudly, completely interrupting the class, to inform us all that he had the flu and was feeling rotten. He wouldn't stop complaining throughout the whole class. He complained about his headache, runny nose, sore throat, and the heaviness of his eyelids. I can't say for sure how bad he felt, but none of those present were in any doubt that he was experiencing the worst bout of flu of his life.

A few chairs to his right there was a person who was clearly experiencing pain in acute episodes. Suddenly she would disconnect from the class, bring her hand to her face, and close her eyes. Maybe she had a toothache. I will never know. She did not complain in the slightest. She didn't make it public. She didn't talk about it to anyone. I know beyond a shadow of a doubt, after analyzing her behavior and the expression on her face, that she was experiencing a great deal of pain. Now, in the eyes of those present, who was suffering the most pain? The person who was complaining, or the person who was trying to manage their pain discreetly?

We are often incapable of controlling pain, but we can control the expression of suffering. Depending on the expression that we adopt, we will be communicating and sharing our pain and involving the people around us in it. Doing so is normal, and is even beneficial, because when we share our pain, we awaken empathy in those who can help alleviate it. So if we try to estimate how much people are suffering based on their facial expression, it is likely that we will be mistaken. Shared pain does not hurt less. Quiet pain has no reason to hurt more. The truth is that we know little, too little, about how much others are hurting in life.

When Pain Becomes Perverse

Some people, in order to gain attention, like to adopt one of the oldest and simplest tricks in the book: faking pain. We can see it all around us. The soccer player who throws himself to the ground and writhes in pain, the child who knows he's going to get told off by his parents, the partner who doesn't feel like making love because they are going through a stressful period, and many other everyday situations.

Victimism is based on the expression of pain, often fake, which demands consideration. The victim asks for payment from the other person in exchange for their suffering. It is common behavior, of course, but that does not make it any less toxic or cruel because, if you stop to think about it carefully, you are actually playing with the emotions and worries of people around you.

When a loved one feels pain, we suffer with them, we cry with them, and we feel their pain. Without realizing it, our mirror neurons and our capacity for empathy cause us pain. Literally. Yes, exactly what you are reading. Maybe the intensity is less than for the person who is experiencing pain. It might be different. It might be partial, but in any case it is not insignificant.

Don't forget

- Don't concern yourself with being happy; instead focus on being strong.

- Come to terms with the fact that adversity is part of life. Do not avoid it, do not ignore it, do not reject it.

- We must train to strengthen our ability to cope and rebuild in the face of adversity.

- If you transform adversity into a challenge, you will find it easier to tackle.

- Not all of us suffer in the same way.

- The one who cries most is not necessarily the one who suffers most; do not mistake pain for the expression of pain.

Sokei didn't know if what hurt more was the sadness or the disappointment. He felt the weight of guilt on his shoulders. Why did he have to open the tongs that held his bowl?

What Hurts?

In all professions, including psychology, you'll find two kinds of professionals you will be able to recognize easily by the way in which they deal with problems (or cases, when talking about psychologists). Imagine that your car tire bursts and you go to the mechanic. A "type 1 professional" (I must confess I love this neutral and elegant euphemism, which I use to avoid calling him "reckless and unmotivated") will simply change the tire. You'll find these kinds of type 1 professionals everywhere: the doctor who prescribes an antacid for a stomachache, the dietician who simply photocopies the latest fad diet, the shop attendant who shows you only the item that is easiest to reach on the shelf, and the psychotherapist who simply tells you to delude yourself into thinking that what is happening to you is not that bad and that there are people who are worse off. But, fortunately, there are also "type 2 professionals," those who enjoy what they do, who educate themselves, who are inquisitive and energetic, and who treat their clients with the respect, professionalism, and love they deserve.

Type 1 professionals go to work hoping for the hours to pass without them running into too many problems, while type 2s love each and every one of the clients they see because their profession is their passion. A type 2 professional will seek the root of what is happening to you. A mechanic will analyze the car's suspension and detect a malfunction causing abnormal wear in the tire. A doctor will analyze the source of that stomachache and discover you are allergic to gluten. A dietician will analyze the reason you are overweight and check your food intake, your metabolism, and your endocrine function. A salesperson will analyze your body shape and select the garments most flattering to your figure. And a good psychotherapist will analyze the source of your suffering.

We suffer for many reasons, and depending on the source of the suffering, we will have to vary our approach. But let's go step by step; let's first identify the different sources and causes of suffering.

Adversity Hurts

Emotional pain arises from adversity. Every day we face hundreds of kinds of adversity, if not thousands. Adversity is a situation that is not favorable, or even contrary to our interests, whether it's a setback, a misfortune, or a tragedy. We try to live a placid life, unaware that adversity is not only common but that it's even necessary for correct psychosocial development.

Properly managed pain allows us to learn and grow. We often try to cheat ourselves or conceal pain with medication, and by covering it up, we do not allow ourselves to tackle the problem head on, resolve it, and grow, feeling stronger and more confident. Stop trying to convince yourself that what you are experiencing is not that terrible, that there are people who are worse off than you, or any kind of argument along those lines, and start accepting that adversity is part and parcel of life. It is an opportunity to grow and gain in confidence. Adversity does not have to be negative if we transform it into a challenge to be overcome.

Frustration Hurts

Emotional pain also arises from the frustration we experience when our expectations are not met. What are our expectations of life? What do we think it will be like? We have some uncertain and poorly adjusted expectations. We set ourselves goals that are not realistic and that do nothing but cause us more suffering.

An unrealistic expectation will never come true. You might think that, one day, someone will do something for you. It will not be me who shatters that illusion, but I encourage you, while that is not happening, to focus on doing something for yourself, such as managing your expectations of the future, the people around you, and the world.

Other people also set expectations for us that we internalize and make our own. They tell us what we must be like, what we can expect, and when we must be successful. And we believe them. We form an idea of the world and of life based on scraps of reality, advertising slogans, famous phrases pronounced by some wise person, slogans read on social media, litanies copied over and over, hopes, fears, and desires. And this idea of the world, this constructed image, we take for real, mistaking reality for what we desire—and of course, what we desire might never come true. And when it does not come true, we suffer. It is a gratuitous kind of suffering that we could have avoided altogether.

In part 3 of the book I will show you different examples of how you can repair what is broken. But until then, my best advice is that you learn to set realistic expectations and that you recalibrate any existing ones, readjusting them to reality.

What Do You Expect Will Happen?

I want to share a personal example with you. In May 2016 I ran the Transvulcania, a prestigious mountain race that crosses the beautiful Canary island of La Palma from south to north, summiting all its volcanoes and covering 78 kilometers over 8,400 meters of accumulated elevation gain. When I arrived on the island, I stayed at the same hotel as the elite runners, where the topic of conversation was our planned times for the race. Twenty years ago, it might have taken me ten hours to complete it. But on that occasion, having scarcely trained, if no physical problem arose (which was quite unlikely), I might have been able to complete it in about twelve hours with a lot of effort.

In the end, it took me fifteen hours, which was the time I had said to those who asked me. Where did that expectation come from? From reality. The reality was that I had not trained enough because I had a limited amount of time to do so. The reality was that I am one or two kilos heavier than I was twenty years ago, that my body is more worn out, and that my motivation in terms of enjoyment versus suffering has also changed a lot. So after this analysis of reality, I decided that five kilometers per hour was an acceptable pace that I could maintain over many kilometers. I set arrival times for each control point to have a reference, and I started running.

As it happened, I felt good in terms of strength, and the pace I maintained was slightly above the one I had expected, especially uphill. If I could keep that up, I could finish the race in around thirteen hours without any trouble. But suddenly a minor physical issue cropped up, something I was aware could happen. Later in the race, the accumulation of kilometers started to wear on my joints, my lack of training, and the fact that I was unused to this effort. I managed to maintain a good pace uphill because I was doing well at the muscular level, but downhill I was not able to run. At the end of the race I fixed the pace at five kilometers per hour. What happened? Did I get frustrated when I had to revise my pace down? Not at all. My more realistic expectation told me that what was happening was what I had expected to happen. There was no frustration, no pain, and no suffering, and I was not hit hard by reality. What was bound to happen had indeed happened. With no bitterness or disappointment.

But what if I had harbored any expectations that I could complete the race in twelve hours? Well, I would have experienced frustration, pain, and possibly helplessness. In the case of the Transvulcania, as in life itself, a well-adjusted expectation is the difference between going on and giving up, enjoying and suffering, building and breaking. Contextualize your expectations in the reality of the situation instead of adjusting them to your desires because that way you will save yourself a great deal of suffering and pain.

Disappointment Hurts

Emotional pain might also arise from disappointment. We often do not see reality as it is but as we would like it to be. People are the way they are, not the way you want them to be. Life is the way it is, not the way you would like it to be. Things are the way they are, but we often do not want to see them exactly as they are, and we create a completely distorted image of reality.

We trick ourselves regarding our partner, our marriage, our work, our car, our decisions, our desires, our children, and our future. We want to think that things are going well and that the problems we have will magically fix themselves. We put our life on hold for an apparent happiness, we refuse to see our problems, we sweep them under the carpet with a good dose of self-delusion. When reality rings alarm bells in the form of anxiety, misgivings, or sadness, instead of analyzing what is actually happening to us, we look for something to distract ourselves.

But reality insists and shows us again its most truthful face, and we again deceive ourselves, not wanting to admit the evidence. We have to make the delusion more resistant; we have to reinforce the facade. The decor we live in starts to peel at the corners, and in that moment we do everything in our power to deceive ourselves further and move to the next level. And we go on until the lie completely comes apart, until the stage set we've been living on collapses, until the movie we're inventing comes to an end. And when this happens, we experience a great deal of pain and suffering.

Why Do We Delude Ourselves?

When we do not like what we see, we can do one of three things: accept it, modify it, or delude ourselves. Accepting or modifying reality requires a huge effort of willpower and a great deal of maturity and responsibility, whereas fabricating a stage set and living a lie is a lot easier. For that reason, many people live a lie, a kind of fairy tale without a happy ending. But as it happens, all fairy tales eventually come to an end, despite our attempts to postpone it, and when they do, they always leave a trail of pain and suffering in their wake.

Disappointment occurs when knowledge of the truth dismantles an error or delusion. And although the truth will set us free, it hurts to know that no one but ourselves has been deluded. Taking a reality check will hurt, but it will provide you the best foundation to start constructing a sound building that will allow you to be much happier than you would be if living a lie.

Self-delusion is not a valid choice because it only provides you with superficial happiness. And this happiness is focused on the short term.

Change Hurts

We find it hard to change, but that's because we start from a root idea that is false. We look for stability, thinking that it will give us safety and happiness, when life is actually unstable and ever changing. We try to control the uncontrollable, we want to set the brakes against dizzying change, we try to construct parapets that will protect us from what cannot be controlled, and along the way we pay a high price: we waste our energy and we feel insecure and weak. That's why, until we accept that the only reliable thing, the only thing we can build a healthy life on, is change, we won't be able to feel strong and safe.

Life is change, and the happiest person will be the one who is prepared to manage it. The fact that life is change is good news because it tells us that everything can change; even the worst misfortune will eventually come to an end if we work in the right direction.

Ultimately, learning to manage change is not that complicated. What's more, on many occasions we believe that a change will be worse, when we do not know for sure how things will pan out. We jump to conclusions, we dig in our heels, and we miss the chance to take advantage of the positive consequences of change.

Types of Change

There are different types of change: for the better, for the worse, or uncertain. When we sell an old car to buy a new one, the change is for the better, obviously. When we move out of a new house to live in an old house that is lying in disrepair, that's a change for the worse. But there are many changes that are uncertain in nature, that will see a positive or negative evolution depending on how we handle them. Changing our job, partner, or place of residence will not necessarily entail negative consequences; however, if we experience these changes negatively, we could make our worst nightmares come true.

The truth is that we react badly when faced with an unexpected change, which leads us to suffer, often briefly, yet still with a great deal of pain.

In the same way, sometimes we suffer ahead of time for an expected or anticipated future change; that is, sometimes we suffer for things we believe will happen after a change, even though they never end up happening.

We Suffer Because of Our Judgment and Thoughts

Without a shadow of a doubt, our best ally when it comes to living fully and being happy is our mind. We have the capacity to think, a great evolutionary achievement, but we often think too little and badly, wasting the huge potential we have.

I've heard it said more than once that thinking is exhausting and leads nowhere. When I hear these kinds of statements, I usually ask my interlocutor whether what they mean is thinking or worrying, which are not the same thing. We tend to invest a lot of time in worrying and ruminating on a subject like a hamster on a wheel—but that has nothing to do with thinking. Thinking, when done right, is a productive, creative, or practical endeavor. Few people know how to do it well, but contrary to what it might seem, learning to think is easy, and all it requires is a bit of practice.

When we talk about thinking properly, we should highlight the role of a mistake that is all too common when analyzing our reality, which leads to suffering: mistaking what is possible for what is likely. This happens when we believe that anything can happen, without taking into consideration the likelihood or probability of it occurring. The lottery is an example that illustrates this well. There is a possibility that we might win the lottery; of course there is. But it's not about whether we can win it; what should guide our conduct is how much of a probability there is that we will win it. The truth is that the probability is low, and no matter how much effort you put into buying plenty of tickets to try and increase that probability, you should not entertain any illusions because the likelihood of you winning will continue to be low. The possibility still exists, that's true. You can continue to dream, hoping for the possibility. But if you want to be happy, stop waiting for a miracle to happen and start working to achieve your goals.

When we don't think things through or when our thinking is distorted, we can end up suffering a great deal. Our judgments tend to be partial and rushed, which leads us to create partial views that are not focused on reality, which at the same time leads us to suffer. Learn to think properly, and you will be happy.

We Suffer Because of Reality Itself

Sometimes life is painful; that fact is unavoidable. We try to live in a fairy tale, but that's not possible; the idea is absurd. When a loved one dies, when we are diagnosed with an illness, when we see a child suffer, when we see a child cry every day, several times a day, we encounter the darker side of life.

However, we can control part of that suffering if we learn to analyze life, to make good decisions, to self-motivate, to recognize the emotional state of another person, to be enthusiastic, and to manage conflict. If we do, our life will be more rich and satisfying, and we will be able to live in a better way. It's about activating our emotional strengths in order to face up to each one of the things that life brings because we cannot change them, but we can learn to handle them so as to minimize their impact. To paraphrase the Serenity Prayer, wisdom consists in changing the things that can be changed, accepting the ones that cannot be changed, and, most importantly, learning to tell the difference. So I encourage you to work and develop each and every one of the different strengths that integrate the concept of emotional strength.

Emotional Strength

Emotional strength facilitates and protects our happiness and emotional well-being. Each strength responds to a technique, a strategy, or a resource that will help you achieve your objectives and live life fully. The nineteen emotional strengths are listed below.

- Incorporate emotions into your life.

- Correctly interpret your emotional state.

- Give a name to your emotions.

- Learn to identify the emotional state of the people around you.

- Manage your emotions and their expression.

- Persevere in achieving your objectives.

- Manage adversity.

- Balance your self-esteem.

- Do not depend on external motivation.

- Gain in responsibility.

- Choose a positive attitude.

- Choose your own path.

- Seek quality relationships.

- Develop your ability to communicate better.

- Cooperate with other people; develop compassion.

- Manage conflict.

- Live in a goal-oriented way, and make decisions in accordance.

- Ask for help if you need it.

- Enjoy the opportunities that life brings.

We Suffer Because of Our Imagination and Our Fears

Our suffering can arise from imagination. We dream up catastrophes and problems that will never happen, and yet we suffer because of them. We suffer for what might happen to our children. Our mind speeds ahead and anticipates a thousand illnesses, a thousand accidents, a thousand problems. The future, imbued with fear, hurts. It hurts a lot. We hurt from what has never happened to us, we hurt from what might come, and we hurt from what has not yet been—from something unreal.

Although those visions are not real, the unsettling pain we feel definitely is. And that pain is born from a fantasy or assumption that wreaks havoc on our body, stresses and alters it, destabilizes it, and leads it to suffer in exactly the same way that it would with real pain.

Take a moment to analyze the distorting effect that fear and our own desire have on our thought processes. We have a lot of trouble seeing reality for what it is, and we tend to add a bit of spice in the form of our own desires. I remember one day when my daughter, on the way home from a new school, explained to me in the car how well it had gone. She told me that a girl had said to her that she was happy she'd started going to that school, that she loved playing with her, and that they would be good friends. When I asked her whether what she was explaining had actually happened or whether it was what she would have liked to have happened, the answer was clear: my daughter had just mixed reality with her desire. She did not do so consciously—she wasn't trying to deceive me or to deceive herself—she just added a bit of spice to the facts. If we look at the context we will see that my daughter had just started at a new school and was perhaps worried about not having friends, feeling rejected, or ending up alone.

On the other hand, when we mix our fears with reality, we are limiting ourselves. Fear paralyzes us and limits us because it causes us to anticipate things that might never happen. Fear is a bad counselor, and it's important to learn to identify when it's playing a dirty trick on us. If in that summer of 2014 I had not managed my fear of writing a book, of trying something new that I had never done before, today I would not be sitting here writing my second book. Being afraid is normal; allowing fear to have the run of the place is not.

We Suffer Ahead of Time

There is a kind of pain that is born from the anticipation of something that we know will happen but has not yet happened. We suffer a lot for things that have not yet happened. We anticipate, in excruciating detail, the pain of a visit to the dentist or a planned surgery. We spend several months suffering the pain of giving birth. We suffer for the death of a loved one months before cancer takes their life. We suffer for things that do not yet hurt, in such a way that when real pain does arrive, our body and mind are already exhausted.

Our bodies are wise; this we have said already. Our bodies and our minds feel the impulse to repair the damage detected. When we feel pain, we activate a repair system with the objective of recovering the balance lost. But we must take care not to end up like Peter in the tale of "Peter and the Wolf": he warned so many times about the wolf coming, without it being true, that when it did truly arrive, nobody believed him. If we activate the alert mechanism in the face of pain ahead of the time, then, when we need it the most, we won't have any resources left to cope with it.

Sources of Emotional Pain

- Adversity

- Frustration

- Disappointment

- Unexpected change

- Judgments and thoughts

- Reality

- Imagination

- Fear

- Anticipation

As you will have seen throughout this chapter, suffering and adversity are part and parcel of life. In this chapter I have analyzed the different sources of pain and suffering that we will have to deal with every day. We have seen that some of them can be controlled and some of them cannot.

I encourage you to do an exercise. Analyze the pain you are experiencing and try to identify its source. Don't leave it for tomorrow. Don't turn to the next page. Don't start a new chapter. Just pick up a notebook and a pencil, find a quiet place, and reflect. Take action, because it's up to you to do something about this. Nobody will do it for you.

Don't forget

- Properly managed pain allows us to grow.

- Thanks to pain we can foresee and avoid future complications.

- Manage your expectations of life.

- Analyze whether you are deluding yourself, and if that is the case, do a reality check.

- Accept that life is change and that you must be prepared to deal with it.

- Stop worrying, and transform your worries into action.

- Don't mistake what is possible for what is likely.

- Appease your imagination; give it a constructive outlet.

- Don't anticipate what has not yet occurred.

The morning sun lit up Sokei's face. His eyes were open, but his gaze was vacant. What was Sokei looking at?

Why Me?

Perhaps he was looking for an answer.

Sometimes, and for some people, there is no answer to this question. Sometimes chance plays cruelly with our pain for no apparent reason. Life is a succession of coincidences and reactions that can be bitter at times.

On March 24, 2015, 144 passengers boarded a plane from Barcelona to Düsseldorf, unaware of what destiny had in store for them. On board were also four crew members and two pilots. At 10:01 a.m., the plane was taking off from the airport packed with lives, dreams, and hopes; thirty minutes later it started to descend, and eight minutes later it disappeared off the radar. The people onboard that plane met a tragic fate; none of them, including the pilot, could have imagined that the copilot's intention was to crash the plane into the mountains. That morning in late March, the beautiful French Alps were witness to one of the worst aviation disasters in European history.

The accident attracted a huge amount of media attention. Although everyone echoed and communicated the facts, in reality, those who were truly affected were the families of each and every one of the people traveling onboard Germanwings Flight 9525. I imagine the pain they felt, and also the question that must have come up time and again in their minds when trying to find a possible explanation for the inexplicable, to justify the unjustifiable, to understand a tragedy that has no meaning: "Why me?"

We need answers to alleviate the pain that allow us to understand the reasons behind the suffering, even when there might be none. We cannot understand why our lives have turned on a pin in a matter of minutes. What reason could there be for such a tragedy, and why did it have to happen to me? There is probably no reason at all. A cruel whim of fate caused over a hundred people to tragically lose their lives, and no matter which way we look, we will not find an answer that eases our pain and suffering.

Don't Explain Things in Terms of Guilt

Don't look for coherence; it simply doesn't exist. There is no logic that can explain suffering, abuse, adversity, or tragedy. Sometimes, when we cannot find an answer, a delusional thought process is set in motion in which we imagine ourselves to have caused our own unhappiness. We believe we deserve it, and we are to blame for some reason we imagine or are unaware of. We seek answers and sometimes even end up distorting our past to make it coherent. But now, dear reader, in this moment in which you are trying to overcome adversity, the past does not matter—what matters is your present and future.

The Germanwings 9525 accident was completely unexpected; it did not fit into the imagination of any of the passengers or their relatives. But could it have been avoided? The case we are looking at is difficult to comprehend. Theoretically, with proper periodic psychological testing of the pilots, the risk could have been detected; in theory, a good supervisor should have been able to identify the risk, and in theory with a good process of control that terrible accident could have been avoided. But the theory does not always apply, and reality is cruel and wayward.

Often there is no answer that can bring peace to a heart that is afflicted by tragedy, but we still try to find explanations because we need them, and, when we cannot find them, we make them up. Our brains cannot bear certain information gaps, especially when we have to explain situations that have a high emotional impact, events that have changed our lives. We tend to complement the information available according to our needs and our current situations. That way, we create an answer based on our conceptual framework and our emotional state, which is why the answer in question tends to be biased, partial, and often puts the blame on someone or something. "It's a punishment," "It's a divine message," "It's one of the trials of life," "I've done something wrong," "I offended some cruel god," and so forth; these and many other answers flutter around in the minds of those who need to explain the inexplicable, but the problem is that depending on the explanation that you give to the tragic event that has taken place, your suffering might drag on for longer.

Life is not the way it is, but the way you think it is. If you believe that some superior entity or fate has punished you for what you've done, you will be condemned to suffering doubly for the rest of your life. On the one hand, you will be suffering from a wound that you must manage, clean, and heal; on the other, you will be suffering from the guilt and punishment that is self-inflicted for no reason.

Throughout this chapter I intend to help you manage the answer to what has happened to you or the lack of an answer to your suffering. Come with me, give me your hand, but most importantly, open your mind and see your suffering face-to-face if you want to tackle it and rebuild your life.

Sometimes There Is a Reason

Sometimes there is a reason. Often, without being aware of it, we behave in certain ways or make decisions that lead us directly to suffer pain. That is why it is hugely important to learn to make decisions. I'm sure you know someone who makes their life complicated through the decisions they make. I remember when someone told the story of how they had wrecked their car in an accident because they were looking at their phone:

"Well, I was unlucky because I usually check it often while I'm driving. Who would have thought that I could have such an unfair accident?"

"You mean it wasn't your fault for getting distracted?" his interlocutor asked.

"Of course it wasn't my fault!" responded the protagonist of the story. "It had to happen to someone, and it happened to me."

Allow me to raise doubts about this person's "bad luck," and to use his example to illustrate the difference between a tragedy that has no reason or explanation and a tragedy that was "asked for," whether we were aware of it or not. The protagonist in this example was not unlucky at all. In fact, it's not unreasonable to suggest that he had been extremely lucky until the moment of the accident. Let's say he was buying tickets to a raffle every time he checked his phone while driving and that, in the end, after much persistence, he won the prize. My best advice is that you analyze whether the adversity that you are suffering has anything to do with your decisions and your way of acting. Don't punish yourself, don't blame yourself, just analyze and learn so that you don't make the same mistake again. Think about what you do and the decisions you are making, analyze your risky behavior, and take care of your diet and your habits, but also look at the things you don't do and the decisions you don't make because these also have consequences. Likewise, don't attribute to yourself coincidences that you have nothing to do with. Sometimes things happen to us by chance, as I have already said, but if you believe that you have done something to deserve it or to provoke it when that is not the case, you will be suffering for no reason. Once again, the balance lies in a measured approach.

Look at the Decisions You Make and at the Ones You Don't Make

We don't give due importance to the decisions that we avoid making. We believe that waiting is the best thing to do, but when we wait, all we are doing is postponing the inevitable and, what's worse, allowing it to continue to complicate the situation that requires the decision we have been avoiding. Don't forget that the decisions we don't make also cause us pain.

You Are Not to Blame for
Everything That Happens to You

One of the favorite control mechanisms for "toxic" people is guilt. If you have spent time with a toxic person, you will be well aware that you are to blame for practically everything that goes wrong in the world. If they burn the food, it's your fault because you distracted them; if a plate breaks, again it's your fault because you didn't put it properly in its place; if they have a headache, of course, it's your fault because your irritating voice triggers their awful migraines. We could make a list of the most unbelievable attributions of guilt in history. Maybe one day I'll even write a book collecting the most outlandish blaming maneuvers you can imagine.

At a cultural level we also use guilt to control people's behavior. Depending on the education you might have received, it's likely that you assume responsibilities that might not correspond to you. I remember the case of a person who came to my consulting room because of an anxiety disorder. The origin of this disorder was nothing other than bad guilt management because she felt responsible for absolutely everything that was going on around her. She spent her evenings trying to come up with a plan to eradicate all the poverty in the world. During the day she picked up all the stray cats and dogs she found in the street, whether they were abandoned or not, and invested hours in publishing their photos and housing them with adoptive families or shelters. At work, she took on all possible tasks and all the impossible ones, too. Her work colleagues, aware of how easy it was to make her feel guilty, toyed with her emotions and assigned her all the work they could. But her suffering didn't end there. At home she felt guilty about everything. Her life was a compendium of "shoulds": she should be able to cook better, keep the house tidier, buy a bigger house, get fitter, be sweeter, and much more. I encourage you to look at how you interpret your experiences and what role guilt plays in your life because it's likely that your attributional style might explain part of your suffering.

What Is Your Attributional Style?

The psychologist Bernard Weiner developed the theory that when something happens to us, anything at all, whether expected or not, when we achieve something or when the thing we were expecting did not happen, we look for the reason and the causes of what happened.[1] This development is important because it allows us to become aware of how we interpret reality and how our conclusions affect us, whether they are correct or not. Thanks to Weiner's theory we can learn and improve our analysis process and, as a result, be wiser and happier. But let's start at the beginning, with our causal attributions.

We usually make an attribution of a cause for what happens to us and what does not happen to us. We formulate our own theories based on our learning and experience. But the most important part of this concept is that, depending on the quality of our attributions, we will either be happier or unhappier.

The fact that we formulate a theory of causation for the events doesn't mean that it is true. We might make mistakes (in fact, we make many mistakes), and each time we make a mistake, we suffer or cause suffering in other people. In the next few pages, I will analyze the main sources of error, and I will provide tools so that we can formulate the most correct and adaptive theories about the causes of what happens to us.

The first evaluation we carry out deals with the origin of the cause, which can be internal or external. If we conclude that the cause is external, we will believe that we are not responsible in any way for what has happened. In contrast, if we believe it is internal, we will conclude that we are partly responsible for what has happened. This evaluation is directly related to the management of accountability and guilt. Often there are people who would rather make external attributions and thus eliminate any kind of responsibility and guilt. Those who attribute the origin of the cause to another person are making them feel guilty for something that in reality does not depend on them. If you are able to appropriately identify the origin of what happens to you, you will be able to eliminate the guilt in your life and live responsibly. You might put the sinking of the *Titanic* down to the presence of the iceberg, or to the captain getting distracted, or simply to bad luck. Whichever one you believe, the key lies in correctly discerning the root cause of what happens to us, admitting our responsibility, and not blaming ourselves for what lies beyond our control.

The second one of the evaluations regards the amount of control we have on what is happening. If we believe that we lack the capacity to control what is happening to us, we leave our lives in the hands of chance, and we will look for a protector, adopt peculiar routines, and become superstitious. Basically, we can't control everything that happens to us, but we can control a lot more than we believe we can. So, again, the best strategy consists of learning to properly discern what we are able to influence and what can be controlled by us up to a point, from what is absolutely beyond our control. In many cases it should suffice to transform what you believe you have no control over; for example, if you lead a healthy lifestyle, you are positively influencing your future health, but if you believe you have no control at all, you are leaving it up to fate and you will not follow a single guideline in terms of health and hygiene.

Allow me to add an aside here. Be careful with the false belief that our minds are capable of everything, that we control things, that we are able to do it all, because this is the source of countless frustrations, problems, and accidents. In fact, most "fail" videos that circulate on the internet are the fruit of a causal attribution in which we believe we can control something that in actual fact we have no control over.

Finally, the third evaluation we conduct is about whether what happens to us is fixed and will persist over time or not; depending on how we see it, we will appraise our situation differently. When we believe that something is fixed and that it will not change, we cannot do anything but resign ourselves, grin and bear it, or suffer in silence, when in reality, life is a succession of phases. You can have an impact on bringing one phase to an end and starting a new one that is more motivating and more in line with your interests; few things in life last forever. Again, if you are capable of correctly analyzing and distinguishing between what you can and cannot change, you will make better decisions and better manage daily life and adversity.

It's important that you learn to analyze what attributions you make regarding what happens to you and to learn that causal attributions are affirmations, functioning as an internal language that affects our way of thinking, feeling, and doing; our self-esteem; our motivations; and even our health. But be careful because causal attributions are subjective, which is why they carry an elevated risk of distortion. Depending on our analysis skills, we will make better or worse attributions. Fear, our complexes, and our self-esteem all have an influence on them.

What have we learned from Weiner and his theory of causal attributions? Depending on whether our theories are correct or not, we will be happier or more unhappy. Depending on the causal attribution that we make, one fact can have different meanings. I encourage you to review and optimize your attribution system because your capacity to understand, face up to, and manage adversity depends on it.

We Are Vulnerable Beings

I remember a conversation with an Australian woman in which she was explaining to me that, in general, Australians tend to live intensely and with large doses of vitality and energy. She told me that, in Australia, death was always around the corner because they have the largest concentration of poisonous or deadly animals on the planet. "We have deadly spiders that might be hiding in your shoes, snakes whose poison could kill you in seconds wandering around gardens and pools, crocodiles everywhere, in a lake, river, or the sea, you name it," she said. And she went on to describe one by one each of the risks she had to deal with every day. "We Australians live side-by-side with death because we put our life at risk practically every day, and our awareness that we could die at any moment is what allows us to celebrate life with joy and intensity." Many Australians feel the fragility of human life has conditioned their character in such a way that they not only do not give up but—aware of this fragility and timelessness—they have decided to live life to the fullest.

We are vulnerable, and we live in a hostile environment. We are continually exposed to physical pain, every day, several times a day, but also to emotional pain. We are extremely fragile. Any day, a car might not stop at a red light and run us over. Any day, the roof of our house might cave in and leave us trapped in the rubble. One of our arteries might get blocked and leave us in a vegetative state, or we might fall and end up in a wheelchair for the rest of our life. Any day, a meteorite might fall on our head, or we might be attacked by a shark while paddling in the sea, or we might get struck by lightning. I have not said anything here that is not possible or has never happened. Well, maybe the part about the meteorite has never happened, but we can't confirm or deny it with any certainty.

Any day we might experience the greatest and most unexpected of tragedies. But what really matters is not what could or might happen to us—which can be just about anything—but what is actually happening to us. When we speak about misfortune and adversity, we must speak about probabilities, not possibilities, namely the likelihood that any of the adversities we are exposed to might occur. Is there a chance that a piece of space debris might fall from outer space and split my head open? I don't have the evidence to deny it. However, if I am going to be afraid of anything, in my case it would be the cows I meet in the mountains when I'm out for a run because it's far more likely that I will be trampled by a cow than get hit by a piece of space debris.

So, if you ever ask yourself, "Why me?" remember that we are fragile; that we live in a hostile environment; and that sometimes, with the behaviors and the decisions that we make—or don't make—we are taking risks that can lead us to adversity. However, at other times, the cruelest fate hits us with adversity.

Building a Wall Is Not the Solution

"Some people think that the solution to live more at ease is to build a wall to defend themselves. Do not make that mistake; the wall will defend you from exterior aggressions, but it will also prevent you from enjoying the wonderful things around you. If you build a wall, you will prevent disappointment, but you will feel bitterly lonely. A wall can protect you from fear of change but will create an inability to adapt to different situations. The wall will provide you with safety, but it will also make you a person who is dependent on its protection; it will make you insecure and fearful of what will happen when that wall disappears. I encourage you to build, instead of a wall, a library full of resources to help you maintain the level of emotional strength that you need."

I've allowed myself here to quote a fragment from my first book, *Emotional Strength*, to illustrate the way in which sometimes we attempt to protect ourselves by adopting strategies that are damaging, and how, when we wear armor, we build a fort or disconnect emotionally from the people around us and from reality. Building a wall is never the solution because it will not protect us from that pesky space debris looming above our heads. Don't forget: prudence is good, fear is not.

Enter Constructive Resonance

We must work on things that have happened and their mental representation. We cannot turn the page just like that; we cannot close our eyes to what has happened and continue to live as if nothing ever went wrong. What happened will not go away on its own; we must manage it and pay attention to it. What happened will always exist, whether we like it or not. However, if we are able to heal the wound and give it the right meaning, we will be able to learn from what happened instead of experiencing it in such a traumatic way.

What did the event mean to you? How did you experience it? How did you interpret it? I encourage you to review your conclusions. Some of our thought processes are perfectly reasonable and coherent but completely biased, and they tend to cause a lot of suffering. On the surface they are good and normal, and most importantly they provide us an answer (the answer we need to hear), but in reality they are false. Don't forget that what happens is as important as the way in which we interpret what happens. We give a meaning to events and latch onto that interpretation, sometimes even distorting reality to make it fit with our idea.

We are the result of the explanations we give ourselves and the ones we fail to give. That said, the explanations we give ourselves and our rationales are always created within a mental frame of reference.

What happens if this framework is negative? Then our reasons and our arguments will be negative, our fears will dominate our attention, and we will focus on the negative, thus missing out on the opportunities that life brings us. We will see life through our negativity bias, and we will interpret what happens to us in terms of guilt and in a negative way. And what if the framework is positive? In that case our reasoning will be contaminated by a naive optimism in which our desires will obscure our analysis process. When we buy a lottery ticket, our framework is positive but mistaken because we believe we are increasing the probability of achieving the thing we desire despite our scant capacity to influence reality.

So what frame of meaning must we provide our mind? The mind will function in an optimal way if its frame of reference is receptive and constructive. And how does the mind function when governed by a constructive conceptual framework? At its best because this is the best of all possible scenarios. It's not about doing just anything, but about doing something constructive, something with meaning. Don't work just for work's sake, work on something with meaning. Don't run just for running's sake, do a physical activity that has a meaning for you. Do something that will make a difference to you, to the people around you, and to the world in which you live. Don't do anything without thinking about what it means. As you will have been able to deduce, things that have meaning will bring you closer to happiness.

The key to a constructive frame of reference is to ask ourselves about what is happening without rushing our conclusions. We adopt the gaze of a curious child who is discovering the world with the attitude of an explorer. This constructive framework allows us to analyze the tragedy that we have suffered from a certain distance, trying to understand what happened to us, and learn from it.

In a constructive framework there is no room for guilt or for naive optimism. A constructive analysis is a well-adjusted and coherent analysis, free of distortions and selfishness. My best advice is that you review the conceptual framework you are living by so that you can migrate toward a better one, one that is better adjusted and that allows you to live a happier life and to interpret events more correctly. Enter constructive resonance to be able to enjoy everything that is beautiful that life offers you, and to be able to manage and learn from the trials and challenges that it brings.

Don't forget

- When we talk about risks, it's not about seeing possibilities but evaluating probabilities.

- You never know what risks might come in the future, so take advantage of the present moment to live intensely.

- Focus on enjoying the present because the future is uncertain and beyond your control.

- Learn to analyze different risk factors and make the decisions you need to make.

- Live prudently but not with fear.

- Be careful about how you interpret what happens to you. If you don't have an explanation that brings you peace, don't make one up.

- You must work out what happened as well as your mental representation of what happened.

He didn't want to cry. He could not cry for a piece of ceramics.
Ultimately, it was nothing but a piece of clay. No.
It was not a vulgar piece of clay.
It was much more than that.
But who would understand that?
Who would understand him
crying over a piece of clay?

How Do We React When Facing Adversity?

Not All Adversity Is Equal

Emotional pain arises from adversity; that much is clear. But what is adversity to you and to me? I remember a conversation with a friend in which I explained to her that I was going to put my daughter in a different school, to which she responded, "That's so hard! I remember the panic I felt when I left my school to start high school." This woman had never changed schools and had not been educated in the culture of adapting to change, nor had she been given the resources to meet new people and expand her social circles. Thus, changing schools can be conceived as something difficult or, on the contrary, as a new opportunity to expand your social circles, experience a new reality, get to know yourself better, and connect with the resources that are available to us all to adapt to change. In other words, as an opportunity to grow and to feel stronger and more confident.

There is no universal adversity because depending on the meaning that adversity has for each one of us, we might not suffer at all, or we may suffer a great deal. Allow me to give you a clear and direct example to help you better understand this concept. Let's imagine the death of a loved one; concretely, that of your partner. It's possible that your partner is a mainstay in your life, someone you have loved and with whom you have enjoyed a long, intense, and rewarding life together. Of course, this death might cause you a great deal of pain. But it is also possible that it will not.

Let's imagine that your partner died after a long battle with an illness or dementia. During months or years you have seen how much they have suffered. What's more, you have suffered by their side, every day. It is possible that, when they die, you feel a mix of intense emotions, a wide palette of emotions ranging from pain to relief. Not relief for you but relief for your partner, who has at last ceased to suffer that unbearable illness. In fact, what I have just described is a frequent consultation I receive from partners of people with Alzheimer's or Parkinson's or any kind of dementia or degenerative disease. When the person you love deeply dies after suffering for a long period, it's as if the hand that was clutching at your soul has become unclenched, allowing you to breathe again. It's difficult to imagine. Those of you who have experienced it understand it perfectly; it's often the case that, despite having loved your partner madly, their death is not that painful.

But let's consider a different scenario. Imagine your partner is the devil incarnate. Imagine that you have had no choice but to continue living with your partner despite life together being hell. Imagine that you are totally dependent on your partner, a partner who is abusive and brings you the most intense suffering imaginable. In this case, your partner's death will not cause you pain of any kind; on the contrary, it will mean liberation from pain. So, as you can see, not all adversity is the same. An event that means suffering for one person is not the same for another.

But there is more still. You yourself might consider something adversity at a particular period in your life but not so at a different time. Let's imagine you get fired from work at the age of twenty. Of course this will have an important impact on your life, but now try to imagine that you get fired from your job at age fifty, with children and a mortgage to pay. As you'll be able to deduce, the context in which you live can influence the way you experience a specific event as adversity. In reality, the consequences of being fired at twenty are not the same as those of being fired at fifty, and these circumstances will end up determining the value and meaning of adversity.

Therefore, the same event will not necessarily hurt the same person in the same way. The context, our interests, our concerns, and the areas in our life that are vulnerable to suffering change throughout our lives. We go through different phases with different interests. Our priorities change, and what did not seem important to us yesterday is crucial today. We grow up, become more mature, and feel stronger, but we also have more fears. At certain stages in our lives, we might feel weaker, more vulnerable, and more afraid of suffering. Therefore, we can't predict how we will react based on a past experience because it's possible that our context has changed, perhaps imperceptibly but enough to cause it not to hurt as much. I would like to share some reflections that I hope will lead to the construction of a framework within which to situate adversity.

How Does Adversity Affect Us?

Why does being fired represent adversity to one person but not to another? The key is in our self-sufficiency expectations because it is upon these that our sense of security or insecurity depends. If we believe we can face adversity, we will be placing ourselves in a position of advantage regarding that adversity. But if instead we believe we are helpless, we will react in terms of loss and bereavement.

Remember: if your expectation of self-sufficiency is positive, adversity will be nothing more than a challenge. Don't underestimate yourself; don't overestimate yourself either. Appropriately assess your ability to cope.

Creating Parameters for Pain

The pain we experience is a completely subjective reaction; however, we can say in general that a splinter is less painful than giving birth, that the death of a public figure is less painful than that of a loved one, and that the pain caused by a broken bone is a lot more intense than that of a sprained ankle. When we try to create pain parameters, I propose talking in terms of four aspects: intensity, duration, prognosis, and impact. Let's look at each of them in detail, starting with intensity.

By intensity we might understand the degree of strength with which a phenomenon is manifested. In other words, the greater the intensity, the greater the suffering; the lesser the intensity, the lesser the suffering. As with physical pain, emotional pain can have different kinds of intensity. Not everything hurts in the same way. But why do some things hurt more than others? What causes one kind of emotional pain to be more intense than another? Well, it depends on the emotional attachment to the source of the pain. What hurts more intensely is what directly affects us or the people we love; the pain of our child is more intense than the pain of a stranger. What hurts more is what affects our greatest aspirations and objectives; the more important an expectation is to us, the more intense the pain associated with failure, adversity, or unanticipated hurdles will be. We are more easily hurt by what affects our desires or fears, and the more intense our desire, the more painful our frustration when we do not achieve it. The emotional involvement determines and explains the intensity of our pain. The greater the emotional involvement, the greater the pain.

Another aspect that we must take into account when creating parameters for pain is its duration. There are kinds of pain that have a specific endpoint, whether they are more or less intense, but there is also lasting, muted, continuous pain—a damaging kind of pain. We all have a specific pain threshold that can vary from one person to another, or from a specific time period to another, depending on parameters such as our emotional state or our context. This threshold of pain tolerance allows us to cope with our day-to-day life and keep going despite the pain, when the pain is tolerable. But paradoxically, this tolerance to pain is the entryway for muted and continuous pain, which takes advantage of any little crack to seep into our lives. It enters little by little, stealthily, in silence, and without us noticing it settles into our life, gaining power and distorting and constraining our experience.

Sometimes we try to compare the pain we feel and to rank it. Which do you prefer: unbearable but short pain, or more moderate pain that lasts longer? It's difficult to answer that question. What we can say is that whatever the intensity of the pain, any pain that persists over a long period of time is like a kind of torture, which in the end has a high emotional cost, ultimately severely affecting each and every one of the areas in our lives. Those who suffer fibromyalgia or rheumatic illnesses know all too well the effects of this continuous, long-duration pain on their bodies and spirits.

Another one of the aspects that will allow us to understand the impact that pain has on our lives and that is closely related to its duration is its prognosis. Pain might have a positive, negative, or uncertain prognosis—that is, its evolution might improve or worsen, or it might be unknown. The best-case scenario is pain with a positive prognosis because, no matter how intense it is, if you know that one day it will end, it will give you a positive temporal perspective that will help you to counteract the pain and find the energy you need to overcome it. If you are aware that your pain has a sell-by date, you are in a better position to bear its terrible consequences.

On the contrary, if you are suffering pain with a negative evolution, you know things will get more complicated. That's why you will need to create a contingency plan, to opt for compensation. Don't do what many people do, which is to abandon themselves to suffering without further ado. I suggest that you don't give up because when faced with pain you can do more than just put up with it. I understand that it's not easy to imagine new activities or connect with new resources or interests that make up for the pain that you are suffering and that you know you will continue to suffer, but if you analyze the situation again with a fresh perspective, you will see it is possible to do something about that painful situation. I encourage you to compensate for that pain by enriching your life, seeking out new things to look forward to and new activities that generate positive emotions. Try to imagine the pain, whether it is physical or emotional, as a payment from your bank account. Every day, every week, or every month, your pain withdraws a specific amount of well-being from your bank account, inevitably, always at the specified time. But if you are capable of paying well-being into your account, it will never go into overdraft, and the quantity of well-being that has been withdrawn by pain will not throw your daily life off balance—or in any case, you will be able to redress the balance.

Learned Helplessness

In the 1970s, Martin Seligman worked on a key concept of psychology—learned helplessness—that works along the lines of giving up the fight because the frame of reference available is that "whatever I do, it will not make a difference."[1] This phenomenon is a logical consequence of a negative pain prognosis. When you believe that you cannot exercise any kind of influence on the pain you are experiencing, it's easy to conclude that whatever you do, you will not be able to control that pain, in which case you will abandon your struggle and become despondent. But as we have just seen, despite being powerless to stop the pain that is torturing us, whether it is physical or emotional, there are things we can do to manage the impact it has on our lives and to compensate for it with moments of well-being.

Conversely, we might find ourselves experiencing a kind of pain whose evolution is uncertain. If this is your situation, I encourage you to try to shed some light on it, if possible. And if the evolution of your suffering truly is uncertain, take it one day at a time without anticipating anything, either positive or negative. We don't know what will happen, so it makes no sense to speculate. If we believe that everything will go from bad to worse, then we will enter into negative resonance and we will end up suffering for things that might never happen. If instead we create the illusion that everything will go well, we will be inflating a balloon that might explode at any moment, causing us great disappointment and adding to the pain in our lives. Therefore, when we don't know how things will go, the only thing we can do is to focus on the present, analyze the way in which things are evolving, and adapt as quickly as we can.

The last aspect we must analyze is the impact that pain and suffering have on our lives. By impact we mean the repercussions and consequences on the different areas of our lives. The impact might be low or high. There are kinds of suffering that can be experienced without any major consequences, but there is adversity that completely knocks you out, preventing you from being able to think, work, rest, or even live. Sometimes adversity comes into our lives, turns everything on its head, and leaves us at a loss for what to do or where to go.

"I've Been Through That, Too, and I Got Over It"

Sometimes, with the best of intentions, someone approaches us and drops this phrase. They might be a lovely person, but they might also be misguided. No two experiences of pain are equal, which is why it is difficult to compare two different situations experienced by two different people. The small variations when it comes to the intensity or duration of the suffering are enough to explain the different reactions when different people are faced with the same kind of pain. However, the impact of adversity is the key element that will mark the difference and determine the way in which pain will affect us.

Do We Know How to Manage Adversity?

By now we have learned a bit more about pain and adversity, but how do we react when faced with adversity? Well, often without thinking, in an impulsive and not rational way, and without in the least bit analyzing the adversity, context, and potential alternatives that might be available. We are not aware that the way in which we react to and deal with adversity has an effect on our likelihood of success, so it is worth dedicating an entire section to the management of adversity.

Some people react with an emotional outburst in the form of anxiety or sadness. When adversity comes our way, it tends to do so at the worst time, ruining our immediate plans or our nearest future. Suddenly, adversity barges into our life and causes a high emotional impact of unimaginable consequences, paralyzing us, reducing our ability to think, and affecting each and every one of the different areas of our life, from our sexuality to our work. When we are under the influence of an intense emotion, our levels of cortisol and adrenaline go off the scale and wreak havoc on our vital functions and our ability to think, analyze, be creative, and solve problems, as well as a long list of cognitive functions. When we feel in such a strong and intense way, we might even become ill: when sadness becomes chronic, it can lead to depression; when anxiety becomes chronic, it can result in a generalized anxiety disorder. When we become blocked or ill because of the intensity of our emotions, we are placed in a position of disadvantage when it comes to managing and facing the adverse conditions that require the best version of ourselves.

Other people react to adversity with surprise, as if they were thinking: "Wow, I had no idea that smoking three packs a day could lead to lung cancer"; "Gosh, how could I predict that one day they would discover at work that all I do is download movies and I would get fired?"; "Oh god, I had no idea my son could suffer a brain injury like that from playing rugby, and it was me forcing him to play"; "Oh my goodness, who would have said that one day I'd have an accident while climbing a mountain at an altitude of more than eight thousand meters?"; "I cannot believe it—how was I to know that my partner would get fed up with my new obsession for triathlon?"; "Wow, my partner took my infidelity badly—I mean, it's the one and only fling that I've had in my entire life." Ultimately, their belief is that what has happened has nothing to do with their own actions, and they are caught off guard. Sometimes we are too naive or purport to be. We deliberately, sometimes unnecessarily, take risks, and then we are surprised when we win the lottery we have been playing. We spend our lives not assessing the consequences of our actions, even cheating ourselves, but when reality eventually catches up with us, we react with the attitude of someone who has fallen into a trap.

There are also people who become angry, who get monumentally upset, with a huge explosion of uncontrollable rage that distorts their view of reality. When we become angry, sometimes it can be at ourselves, but that is not frequently the case because we would rather be angry at someone else, at a scapegoat on whom we can place the responsibility of what is happening to us. We blame the mechanic who fixed the motorcycle, another driver who made us nervous, the guide who didn't check the time, the gin and tonic we had, the pressure we were under, or life. What difference does it make? As long as I am not to blame, I don't care how outlandish my pretexts are. This is an easy strategy, but it is also naive and ineffective for two reasons. The first is that when I blame someone else, I have no responsibility to assume, nothing to improve, nothing to learn, and nothing to correct. I sleep fine at night, true, but I overrun the costs for those around me and for myself because it's possible that I might repeat the same mistake again. The second reason is that where there is rage, there is guilt, and where there is guilt you will find punishment and abuse, whether it is directed toward ourselves or toward the people to whom we attribute the root of the problem. This way, I get away with controlling, punishing, and torturing the person I believe to be the source of all my ills because I have a justification that absolves and protects me. It's all their fault! And while I abuse someone or act as an avenger, I don't have to assume any responsibility that corresponds to me. When anger and resentment become chronic, our lives become dark, and we make ourselves and the people around us bitter.

Some people feel fear when faced with adversity—a cold, hostile, and cruel fear that paralyzes their blood, their life, and their ability to think straight. In the same way that a rabbit freezes in the headlights or a fox starts running erratically to escape from its hunter, the fear of adversity exposes us to the consequences of the problem and causes us to act without rhyme or reason. Worry takes over our lives, and we start going around in circles, unable to make a decision. And while we worry, we do nothing useful to manage adversity, its causes and its consequences. Anxious and tired, we lose our mental agility, everything becomes confusing and dark, we lose sight of all the resources available to us to tackle adversity, and we become small and insecure, incapable of fighting against it.

A few pages earlier I spoke about the phenomenon of learned helplessness, which consists of believing that nothing at all can be done to reach an objective. We often need an additional impulse, some extra energy to allow us to draw out strength from our weakness and cope with challenging situations wearing our best smile, and this energy is born from hope and excitement. But what happens when we lose hope? Without hope we don't have the slightest probability of success. If I believe that "no matter what I do, it will not make a difference," I will limit myself to doing nothing and hoping for a miracle. And while I wait, I won't be doing anything to solve my problem and put an end to the adversity that is causing my suffering. Learned hopelessness has its origin in the teachings we extract from our past experiences; so, if you want to liberate yourself from that heavy load, you must start by reinterpreting what happened and the conclusions you draw with respect to it.

We cannot think of adversity without considering the concept of pressure. All adversity requires our immediate attention to be resolved, which generates a kind of pressure we must eliminate. This pressure is what drives us to action. If it did not exist, in many cases we would do nothing at all. However, some people don't know how to handle that pressure—they feel ill at ease, are unable to bear it, and decide to adopt the worst of strategies: self-delusion.

Self-delusion can manifest in many ways, but none of these is a valid coping strategy. It is based on the inability to have a negative self-image, which is why we prefer to distort reality instead of having to come to terms with our errors or inabilities. Ultimately, it's a lot easier to delude ourselves, to look the other way and pretend rather than to admit you have a problem and that you don't know how to solve it. When we deny we have a problem, we cannot create parameters, study, analyze, and tackle the situation. And when we don't do anything to tackle the problem, we leave the solution in the hands of chance or the goodwill of the people around us.

Self-Delusion

We cheat ourselves every day, several times a day, believing that it is a good strategy, but it is not. We cheat ourselves on minor details (for example, I tell myself that it will be fine if I arrive ten minutes late) but also on more serious things (for example, I will not be able to find a better job than my current one).

Self-delusion is a common strategy, which doesn't make it valid; it's extremely toxic because it paralyzes us, preventing us from taking action. There are different kinds of self-delusion:

- "There was nothing else I could have done." This is the most complacent and immature self-delusion of all. In addition to doing nothing, we shrug off responsibility and rest on our laurels.

- "There are people who are worse off than me." To me, this is one of the worst ones, especially because you are paying selective attention. Of course there are people who are worse off than you, but there are also people who are better off. Perhaps if you looked at people who are better off than you and learned, then you could evolve, become more mature, and solve your problems.

- "Whatever I do, it won't make a difference." Maybe you have made attempts in the past to solve a problem, but perhaps what you did was not appropriate or you didn't execute it properly. If based on that, you conclude that you have done everything in your power and that it still didn't work, logically the conclusion you will reach is that no matter what you do, it won't make a difference. I encourage you to reassess your conclusions because often there are at least one or two more things you can try.

- "Time will fix everything." Time alone will not do anything. You will be better off if you take control because otherwise you will be leaving your future in the hands of chance.

There are many ways to react in the face of adversity—as many as there are people. You might have seen yourself reflected in some of the things I have said. It's even possible that you have different responses to different problems. Although I have listed only the most common ones, what's important is that you analyze the way you respond to adversity because, by doing this, you will be able to anticipate how to tackle it.

I would like to share with you the results of Max Watson's research on coping strategies in the face of adversity.[2] In his research, Watson isolated some key factors and analyzed how they can influence or determine our success when managing adversity. According to him, there are four key elements that predict our success or failure when attempting to overcome adversity. The first refers to the way in which we interpret adversity—in other words, the meaning we give to the events we experience. The second refers to our perceived control over adversity—that is, the belief that we can do something or that it is impossible to do anything to manage adversity. The third is about our appraisal of the evolution of adversity, and, finally, the fourth factor analyzes our emotional response, as well as its intensity regarding the problem.

Based on these parameters, Watson proposed five types of response in the face of adversity. As I explain the different strategies, I suggest that you self-analyze with the objective of recognizing your dominant style.

The first of the styles has been labeled the "fighting spirit." People with this style interpret adversity as a challenge, and when they are faced with it they believe there is no better alternative than rising up and tackling the situation. In addition, they perceive an elevated degree of control when confronted with the situation they are experiencing; they have an optimist's attitude toward the evolution of the problem, and they adopt the role of the protagonist in the resolution of the problem or adversity. This is without doubt the best coping strategy, the one that will give us the best chances of success and will put us in a better position to overcome the adversity that is tormenting us.

The second of the styles is avoidance or denial. Those who present this coping style don't see any threat in adversity; they have a naive view of adversity and reality, tend to minimize the problem and its consequences, and do all of this with a calm emotional tone. In other words, they are too laid-back.

Fatalism is the third coping style that Watson so accurately described. Fatalist people perceive adversity as a moderate threat but at the same time cannot conceive a single possibility of control, either over adversity or over its causes or consequences. As a result, they adopt a resigned attitude that leads them to the most passive stance possible. Because they believe they cannot do anything, they decide not to get in the least bit involved in resolving the problem.

The fourth style comprises defenselessness and hopelessness, which lead people to see adversity as a terrible threat, without the remotest possibility of control. When faced with this panorama, the only choice is to adopt a pessimist's attitude toward the evolution of the adversity, which causes them not to get at all involved in solving the problem, an attitude that leads to depression.

And, finally, there is anxious preoccupation, a style that is characterized by perceiving adversity as an unsurmountable threat; what's more, everything around them feels like a devastating threat. People who predominantly adopt this style live in the most absolute state of uncertainty and tend to compulsively seek the security they so desperately need.

Now that you are familiar with the different styles when coping with adversity, take a moment to consider how you tend to respond in the face of adversity. Do you recognize yourself in any of the descriptions?

Can We Learn to Manage Adversity?

Of course we can. In fact, it is an emotional strength that should be taught as part of the school curriculum. We are obsessed with teaching our children to compete and be tough, but we don't realize that what they really need is to learn how to live, to listen to themselves and others, and to acknowledge each other. What if instead of teaching your children to compete against other people, you taught them to connect with them? If instead of teaching your students that the other people were adversaries, you showed them they were allies? If you taught your students to view the people in front of them with curiosity and compassion? If instead of teaching them to ignore adversity, you provided them the resources to recognize and manage it?

Turn adversity into a challenge and the fighting spirit that you need will emerge from within to help you overcome the problem, rebuild your life, and emerge stronger at the other end. When life knocks you down, evaluate the physical, psychological, emotional, and social damage that the blow has caused you, dust yourself off, and go back into the fray recovered, wiser, and with more resources.

Don't forget

- Your expectations of self-sufficiency determine your assessments of adversity.

- Emotional pain might vary in intensity, duration, prognosis, and impulse. The same kind of adversity can affect different people in different ways, or the same person might be affected differently at different times.

- The fact that you are experiencing pain does not mean that you cannot compensate for it through focused actions.

- The way in which we tackle and manage adversity affects our likelihood of success.

- Transform worry into action.

- Reinterpret adversity and learn from it.

Sokei faced two choices: either to repair the bowl or not. Did he really want to suffer again, reencountering the image of his own shattered spirit? Would it not be preferable to place the broken pieces in a drawer and not have to look at them again? Sokei was thinking from a place of pain. Suffering is a bad adviser. He closed his eyes again to be able to see things clearly.

Can Life Be Rebuilt?

It was a stiflingly hot summer's day. I decided to head to the river to do some white-water rafting to cool down and have some fun. Between Llavorsí and Sort, in the Catalan Pyrenees, there is a large concentration of rapids, and in the summer there are many people rafting, kayaking, or simply diving into the river with a rubber ring! Anyway, as I was on my way down I met a couple who had dived with an enormous inner tube from a truck wheel, and they were in trouble. They were trapped by a current on a bend of the river that was inaccessible from the land. After seeing the fright on their faces and realizing that at the end of the countercurrent they would meet with a fallen tree, I decided to initiate a rescue operation.

I went up to where they were and noticed they were hooked to a submerged branch. I got off the kayak and freed them, but suddenly I saw the water turn red with blood, my own. The cold water of the river had masked the pain caused by a rock when I scraped my shin jumping off the kayak. After the couple was safe and sound, and I was calmer, I examined the wound; it was a deep gash of about twenty centimeters.

What a nightmare! I still had at least an hour of river descent, and then I had to get to Llavorsí to fetch the car. I thought about continuing down the river to the hospital in Tremp, but the truth is that when you live, work, and go adventuring in the mountains, accidents are the order of the day. After the ordeal, when I finally arrived at the caravan I was staying in, I realized that the wound had already started to heal. The inflammation had gone down, I was no longer bleeding, and the pain had subsided a great deal.

As mentioned previously, it's the "drive to repair" that causes our body to heal a wound. Being alive in a biological body entails the possibility of being wounded. We should not aspire to be invulnerable, live a safe and easy life, or stay at home out of fear of injury. Instead, we must learn to be stronger, heal our wounds, repair what is broken, and rebuild our lives.

The Drive to Repair

When someone is injured, the repair process is set in motion—a chain of complex biochemical reactions that will disinfect, regenerate, and heal the wound. The human body feels the drive to repair from any injury received, and it activates a system of alarm and repair that involves practically all of our vital functions. It is equipped to cope with major injury and physical trauma. It can repair burned skin, regenerate cells, heal a fractured bone, rebuild a damaged area, and even replace lost brain function. In my case, my injury healed within a couple of weeks, leaving me a scar that reminds me that even the worst disasters can be overcome. Therefore, the drive to repair is inherent to our nature, intrinsic to our bodies, and necessary for life.

But this drive to repair is not exclusive to the body because, just like our body, our mind feels and has the drive to repair our emotional wounds. It's that simple. We already have the answer to the question that gives rise to this chapter: Can life be repaired? Yes, no doubt about it. And, what's more, we are designed for it.

The Suffering Paradox

Unlike what happens with our bodies, sometimes we don't allow our mental repair process to complete itself, and we interfere in such a way that we remain hooked on our emotional pain. It's as if, perversely, we enjoy suffering. It's difficult to understand why we clean and disinfect a physical wound in order to heal it, yet don't do the same with our emotional wounds to prevent them from becoming infected and ossified.

Why don't we heal our emotional wounds? Why do we close our eyes and ignore what our soul is begging us to see? There is no simple answer. In some cases we have become disconnected from our emotional strength and the resources available to cope with adversity. In other cases, the reason is that we have overstretched ourselves to the point that we are unable to connect with our own resources. Sometimes we have lost perspective, and we deceive ourselves with the pain that we feel. Some people have internalized the idea that we have come to this world to suffer, and for that reason, do nothing to stop their suffering.

The Sleeping Giant

If you will allow me, I am going to use again the analogy of physical repair of a wound to illustrate a new and crucial concept. Usually, your body does not keep sending unmistakable signs that it can heal itself. Instead, it is discreet about its own potential. The body feels at ease because it knows that it has available a whole arsenal of tools ready to be deployed. And meanwhile, it keeps on living, ignoring any fear of injury.

Your body is prepared to resolve any wound or fracture, but it won't enter into action until we need it; it won't wake up until there is an injury. In the same way, our mind has everything it needs to repair the emotional pain and, just like our body, it doesn't constantly tell us it is prepared and ready. However, unlike with physical pain, we feel insecure about our ability to heal our emotional pain.

Don't forget you have everything you need to repair a wound but that you won't set the process in motion until you need it. I understand that you might be afraid and might even believe that you cannot overcome something, but you shouldn't worry. Conserve your energy and strength for when they are needed. If you live in a sea of fear, you will continually dream up scenarios that begin with "what if," and you will be weakening your body and soul, making them more vulnerable.

Can you imagine what would happen if your body started reacting against all potential threats? Imagine if, when faced with every little possibility of risk, your body activated its alarm system and sent antibodies to attack the invading enemy. You would become ill, without a doubt. Well, what I just outlined happens to many people; in fact, autoimmune diseases are the result of an attempt to attack and repair our immune system against a nonexistent disease. This overreaction is dysfunctional and causes significant disturbance to our health. In the same way, cognitive and emotional overreaction to imagined or feared dangers causes a great deal of dysfunctional disturbance in our daily life, such as the inability to concentrate, memory problems, sadness, anxiety, limiting fears, and a long list of symptoms that can lead to major disorders. With every unfounded alarm, we suffer unnecessarily; with every additional effort to protect ourselves from a nonexistent threat, we consume a quantity of energy that is difficult to recover.

The Reconstruction Process

Rebuilding your life is a complex process that goes through different phases. When you receive the blow that throws you off course and shatters you into pieces, it's difficult to see things clearly. The first thing that happens with a nonphysical wound is a kind of emotional exhaustion that clouds your judgment and senses. You are incapable of thinking clearly; pain takes over your life and your whole being and expands toward your past and your future. Your attention becomes partial and biased. You look ahead toward the future, and you see nothing but loneliness, fear, chaos, and sadness. You look back and cannot understand anything. And in the midst of all this despair you forget to look around you to see if there is anyone you can trust—someone you can rely on. There is always someone, but you can't always see them. Sometimes it's a friend, partner, or relative, but it can also be a psychotherapist.

Just as you don't need to go to the doctor for a minor cut with no complications, you don't need to see a psychotherapist about a minor mishap. However, if what seemed like a simple wound becomes complicated, or if it involves major trauma, we should not hesitate to visit a specialist in order to ensure a speedy recovery, minimize our suffering, and reduce the risk of complications. In the same way, if you see that your emotional wound is worsening, escaping from your control, or not evolving in the way you would like, you should immediately seek help from a reputable psychotherapist because they will support you in recovering the perspective that you will so desperately need to be able to rebuild your life.

It is also true that some people might find the perspective they need simply by understanding some basic psychological processes. That's why both in this book and in *Emotional Strength* I have put all my efforts into bringing psychology out of the consultation room and making it accessible to you.

But let's get back to the topic at hand, the analysis of our emotional wounds. At the beginning we don't understand what has happened; we just feel a mix of intense emotions. Pain is mixed with fear, sadness with frustration, and resentment with disappointment. Our thinking becomes cyclical, we're unable to focus, and we lose sleep. Little by little, within a few days, emotional exhaustion starts to give way to a more settled state in which we are able to gain a clearer understanding of what happened. At first, our vision is blurry, like when we have just woken up. We open our eyes, and we need to close them again. We slowly start to see things more clearly. Shadows become defined silhouettes. The confusing elements become distinct, and we start to see the reality that we were unable or unwilling to see at the time.

In this phase, we start to gradually work out what has happened and how we feel. We put events in order, we organize the facts, and we start to feel able to make some decisions. However, some people, in order to avoid seeing a reality that is painful, prefer to close their eyes again, thus blocking the healing process. It's in exactly this phase when we decide to remain anchored in pain. Victimism, anger, and incomprehension swirl around in our heads, emotions that will become moods, and moods that will end up causing greater damage.

Finally, one day, if we have not decided to close our eyes again and live in our imaginary world, the healing phase, the most important one, begins. This is when we have to close the wounds. Life has changed. It won't be as it was before, but it might be even better. Come to terms with change. The fact that you come to terms with something doesn't mean that you like it, but it is still necessary to find acceptance in order to start to heal.

Adversity Is Nothing More Than a Challenge

You have been born again. Every day, we are born again. We go to sleep without knowing for sure whether we will wake the next morning, so every morning is a rebirth, a new opportunity. Every morning, every week, every month, every season, and every year is a wonderful opportunity to start over, to rebuild our lives, and to transform adversity into a challenge.

Challenges are stimulating and motivating and help you to bring out the best in you, whereas problems and adversities have a negative connotation that tends to block us and limit our creativity and our potential to develop. Transform adversity into a challenge, and you'll activate the drive to repair swiftly and effectively.

If you have been broken, that's all right, because you can always go back and rebuild yourself. In fact, rebuilding yourself is a necessity. And after you are rebuilt you will be stronger, you will become aware of your own resources, and you will feel more secure and better positioned to face new challenges. But rebuilding yourself is not enough;

you must also learn from what happened, close a chapter, and make your wound beautiful. You know why? Because our gaze always gravitates toward the wound, which is the weakest point we have, the link at which our chain broke.

Contrary to what it might seem, the rebuilding process is quite straightforward. The method that I suggest and explain in detail in part 2 of the book starts by collecting the pieces of our broken soul and moves on to a detailed analysis of the situation, which will allow us to learn from what happened. After this, we will connect with our emotional strength because that is the resource we most need in rebuilding what is broken. Last but not least, we will make our scars beautiful so that we can view them not with nostalgia or pain but with the joy of someone who realizes they have proof of their own strength. We will cover our scars with gold so that when we look at them, we realize that by overcoming adversity we have grown, become more beautiful, and gained in strength.

You need to reinterpret that wound, which can only be done through a therapeutic process. It's important that you go through this process because it is likely that memory of the event will revisit you at some point or another in your life, and you must be prepared for when this occurs. The memory of what you suffered sometimes crops up when you least expect it and will inadvertently inflict pain. When we look back we distort our memories, and victimism and self-pity take over.

We cannot adopt a passive attitude and allow for negative emotions to take over our lives and our moods, dragging us into a cold and dark place. We can and must get to know ourselves and understand the events we experienced in order to manage those negative emotions that are calling for our attention. It's important to know where you are and what you have lived through and suffered, but it's also important to know where you are and where you want to get. There are always destinations, always alternatives, and always more possibilities, but to be able to reach your new destination you need to heal first.

I know you are afraid. I know you think you cannot rebuild your life, but I also know that you are thinking from a place of pain. I know that you're mistaken and that you can be happy again.

Don't forget

- Living brings with it the possibility of getting hurt, but don't worry—our bodies and minds have already foreseen this and are equipped to heal physical and emotional wounds.

- We can learn to be stronger and develop strategies for repairing what is broken.

- Don't remain hooked on pain; allow your mind to activate the drive to repair. Don't become blocked with ill-adjusted beliefs and ideas.

Part Two

"I want to mend the bowl!" Sokei told Chojiro, his gaze serene, decisive, and firm. "I'm sorry it took me so long to reach a decision," he continued.

Kintsugi: The Art of Repairing Our Lives

"Dear Sokei, do not be sorry about things like that."

You need to regain control over your own life and your emotions because this will be the basis for your recovery as you develop trust in yourself and in your capabilities. The time has come to relearn how to live a different life, to breathe freely, and to walk in the direction you choose. You have to rebuild yourself. Sometimes you will have to do it on your own, and sometimes you will have help, but whatever the case, do so free of the heavy load of the past, enjoying the experience and the sensations and actively seeking it. If you don't rebuild your life, the crisis, adversity, or drama that you have experienced will be your reference point, your measurement unit, the center of your universe—and, without you realizing it, will govern most of your choices, memories, fears, and desires.

Your life will not spontaneously heal. Don't wait for something to happen merely by dint of desiring it because desire alone is not enough to heal our lives. Action will be what brings you a better life, helping you overcome adversity. Are you ready to take action? Are you willing to rebuild yourself?

Don't Wait until You Hit Rock Bottom

We often need to hit rock bottom to gather momentum again, to start to fight for a new life, and to realize that we must radically reorient our destiny. Change is not easy. And neither is accepting the possibility that we are responsible for the state we find ourselves in.

Many of humanity's greatest advancements have been achieved by people who have hit rock bottom, people who could no longer cope, and people who in the midst of their deepest suffering had no other choice but to stand up again—no other alternative but to pick up the pieces and rebuild their lives. But don't wait until you hit rock bottom to activate all the resources available to you. Don't wait until you reach the limit to find the energy required to rebuild your life. You might already have seen signs that you need to make a change in your life, that you are suffering because of things that can be changed, and that you could be living a different life. Don't ignore these signs; don't try to drown them out with noise, possessions, or adventures. Stop and listen to what your body and your soul have to say because some people, when they hit rock bottom, find themselves unable to rise again.

Don't Remain Anchored in Pain

People don't tend to die from falling into a river; they die from not getting out of it in time. By the same token, we might have fallen into the river of adversity, tragedy, or problems, but we need to make sure we get out of it and avoid staying anchored in suffering. We all need time to put together the pieces of the puzzle of a tragedy or a problem, time to reflect. Sometimes we are slow to react, too slow. When disaster strikes, the most natural thing is to be in a state of initial shock, disoriented and stunned. But after that brief period, we have the obligation and the need to start rebuilding our lives. Let me share an anecdote with you that illustrates this phenomenon. It was mid-July and several families were on a day trip into the Pyrenees. After a short trek we reached our destination, a beautiful lake surrounded by steep mountains. We had been hiking for a couple of hours and were hungry, so the first thing we did was find a place to sit, set up camp, and recoup our strength. We looked for a good vantage point from which we could watch the kids as they went back and forth from the lake, and we laid out the spread: Spanish omelet, olives, and a few cheese wraps. Nothing beats outdoor dining! (My favorite restaurants are all part of the same chain: a place in nature with a great view.) As we ate we chatted away, except for one person, one of the dads who wouldn't stop whining. Apparently he had sat near an anthill, and every so often he felt an unpleasant sting caused by an ant bite. "What's wrong?" his wife asked. "Nothing. These ants, they're biting me." "Sit somewhere else," another friend suggested. "It doesn't matter; I can't be bothered to move now." And he continued to whine every so often.

"What's wrong with him?" asked one of our friends who had just joined the picnic. "Why is he bellyaching so much?" "Because he's sitting on an anthill," replied his wife. "Why doesn't he just sit somewhere else?" she suggested. "Because he hasn't been bitten enough yet."

Herein lies the key! My dear friend decided that the hassle of sitting somewhere else was greater than the suffering imposed by the ants. In the same way, many people won't lift a finger to rebuild their lives until they can no longer bear the pain. However, sometimes, when the pain has become intense, we find ourselves in a worse condition for making the change we need because we are more and more worn out, exhausted, and we have lost perspective. Don't wait for life to be painful enough! The hassle of change is far preferable to the seeming comfort of abandoning yourself to suffering.

Take action. Don't live life as a spectator when you can be an actor. You have the starring role in the movie of your life! Many people just see life pass by, expecting that someday, something will happen and their lives will change, but the real thing is that we can have a high potential to act in our lives and to change what we want.

This belief is the key—the belief that you can take control of your life and thus the decisions that you can make.

Move on to action, and take the first step in rebuilding your life. Reject the scripts that want to typecast you. Go off script. Write your own script. Be the director of your own movie, and start doing it now. Stop living in a black-and-white drama and start living in a full-color feature film.

Take the first step; make the decision to rebuild your life. You have already suffered enough.

Think Differently

Our thought processes are insufficient and inadequate, which is why in this second part of the book I provide some keys to improving our thinking. We tend to jump to conclusions, make mistakes based on them, and then try to justify those errors.

I suggest that you think differently—that you think in simple terms. Simplifying things is no easy task because it involves a certain amount of effort. Simplifying reality is not something banal; on the contrary, it is important because it means a change in attitude that will help us gain in happiness and emotional well-being.

What does thinking simply consist of? Well, it means not needlessly complicating our existence. Are the ants biting? Then sit somewhere else. You don't feel happy in your workplace? Then start planning to enrich your work or change jobs. You don't feel well? Then go to the doctor. The key is to control our thinking—to stop worrying and thinking in circles—and instead take action. It's about transforming inaction into action, abandoning complacency, taking a step forward, and losing our worries so that we no longer anticipate a hypothetical catastrophic future and instead take a more realistic view of what might actually happen.

Sokei picked up the six pieces carefully, but suddenly he realized there was a seventh fragment on the ground—a tiny fragment that he could barely see because of the faint light filtering through a curtain of torrential rain outside the window in Chojiro's workshop.

Pick Up the Pieces

I like climbing. I have climbed a lot, and often while climbing I marvel at how life triumphs in nature's fight for survival. I often see plants flowering in the most inhospitable places, like a tiny nook of a sheer wall of rock. In that place, life fights to show its great capacity to adapt, the same strength with which nature and life have blessed us. Never forget that we can blossom and grow in even the worst of circumstances, but we will not manage to do so until we take action. Do you know what's the first step we must take? To pick up the pieces of whatever it was that broke. Yes, to pick them up. Often we neglect them, we hide them, or we put them away in the drawer of oblivion. This attitude isn't the solution because it won't help you rebuild yourself but instead will keep you hooked on pain, cheating yourself, or ignoring what has happened—all the wrong strategies. I encourage you to pick up the pieces, to take them out of the drawer of unpleasant memories, and to lay them out on the table. We're going to take action, and we're going to do it together.

Do You Know Your Ikigai?

To be able to start rebuilding yourself, you need a how and a why. We will talk at length about the "how" in part 3 of the book, with the help of the different case studies that I have outlined for you. But we can't talk much about the "why" because you must find it for yourself. I can give you a few whys; I can inspire you and even explain the most common ones, but only you can find your own.

You can start by picking up the pieces for yourself, for your partner, or for your children. You can decide to mend yourself for what you have been or for what you might one day become, for nothing in particular, for the life you are lucky enough to have because you must be happy, or even to annoy the person that hurt you. Any motivation you find is good! At the end of the day, the only thing that matters is that you find the driving force and the impulse that will allow you to begin your healing process. I could continue to suggest "whys," but if you don't internalize them, it won't make much difference. But let's go step by step.

Why do you get up every morning? What motivates you to get out of bed every day? In Japan there is a term to describe our reason for living or being: *ikigai*. We all have an ikigai, even if we don't know it. In fact, the search for an ikigai is what will bring large doses of satisfaction and self-fulfillment because when you connect with your ikigai, your life will acquire a meaning. Often we live a life that is full of appearances, possessions that appear to speak for who we are, jobs that provide much prestige but that we don't enjoy, inherited stereotypes, scraps of other lives, and only superficial meaning. But that life full of appearances has a tendency to crumble and fall apart, and, when it does, it's usually in the form of a crisis. For some people, the crisis that tends to happen in adult life is an opportunity to ask ourselves what our ikigai is and what the meaning of our life is. However, when you are suffering, it's not the best time to find a meaning for your life because from a place of lacking everything is harder. Have you ever been to the supermarket while hungry? Well, when you look for the meaning of life while going through a crisis, something similar happens. If you are in an altered or intense emotional state, your judgment becomes clouded and you tend to react impulsively. What else did you expect?

You are suffering! You are suffering because of values and principles that were not working for you, so what we need to do is end that suffering as soon as possible. At times like those, it seems that anything will do. When we seek the meaning of life while in the midst of a crisis, we are a sitting duck for the first alternative or suggestion that appears in front of us; an easy target for devious people who will provide meaning for their own benefit only; vulnerable victims of mystical beliefs, pseudoscience, and alternative theories. When we're hungry, anything tastes good, and when we're suffering, any route might seem rational. I suggest that you don't wait until you are in a crisis to give meaning to your life—the meaning that you truly want, not the meaning that your parents or peers want or a meaning based on ideals that are difficult to achieve. When you discover your ikigai, you'll discover something that will make you brave. You will be happy when your life has meaning, a meaning you have discovered for yourself, but first you must find silence to be able to look for that meaning within.

Have you noticed the noise that constantly surrounds us? We can't bear the silence. We run around listening to music even out in the mountains, oblivious to the fact that we are missing out on the beautiful melody offered by the forest. We enjoy the noise; we flee from silence without being aware that if we don't ever embrace silence we can't connect with ourselves, with our essence, with our dreams and desires, and with our needs. But silence scares us. We insist on making noise so as to not have to listen to ourselves. We believe that noise blocks it all out, but that is not true. Disconnected from ourselves, we work, love, and eat. Always surrounding ourselves with noise, running away from the beautiful silence we so desperately need in order to live in peace.

What is your inner dialogue like? Are you ignoring yourself? What are you trying to silence? The best strategy to enjoy silence might be to attend to the messages your body is sending you. I invite you to delve into the forest and listen to its silence, your silence. Connect with it and connect with yourself. Listen to yourself. Stop ignoring yourself. Noise assumes many forms. Sometimes it takes the shape of a need for recognition, other times of vanity, an inflated ego, aggressiveness, or narcissism. We flee from sadness without realizing that it's an emotion we need in order to live, to evolve. Sadness is nothing more than focusing on our inner silence. This can be a pretty scary thing to do, so we often prefer to make noise instead. Allow yourself to be sad (though not depressed) and listen to yourself. Wisely interpret what you are hearing, and start making decisions. Sadness will help you find the courage you need. Your soul won't become silent until you tend to it.

Your ikigai is your "why," your reason to collect the hundreds of pieces your life and soul have broken into and to begin to rebuild yourself in a wiser and happier way. You are suffering. Your soul has been broken. It's possible that your present is full of sorrow and regret. You might be in pain, but merely having the certainty that you will be better in the future and that right now you already have what it takes to rebuild yourself is reason enough to motivate yourself to pick up the pieces of your soul and to take the first step in healing your wounds. You already have an ikigai.

Look for Your Ikigai

We have already established that at the least you already have one ikigai, a reason to pick up your pieces. But I encourage you to think about what other ikigais you can find. Analyze the meaning of your life up until now and evaluate whether you need to redefine it.

Sometimes, because we have good intentions, we mistakenly believe that our lives consist only of our children, partners, work, parents, or a long list of other things, but in reality, you must never allow all your life's responsibilities to revolve around a single meaning or a single motivation.

I have scores of ikigais! Every morning I get up just because I can. I have lost friends along life's journey, and I believe I am privileged to have the opportunity to continue living intensely. I get up for myself and for everything I enjoy doing. I get up for my wife and for my daughter, for my clients; to go for a stroll, to go for a bike ride, or to get lost skiing in the mountains; to use my talent to remove psychology from the confines of the lecture theater, to learn and teach, travel, smile, and enjoy a kiss and a hug. Each morning I get up for the bear hug I will give my daughter, to feel the sun on my skin, to get drenched in the rain, and to curl up with a good book. I could fill pages and pages with my ikigais. Some of them are more transcendental, others are more epic, and many of them are extremely mundane—but they all give meaning to my existence.

To begin this exercise, ask yourself about the meaning behind what you are doing, where you are living, your work, your partner, your lifestyle, and your vacations. I encourage you to go over each and every one of the aspects of your life and to ask yourself whether they contribute to your happiness. You might not believe me, but I practically always question the meaning of what I'm about to do. What meaning is there in my drinking a cup of coffee? What meaning is there in glancing at the phone while I'm driving? What meaning is there in attending a specific conference? What meaning is there in getting angry?

What meaning is there in writing a book? Every day, several times a day, I ask myself about the meaning of what I am about to do.

Do I Need to Pick Up the Pieces?

We might think that adversity has already passed, that the abuse has ended, and that time will help us put everything in its place, but I'm sorry to inform you that this idea is neither valid nor acceptable. The end of abuse doesn't mean the end of the problem—far from it. The end of an illness doesn't mean the end of the problem. The end of a job-seeking process doesn't mean the end of the problem. The truth is that abuse, suffering, and adversity leave a wound in your soul that requires your willpower and action to heal. If you don't pick up the pieces you will be allowing chance to heal you, which is as dangerous as allowing a chimpanzee to treat a broken leg. It might be capable of setting it straight and even putting it into a cast, but it definitely won't be a finely executed operation. The key here is in the more or less. Are you all right? More or less. But do you mean *more* or *less*? A repair process must be carried out correctly, with awareness. More or less is not good enough.

After adversity has been suffered, its aftereffects might persist over time, for as long as you or someone close to you allows it. Maybe you were mistreated, and maybe you managed to leave the home of your abusive parents, but as long as you do not deal with the past you will continue having nightmares, feeling insecure, comparing yourself with other people, and isolating yourself at the social level. Perhaps you suffered an addiction to a drug and you overcame it, but if you don't deal with your past, you will continue to live dominated by the fear of relapse, blaming yourself for all the pain you have caused and feeling insecure, running away from the phantoms of the past. Maybe you had a bad love affair, but if you don't learn from what happened and close that chapter, you won't be able to love again fully. Don't flee from your fears, your demons, or the monsters that pursue you. Stop, turn around, and look them squarely in the eye.

Pick Up Just the Pieces

Stoop down calmly and start picking up each and every one of the pieces of your soul. Do it conscientiously, taking your time, taking care not to pick up any dirt along with the pieces; don't get them confused. During a breakage we tend to acquire destructive habits, routines that seem helpful on the surface but that actually limit us, attitudes that are debilitating and toxic—ultimately, factors that may contaminate the process.

Suffering never comes on its own. When we suffer, we unwittingly open the door to toxic emotions, such as anger, rage, frustration, resentment, or pain. Sometimes we remain hooked on resentment, and we become bitter or ill. Other times we feel hate, which is understandable and even expected. When anger takes over, we are capable of causing a great deal of pain. Rage is a mix of hate and anger, but directed toward someone or something that locks us in a deadly embrace with our enemy. Frustration, in contrast, is a terrible emotion that mines our self-esteem and self-image. Sometimes these are the only emotions available to us, and they can become like bad habits. But now you can take one step further and give up those bad habits. When picking up the pieces of your broken soul, don't also carry with you those useless, toxic emotions. Pick up the pieces without impurities. Actively decide what you will and will not bring with you when starting this new chapter of your life.

Don't procrastinate by leaving behind any pieces to be picked up later, believing that will make the task easier. I know one person who picked up the pieces after a failed relationship. She picked them all up except one—the piece that, according to her, had caused all her suffering—the piece in which resided her idea of romantic love. I stooped down with her, and I picked it up with my hands. "Don't leave behind a single one," I said to her. "You might need to sand down some jagged edges around the piece that contains your idea of romantic love, but don't give up on falling in love again. Your duty now is to learn how to fall in love with the right person without renouncing anything along the way out of fear."

Collect all the pieces and clean them, so as to keep the final work—your masterpiece—clean. Eliminate the traces of tears, hate, and resentment. Leave victimism, incomprehension, and self-pity on the floor. Leave there each and every one of the toxic emotions that will limit you, all the half-baked conclusions you have drawn out of your pain and suffering, all the beliefs that have led you to the situation you now find yourself in. Make sure you have all the pieces you need. Sometimes we are in a hurry to rebuild ourselves, and we forget that rushing things is never a good idea. Take your time, digest what has happened, lay out the pieces, examine them, and make sure you didn't leave any behind. Put them into order and feel them. Each and every one of them has something to tell you.

Don't put them together any old way. Don't be clumsy or rough. Every piece fits in perfectly with the rest. Don't force the reconstruction; if something doesn't fit, there's a reason for it. Start over if you need to, but don't force a repair if you don't have everything ready and prepared.

You are not a prisoner of your fate, mistakes, or misfortunes. You are the creator of your own life, the leading actor. It is never too late to radically reorient your life toward the life you want, the one you are dreaming of, the one you need. But in order to achieve that you must start to rebuild your life, your suffering, and your present situation.

Don't forget

- Pick up the pieces in order to understand what happened, how you feel, and what you think. This is the first step in gaining a clear picture of what happened and understanding the mental representation that you have formed in relation to the event.

- Don't wait until you hit rock bottom to start picking up the pieces. If you want to feel better, you need to do something; you need to take action.

- The mere fact of knowing that you will be better in the future is already reason enough to start the process of repairing your life.

- The end of the problem doesn't mean the end of the suffering. Problems must be actively closed.

Sokei was kneeling. His hands were together, palm to palm, resting on his lap, as he examined in detail the seven fragments arranged in front of him.

Analyze the Situation

Up until now we have been gaining the necessary perspective. From a distance everything looks better, doesn't it? How easy it is to give advice to our friends, and how difficult it is to take it ourselves. For that same reason it's time to start thinking differently. So let's get started!

The first step in initiating a good process of repair is to understand what happened and to learn from the events. We look back at the past again and again, trying to understand what happened and why it happened, but when we try to analyze our experiences, we tend to do it wrong, in a distorted way, which doesn't help us to create a solid base on which to work. The truth is that when we review what happened, we tend to put some kind of filter in place. As if it were Instagram, our mind has a multitude of filters that are warm, cold, saturated, and blurry and applies them when we review the events and the suffering we experienced. In this way, with the use of a filter, we soften our pain, try to mitigate our memory, and tint it to make it seem prettier or darker.

Sometimes we distort our memories and even our reality, selectively forgetting important elements such as, for example, our own accountability or the unkind actions of someone we love. Other times we don't omit details, we add them. We embellish the truth; we add guilt, which distorts everything; or we add what we would have liked to have had happen.

But no matter what filter we apply, we will be making a mistake. If we soften what happened, it will be the wrong move because we will be introducing a distorting element into our analysis. Contemplating your pain in all its fullness might be difficult, but only in that way will you be able to identify the magnitude of the damage. Imagine for a moment that you had a minor car accident, nothing serious, but when you took the car to the mechanics they looked only on the outside and paid attention only to the material damage on the exterior. You will no doubt agree with me that this damage assessment is not sufficient because it ignores aspects as important as the engine or the steering. Well, the same happens when we are so afraid of suffering that we don't analyze our experience in depth.

So I suggest that you analyze your experiences and the events exactly as they happened, with no added elements and no edits—without softening things, without complicating things, and without filters. It is undoubtedly the case that, if you want to repair your life, you need to analyze what happened and to analyze it appropriately.

Analyzing?

We fear analyzing; we find it difficult to analyze our experiences, and when we do so, we do it wrong. Analyzing something consists of carrying out a detailed examination of the object of our analysis, for which we need to consider each one of its parts separately with the purpose of understanding in detail their characteristics, qualities, particularities, or composition. From this detailed examination we will be able to extract some correct conclusions and sound knowledge. Detailed analysis is the only strategy available to us to try to objectivize our subjectivity.

I am proposing that you gain perspective, and I will help you with some powerful questions, but before that, just let me show you what happens with our perspective when we are suffering. When we suffer, whether it is physically or psychologically, pain monopolizes all our attention and doesn't allow us to focus on anything else. When pain comes in the door, perspective goes out the window, taking with it our ability to reason properly, to analyze events, and to make good decisions. Without the necessary perspective we are doomed to suffer from day to day; we place ourselves in the hands of chance, and little by little we start to lose our capacity to live joyfully and to anticipate the hurdles of everyday life. You need to once again be the master of your emotions and your life—your dreams, actions, and perspective.

When you lose perspective, you become more vulnerable to everything around you, you stop living in the present, and you remain anchored in the past. Remembering the past is an act of the present. Our mind selects certain memories and highlights them or gives them meaning by bringing them to the present and mixing them up with nonexistent realities. What happened is undoubtedly important, but the way in which you interpret it might vary and, on occasion, completely change the meaning of what actually happened. Ultimately, your subjective experience of an event is more important than the event itself. What happened is not as important as your opinion about what happened, the mental representation you have created of what happened, and your own narrative.

Something happened to you (a disappointment, disillusionment, wound, or emotional pain) at some point in the past. Whether it was a few years ago or a few days ago, the fact is you experienced the event from a subjective point of view, which is why you interpreted it in a specific way based on your mood, your assessments, and your conclusions. In addition to that initial distortion, your memory of the past, which is a representation you make in the present about what happened, is also distorted. You reinterpret the memory of the events from the present, and in a way that is biased. Each time you remember what happened you transform what happened. Everything continues to be true, or at least it is to you, but without realizing it, you reorganize and reinterpret your memories, adding new meanings based on your current point of view and emotional state.

You do not relive the actual event but what you believe happened, and that biased evocation can either be of benefit or be a problem. Let's start with the bad so we can end on a good note. The problem lies in the fact that each time you relive what happened, you might be suffering over something you have modified, changed, accented, or distorted. However, the incredible benefit is that at any moment you can work on reinterpreting what happened in order to close that chapter and focus on a new stage that is a lot more positive and fruitful. And here is where our analysis of the events plays an important role. It's important to remember that when you were suffering, you might have made a partial analysis from a place of pain, jumped to conclusions, decided to take radical measures, or have been unable to see any other alternative. Now, if you take another look at the events with the perspective you now have, with the serenity of someone who sees their life as if it were a movie and with the safety afforded by distance, it is highly likely that you will transform that memory and value it in a different way, which is less painful, more constructive, more appropriate, and more realistic. So, let's start analyzing!

The Gaze of Others

We live facing outward and playing to the gallery too much, and sometimes we worry more about others' opinions than about reality itself. It's important for you to analyze your beliefs regarding others' views of what happened to you. But I don't care so much about their opinion or the opinion you believe they have. The key lies precisely in your own beliefs, in what you believe to be true. We infer the meaning behind a glance, we imagine behaviors, and we interpret attitudes based on our own beliefs more than on the actions of the people around us.

I remember the case of a couple where the husband died after a long and painful illness. The woman felt liberated because an end had finally come to the extremely intense and devastating suffering that the person she loved most had been through. In secret, she felt good because her suffering and that of her husband had ceased. But the moment her beloved died, there began a much more difficult kind of suffering, the pain that she believed she had to appear to be suffering in order to dispel the misgivings of the people around her—her husband's family, her children, her neighbors, and her friends. The punishment this poor woman inflicted on herself was as painful, if not more so, as the traumatic experience that she had been through.

So I advise that you ignore the gaze of others and stop trying to please people who might be judging you, that you review what you think others believe, and that you don't try to please the judgment of someone who dares to form an opinion based upon partial and inferred information.

Only you are aware of the full extent of what you have experienced and suffered. People who are empathetic and able to understand how you feel without making you feel judged must be welcomed; the rest must be ignored. You have suffered enough already as it is; don't make things any harder for yourself.

The Powerful Questions

I know that analyzing the past is no easy task, so we will do it together. If you like, I'll suggest an exercise that will act as a guiding thread. Start by choosing something that hurts, something from the past that caused you pain, disappointment, or adversity. Got it? Now I want you to formulate a few questions with me and—the most important part—I want you to respond to them for yourself, calmly and serenely. Take your time; there is no rush. I would rather you have a thoughtful and thorough answer than a quick but partial one. Are you ready?

What Happened?

Here we have the first question: What happened? It seems like a simple question, but don't be fooled for a second! Before rushing to answer, reflect for a few moments or a few days if necessary. I want you to ask yourself what happened, not what you think happened, what you would have liked to have happened, what you thought about what happened, or what your interpretation is of what happened. It's important that you focus on describing the facts. Try to narrate what happened without adding or removing anything, without interpretations, without bias. If the situation is still ongoing, then all the better because memory often distorts reality.

I suggest that you put it all in writing. Write a story, a detailed report on the events, past or current. Imagine that you are a UN envoy acting as an observer and that you are going to do a report on what is happening to you. It will seem like a hassle, but I urge you to put it in writing because in this way you will undo the tangle you have in your head; distill what is real from what has been added; and identify feelings, opinions, and actions. When you reread it, you will be able to correct and adjust your report to provide a more objective description of the facts.

Why Did It Happen?

Shall we move on to the next part of the report? What was the cause of the events? Why are you in this situation? Why are you suffering? I've always been more about fixing the leak than catching the drips. What I mean is, when faced with a problem we can do one of two things: either attack the consequences of the problem or attack the root of the problem. Whenever possible, it is preferable to attack the root of the problem, but in order to do this we need to properly identify it because if we don't, we will be investing our energy in the wrong place and will end up believing that none of our effort was worthwhile.

What lies behind the adversity? What is the origin of your suffering? I remember someone once telling me that the root of all their ills was their mother, when in reality it was that they didn't know how to make decisions. And another case in which the person believed that the source of all their suffering was their inability to manage conflict, when in reality it was down to their lack of self-esteem. Analyze what is causing your suffering, and do it in the form of an objective report—or at least as objective as possible. If you don't know where to start, please go to the powerful questions I've listed, and they will help you. But you must know that sometimes we can't be as objective as we need to. If this is your case, don't hesitate to look for the help of someone who can give you some objectivity about what happened.

Why Do We Lose Our Analytical Skills When Faced with Adversity?

When adversity enters our lives, an alarm signal is activated that places our bodies in a state of alert. The sympathetic nervous system is activated and causes a series of changes at the hormonal level that affect the way we think, act, and feel. The body becomes stressed, the levels of cortisol and adrenaline rise, and we lose the balance that is so necessary to be able to think clearly and keep everything in perspective. Our thought processes deteriorate, and we become avoidant. That way, adversity situates itself at the center of our life, claims all our attention, and prevents us from appreciating the little joys of everyday life.

But what happens when we turn adversity into a challenge? When we eliminate the threat component from our appraisals, our brain activates all our cognitive functions and puts them at the service of our mission: tackling a challenge. We enjoy challenges, we like bettering ourselves, and we like achieving things. In the face of a challenge we become excited and active, and we are capable of developing skills that we didn't know we had. Therefore, always keep in mind that when faced with adversity our thinking deteriorates, but when faced with a challenge our thinking always improves.

How Did You React?

Third section of the report! The time has come to analyze your reaction to adversity. Previously, we looked at different reactions toward adversity. I encourage you to review the earlier chapter "How Do We React When Facing Adversity?" and try to identify the way in which you responded when faced with the events.

If you are capable of identifying your response style, you'll have a much clearer understanding and you'll be in a better position to manage the pain and repair your life. If you are aware of the different reaction styles, you will be aware of your own reactions as they are occurring, and your management of adversity and in particular your reaction will be a lot more effective.

Why Did You React That Way?

Again, I suggest you search for the root cause. Always go back to the beginning and look at the root cause. This process should be like a kind of investigation. Go back in time to identify what was the starting point. For example, maybe you became ill because of your diet, not because of your partner.

When we look at the causes we need to take into consideration, it's easy to try to refute them, or it's hard to accept them. But, dear, be open-minded and investigate without guilt or shame. You have to go to the starting point.

Why do you believe you reacted that way? What led to that reaction from you? Sometimes we attribute the root to external causes—the context, the pressure we were under, or bad luck—but the truth is that the source of your reaction is always in you. Don't forget this: we are analyzing the source of your own reaction.

We always have the capacity to decide; we never lose it. Sometimes we anesthetize it or ignore it, like when we are drunk or use drugs in their various forms. Other times we are simply exhausted. That is where the problem resides. The moment we lose awareness of what is happening, there is nothing more to be done. We tend to lose the notion of time and our awareness in many situations, but if we are capable of foreseeing and anticipating these situations, we will greatly reduce the risks associated with the loss of awareness. If you notice, or others tell you, that you seem disconnected, absent, overly nervous, and so on, the moment has come to stop and reconnect with yourself.

There is only one solution in order to avoid losing perspective: thinking ahead. If you are becoming stressed, you need to hit the brakes. If you feel under pressure, you need to find a solution. If you feel like you are losing control, you need to stop.

The Day I Lost Control

I love the mountains; I live in the mountains, and I work in the mountains. When I'm not in a session with a client, skiing, or hiking, I am working with a company in the middle of the mountains or writing on my iPad in a field, on a hilltop, or near a stream.

If I go to the mountains to write, I tend to hike or run to my chosen spot; then I spend two to four hours writing; and then I run down hell-bent for leather to pick up my daughter from school or tend to some business in the office or for no reason at all, just because I love running.

When I go out to work in the mountains, I try to find steep slopes so that I can gain between six hundred and a thousand meters of incline over barely four or five kilometers. I remember once there was a steep and long slope; in fact, it was a red trail at a ski resort. I was a bit tired, but I was in a rush. I had been writing for too long. But it felt so good!

Anyway, the point is that I ran too fast, I lost control, and I ended up twisting my ankle. Fortunately, it was just a sprain.

It was nobody's fault but my own, and indeed, what happened is the kind of thing to be expected when you lose control. I could choose to believe that it was bad luck, that the stars aligned against me, or that I have to strengthen my ankle, but the truth is that I ran too far and spent all the energy in my quadriceps; my legs could barely hold me up, and instead of going down facing the slope, I started going sideways—and as a consequence made myself vulnerable to spraining an ankle.

I lost control, and it was obvious I would. I could have done many things before losing control, such as set out earlier, pace myself in the first part of my descent, call my wife and ask her to pick up my daughter, leave her in after-school hours, and a thousand other things, but the truth is that the main reason I suffered was because I lost control.

What Were the Consequences of the Adversity?

We've assessed the causes of adversity, but now it's time to assess their consequences. The time has come to analyze the repercussions that the event had on you, your life, and the people around you.

When I work with people with low self-esteem, I usually meet some resistance to following certain instructions. The problem with low self-esteem is that you don't believe you deserve joy and happiness, you place yourself at the bottom of the priority list, and in the end you do nothing for yourself. In these cases, I analyze the person's environment and I look for a motivation that is stronger than any they could imagine for themselves. There is always a child, partner, parent, friend, or pet that we could do something for, and that's my resource. After I have identified that motivation, I explain to my client with low self-esteem, in as much detail as possible, the repercussions there would be for the people around them in terms of their actions and nonactions. Your actions have consequences for you and for the people around you; don't forget that. So now it's time to analyze the consequences of that unpleasant moment. The time has come to ask yourself another question.

What Ideas Do You Have about How Life Should Be?

We often suffer because of the gap that exists between our expectations and reality. Throughout our existence we form an idea of what life should be like. The people around us transmit their beliefs about life, and we incorporate them without any filters.

Analyze your idea about life. How did you arrive at that idea? Life is not as it should be, it is the way it is, and here is where the larger part of our problems and everyday suffering originate. Break away from those ideas and preconceived notions, and instead focus on living fully and enjoying each moment. Don't wait for something to happen; enjoy what is actually happening. Don't spend your time evaluating what should have been; focus on what is. If you want to be happy, I encourage you to revise your expectations of life and to readjust them.

When reality doesn't fit in with your expectations, you can become depressed, angry, or stressed. Instead, it is preferable for you to revise and readjust your expectations. You can even make the decisions and changes you need in order to be happy.

What Did You Learn from the Events?

Let's move on to the last question of the report. Suffering is never in vain if we are able to learn something from it. This question is so important that it deserves an entire chapter—the next one, in fact. Before we get there, let me tell you about a couple of thoughts that I believe are important to consider in your analysis process.

Imagined Suffering

Sometimes we haven't suffered, but we have witnessed the suffering of people who are important to us, and this has a deep impact on us. We form a mental representation of what is wrong, of the source of suffering and pain based on the suffering of people around us. Based on this representation we avoid at all costs the source of that suffering, whether we are right about it or not. If we see important people in our lives suffer—such as your father suffering for work or for love—we will arrive at the conclusion that working is wrong, that loving is harmful.

So I encourage you to revise these notions of yours, these conclusions that you have drawn and the expectations and beliefs that guide your life, which you have incorporated based on what you have observed in other people, and that you put them through a good analysis process. Ultimately, you must revise your ideas and their origin and decide whether it makes sense to keep them as they are or whether they need an update.

Imagine you are walking through a forest where all kinds of vegetation and wildlife thrive. In fact, a forest is a paradise for the most keenly observant people (I love walking through the thick forests of the north-facing side of the Moixeró mountain in Catalonia). However, if you walk through a beautiful forest without departing from the path and with your head down, all you will see is stones, dirt, and mud. We are talking about the same landscape, the same place, with two people traveling along the same path, but one of them has their head down and the other one is looking up; one of them is looking at the ground and the other is looking all around. Depending on where you direct your gaze, you might see flowers or you might see stones.

Attitude is no more and no less than what I have just described. Decide which way to look, what you will focus on along the way, and what you will enjoy of the experience. Reality is what it is. Both travelers are in the same forest, but each will have a different experience based on their attitude. A negative attitude won't change reality, but it will filter it in such a way that we will pay selective attention and pick out only the elements that chime with our attitude. Likewise, a constructive attitude doesn't change reality, but it allows us to experience it fully and with more intensity, enriching our experience and facilitating opportunities to enjoy the possibilities that life offers us. This way, when faced with a problem, challenge, or adverse situation, it's better to keep a constructive attitude because it will provide you the tools you need to solve everyday problems, enabling a better predisposition and allowing you to learn something positive from the events.

Don't look the other way, telling yourself that you can do nothing to repair your life. Look directly at what happened, with your head held high. You have the power of analysis. You have the best brain of all the animals that live on this planet, so put it to work. Stand up tall in the face of adversity, look it square in the eye, and analyze it.

The sooner the better! Don't wait any longer; don't waste time because time does nothing but complicate things.

Don't forget

- Analyze what happened without filters—filters are of no help; in fact, the complete opposite is true.

- Don't stay anchored in the past; stop reliving what happened over and over.

- When we speak about suffering, the subjective experience of the fact is more important than the fact itself.

- Analyze the event again with the help of the suggested powerful questions, which will provide you the perspective you greatly need.

Sokei closed his eyes as he held each and every one of the seven fragments in his hands. "Why did you break? Was it your destiny? Was it my clumsiness? What is it you want to teach me?"

Learn from What Happened

None of our experiences is in vain if we are capable of learning from what happened to us and from the suffering and pain it caused us. But we won't be able to learn from what happened if we don't look back and review our experiences. I know it can sometimes seem painful. I know that looking at the past involves reliving what happened and bringing to mind things we found difficult to forget. I know it's easier to turn away, put things out of our mind, and pretend nothing happened. But believe me, denying, covering up, or hiding what happened will not help you in any way; it will do completely the opposite.

After going through a traumatic experience, we need to transform it to be able to understand and bear it. However, that transformation won't help you learn anything. You need to face the reality, one last time, with neither rose- nor dark-tinted glasses—reality exactly the way you experienced it. That will allow you to learn and grow. Stop running away from your past, stop hiding, stop pretending it's been and gone; turn around with your head held high and look at it one last time. The time has come to learn from what happened so that you won't have to go through the same suffering again.

Let's learn together from what happened to give it new meaning, to understand it, and to prevent it from happening again. You might believe that you have to go through this redefinition process on your own, but that's not the case. You have me, my experience, and all of my goodwill to guide you through this reconstruction.

Ordeal by Fire

Throughout history, in different parts of the world, we can find documentation and examples of different expiatory tests used to prove the innocence of a person regarding a specific act. In the Middle Ages, they were known as the ordeal by fire, which people were submitted to when accused of heresy and witchcraft.

When someone has done something wrong or they believe they have done something wrong, they need to go through an ordeal by fire, or by other means, in order to prove to others and to themselves that they are strong or that they are not guilty of what they are being accused of. The expiatory test, of whatever kind it is, and on whatever continent, usually consists of an act of extreme suffering that, if overcome, might act as a guarantee of innocence or redemption.

Now, what if the person submitting you to an expiatory test is yourself? What is the ordeal by fire you feel you must go through? Sometimes we are our own worst judge, and we put ourselves on trial and punish ourselves mercilessly based on a conclusion that more often than not was not properly thought through. We believe that we deserve to suffer because of an adverse situation that we are experiencing or that we believe we have caused. Without realizing it, we give ourselves over to suffering, we accept as normal a situation that has no reason to be the way it is, and we believe this will expiate us through a kind of self-inflicted punishment.

A New Meaning

Let's start by giving meaning to what happened. Our mind governs everything and yearns to be in control. We don't cope well with uncertainty or a lack of information or clarity. The mind attempts to provide a conceptual framework for whatever is happening to us, to put it into context. When an event doesn't have a high emotional intensity, our minds find it easy to come to grips with it, but when the emotional impact is high, our minds become blocked and don't function with clarity.

In order to understand how this process works, we need to talk about neuropsychology. The human mind is stored in a nervous system that governs every single process taking place in the body. The nervous system is the central computer, which controls absolutely everything that occurs in the body. It's in charge of regulating our heart rate, our breathing, and the rest of our basic vital functions. It also regulates our perception processes, which collect everything the world has to say to us. It allows us to walk, run, feel, love, dream, rest, jump, talk, be sad, and feel the joy of a loved one's kiss.

This computer that is the nervous system depends on some highly specialized cells to accurately perform its tasks. The basis of the precision and power of the brain are the neurons—cells that are capable of processing a vast quantity of complex information intercommunicated through a complex network of connections. The communication process between neurons, based on electricity and chemistry, bridges the synapses and is hugely important because it is ultimately responsible for what we feel, do, or think. Therefore, we can say that everything we experience has an effect on our nervous system, which leads to a series of consequences in the rest of the body—an inevitable and even necessary fact.

Now, the brain, which controls the entire body, needs to understand what is happening because if it doesn't, it becomes stressed, and when it becomes stressed, it sends a series of signals throughout the body that results in stressing the body. We have a natural survival impulse, which is why our brain tends to avoid stress, and the only way it can do this is by providing a specific conceptual framework for what we have experienced, even if it's an incorrect one.

Our nervous system quickly interprets stimuli and sometimes makes mistakes in its proposal of a conceptual framework, but it has no other choice; there is no alternative. The mind wants a framework of meaning and wants it fast, whether it is correct or not, because with a frame of reference the tension of uncertainty disappears and the mind can again relax and calmly occupy itself with other tasks, having eliminated the source of stress that the mind and body were suffering. The mind doesn't want us to be happy; it wants us to stay alive and away from danger—it actually wants to protect us.

Let's review the conceptual framework that you are offering to your mind and, as a consequence, to your body. Analyze your conceptual framework, the way in which you interpret what happened to you, what you experienced, and what you suffered—because your conceptual framework will determine what you perceive. Remember that the brain controls it all, including our senses. If I believe that I am not good enough, I will selectively see things that confirm my perception. When I filter what I perceive, I will have a partial vision of the world, but nevertheless the emotions I feel will be real.

Any emotion we feel has an origin, a detonator, a stimulus that provokes it. Sometimes we are not aware of what is triggering an emotion in us, and we mistakenly identify the stimulus that is causing the emotion, or we might even believe that the emotion arises out of nowhere, erratically. But we are mistaken. Emotions are born from our perceptions and also from our internal dialogue. What is your internal dialogue like? What do you say to yourself? Do you see yourself as not good enough? Do you see yourself as weak? Are you shouldering the blame? If that's the case, then you need to know that you are punishing yourself for no reason. The memory of our suffering alone is enough to cause us more suffering. I encourage you to look at your past, one last time, to analyze the event with the perspective you now have so you can finally close that chapter once and for all.

The Expectation of Suffering

Similar to what happens with memory, the expectation of suffering causes us to suffer from the outset. That's why it's vitally important for you to analyze the event and extract a meaningful lesson, a conclusion, and a new perspective.

I encourage you to change your expectations about the future; these have been conditioned by your past suffering. Abandon the idea that you will not be able to overcome adversity, and exchange it for the certainty that you will be capable of overcoming adversity and misfortune because you already have all the resources you need.

Maybe you suffered in love and decided never to love again; maybe you were betrayed by a friend and decided never to trust anyone again. Review your conclusions, let go of your distorted predictions born from pain, and allow the future to surprise you.

Start with Self-Care

Sometimes we abuse ourselves without being aware of it. We are often our own worst judge. We distort the event through the lens of a negative self-image. We punish ourselves with unrealistic demands, forgive in others what we are not able to forgive in ourselves, treat ourselves badly, don't love ourselves, and try to pass the ordeal by fire to atone for our guilt. Enough is enough! The time has come to break the cycle. Start by being kind to yourself, finding self-acceptance, and allowing yourself the chance to think and talk about what happened.

With the frenetic pace of modern life and the focus that is placed on individualism and unbridled competition, the person must invent their own survival guide after experiencing a traumatic event. It's a shame, but often we can't count on anyone else. Being isolated, we might miss a great opportunity to gain perspective, and we end up doing whatever is in our power to create frameworks of meaning that provide an understanding of our experiences and what actions we need to take to overcome them.

Pay special attention to your inner narratives; to the kind of language you use in your inner dialogue; to the questions you ask yourself; to the origin and the cause of what has happened to you; and to what you must understand, learn, and do to overcome adversity. Not many people will understand you. Few people will want to listen to you, and few people will lend you a hand. But it's almost better that way because they will hardly be able to truly put themselves in your shoes. Most people are too quick to judge, have their own prejudices about what happened, and issue partial and unjustified opinions that can cause more harm than good. To manage adversity we don't need a crowd, so be selective and choose who can truly empathize.

I'll Never Be Able to Forget What Happened

It's not about forgetting what happened, nor is it about remembering it. It's about managing the memories of what happened, to forgive, to archive, and to learn. Don't reminisce endlessly because each time we recall the event, we relive all the negative emotions associated with it. When we remember what happened, we feel the same emotions again, even if they are less intense. In other words, when we remember sad experiences, we will become sad.

Continually recalling the past leaves behind a nasty sediment: the fear of suffering again. So in order to manage the expected fear of suffering again we must process what happened. The past does not determine our future; it's an influence and only that. Fortunately, we can close one chapter to open another. Your past explains many things, but it doesn't have the capacity to determine your whole existence. What's more, if you pay too much attention to your past, it might contaminate the future that awaits you. I am an expert when it comes to discovering people's potential—their virtues and talents—and helping them to write their own destiny; to do that I don't need anything from their past. I have never been interested in the past. There is nothing we can do to change it. When someone wants to work through the past with me, the first thing I do is to define a plan for the future, a work plan. We always fix our gaze on the future, we set goals, and we start working to achieve them.

Learn to let go of the past even if you experienced trauma and even if you suffered immensely. It doesn't matter. Learn from what happened and bring that period to a close. If you live anchored in the past, you won't allow it to be over. Nothing can be done to change the past, so the best thing is to manage your memories. Rid yourself of the negative memories to make space to start a new life.

Change your focus from the past to the present. In order to do so you need to bring your past to a close. Empty your backpack; free yourself of the weight of your past. Throughout our lives we gradually metamorphose, grow, and evolve, so it might be the case that who you become in the future will have nothing to do with who you were in the past.

Who Cares about Your Past?

I don't care in the least. Don't tell me your life story; it doesn't contribute anything to me or to you. You shouldn't care about it either. And I'm not the only one who doesn't care about your past. The people around are not the least bit interested in your past either. Don't tell everyone at the first opportunity what kind of life you lived, all the things you suffered, or the hardships you had to endure. None of the people around you, if they truly love and respect you, should care about your past.

Recently, a charming and lovely man with many virtues told me, just five minutes after we'd met, that he had been a drug addict. "And why do you care?" I replied. "I don't give a fig about that, and neither should you." All I could see was a wonderful person who was still carrying with him the heavy burden of his past. "Why are you telling me that you were an addict?" I asked, to which he replied, "I just thought you should know."

He wasn't a client of mine, and he did not even know what my job was. "But who cares who you were a few years ago?" I responded. "Did I tell you that I once had whooping cough? That when I was little they used to tie me to a chair at school? That once I nearly choked on a popsicle?"

What difference does our past make? Don't you think we should focus on enjoying the present and imagining a future that awakens in us joy and enthusiasm?

Reinterpret your past. You are wiser now, so if you look back, you will be able to reinterpret it with a different perspective. Redefine it. Put your past in order and understand it because we distort our memories. Put your experiences into context. Your context now is different; don't feel unsafe. What happened in the past no longer exists.

Try to understand the events from a fresh perspective. Think of your past as a vague memory that has become distorted over time, reconstructed by your fears and your desires, embellished with brush-strokes of melodramatic tragedy. Your past, a heavy burden that will be with you until the day you die—or not. Carrying your past is like carrying a huge backpack full of stones that prevents you from walking freely. But to walk through life all you need is a bit of water and food, a dream, and a destination—and, in a pinch, you can probably do without a destination.

Forgive Others and Forgive Yourself; Forget and File Away

Forget, forgive, and file away. Keep the pleasant memories, and leave out the rest. Do whatever you like, but stop facing toward the past. Stop remembering, thinking about, or living in the past. If there is anyone who shouldn't care about your past in the slightest, it's you. It is possible to go back and reinterpret the past with the perspective that you now have, but, trust me, there is not much point. Instead of investing time in stirring up vague memories, distorted images, and confusing facts mixed with opinions and confabulations, it's better to dedicate your energy to designing your future.

Be careful with the sentences people have issued about you. Look at what you have internalized. The fact that people have said something doesn't mean it's true. People go around dictating sentences as if they were experts in psychology and forensic analysis, but the truth is that more often than not, they make mistakes. The problem doesn't reside in what people say but in what you believe.

Recognize Yourself, Rebuild Yourself, and Give Yourself a Chance

The past is gone. It explains a few things about your life, but it is nothing more than an influence—don't forget that. There is no reason your past should condition your whole life. Of course, if you are determined to continue to carry it with you, that will be the case, but believe me, it makes no sense for you to do so. There is no basis for the idea that your past dictates your present or your future.

What matters is not who you have been but who you want to be. You might not feel free to be who you truly are in your neighborhood, city, or town. Well, get the hell out of that stifling environment! Leave! Don't think twice. New homes have saved lives. Find a place where you can be reborn; where you can reconnect with your true essence; and where you can build your life free of prejudices, phantoms, and stereotypes—a place where you feel strong. "You're running away," is what cowards will say. They couldn't be more mistaken. It's not running away; it's an intelligent decision. You were born where you were born as a fruit of the purest chance. What sense is there in continuing to be anchored to a place where you don't fit in? Everything is yet to be discovered, experienced, redefined. Connect with your emotional strength and start writing your own destiny.

Your conclusion, after this whole process, should not be fear. Learn positive things, not negative ones. Don't learn that you are powerless. Learn that you have the power to rebuild yourself. Realize that through experiencing a traumatic past, you have become wiser.

Review Any Routines or Habits You Have Adopted

Sometimes we do weird things to prove to ourselves that we are strong, that we were able to overcome a situation, and that we won't make the same mistakes again. I remember the case of a woman who got a new tattoo for each month spent without doing drugs, using the money she had saved, to demonstrate that she had once again succeeded. There was also the case of a young man who, having escaped from his aggressor by running fast, now trained obsessively on the treadmill because he believed his safety depended on his sprinting abilities.

Be careful with the routines you adopt because they might seem positive on the surface but are not necessarily so, especially when taken to the extreme, as in the examples above. If you need to, carry out a symbolic act that reminds you of how strong you have been but never of how much you have suffered. Your routines need to be positive and demonstrate your ability to repair yourself. If you use rituals as reinforcement, make sure you find them inspiring and not victimizing.

The most important conclusion lies in the answer to the following question: What have I learned from what happened to me? You might learn many things, but before incorporating anything as a lesson, make sure that what you incorporate is realistic—meaning that it is free of bias and distortion.

Take positive lessons from the events because your conclusions will become incorporated into your inner dialogue and will go on to form a part of your life's frame of reference. Your internal dialogue is born from your beliefs, your thought process, your upbringing, the people around you, and what you have learned. And this conceptual framework governs your life, emotions, desires, dreams, decisions, and behavior. Review your conceptual framework—your ideas, beliefs, and opinions—which we often mistake for the facts—because that will be what gives meaning to your life and to the events you experience. You need to acquire internal resources, learn new skills, and connect with your emotional strength, and that is something you can achieve only by learning from what happened.

Don't forget

- What happened was not in vain if you are able
  to extract a meaningful lesson from it.

- You are probably your own worst judge. Stop
  judging yourself so harshly, and start to understand
  yourself from a place of love and compassion.

- Review the meaning you gave to what you experienced,
  and update it with a new perspective in a new context.

- Let bygones be bygones, learn from what
  happened, and bring that chapter to a close.

- When you reach a conclusion about what lesson
  you must learn, make sure it is realistic.

- Your conclusions and your lessons learned go on to form
  a part of your life as the official version of the facts.

Sokei dried his tears. He opened his eyes, and a shy smile came to his lips. At last he felt strong; at last he felt confident enough to start repairing the bowl. "What happened in the past does not matter," he said to himself. "What truly matters is what will happen from now on."

Connect with Your Emotional Strength

I have a clear objective: for you to feel strong. And there is no better way to feel strong than to connect with your emotional strength. You have everything you need to be happy. You have everything you need to be able to repair yourself. All you need to do is connect with your emotional strength.

Nature is wise and has provided us resources for our daily survival, for repairing ourselves in the face of adversity, and for healing our physical and emotional wounds. In the same way that physical strength will allow you to take on greater challenges and recover from exertion, emotional strength is the key to overcoming adversity. But let's start at the beginning. What is emotional strength?

Emotional strength is the set of skills, resources, techniques, and competencies that—when learned, understood, and mastered—make us stronger and allow us to be happy and manage adversity. Each time we learn a technique or incorporate a skill into our repertoire, we feel stronger and more confident because we become aware that we have another resource available and that we are capable of generating resources for facing up to everyday challenges. So, in conclusion, our emotional strength comes from the confidence that we will be able to face up to the challenges that appear along the way. I know that you feel insecure, but it's like a kind of faith—have faith in you. I'm giving you all the resources you need in this book, and in part 3 you will find real cases that will help you to gain this faith.

There's no reason to think that you won't be able to overcome adversity. In the same way, there's no reason to think that you will overcome adversity. The only things that we know are that we have to face adversity head-on and that you are learning a lot of resources that you will be able to apply in your life.

So, focus in the now, and let's work with confidence that you are doing okay.

It is therefore extremely advisable that you connect with your emotional strength and that you make use of all its power in order to live in accordance with your needs and desires.

Anything Not Dealt with Will Accumulate

Most people have problems caused by an accumulation of minor conflicts, unresolved frustrations, and unrealistic expectations that have not been met. A low level of emotional strength will of course be a handicap when trying to keep up with the demands of daily life. The difference between a person who is confident and happy and someone who is not resides in their emotional strength.

Emotional strength is the set of resources available to us when tackling these challenges and problems. Don't forget: most people suffer because of their accumulation of minor problems rather than because of a single, big incident of adversity.

Do We All Have the Same Emotional Strength?

Again I will use the analogy of physical strength to illustrate an important concept in connection with emotional strength. Just as not all people have the same physical strength, not all of us have the same emotional strength, but we do have enough emotional strength to be able to respond to the challenges that life brings.

People differ both in their degrees of strength and in their mastery of different kinds of strength. Some people are good at making decisions, but they need to work on their ability to manage conflict. Others are good at identifying their emotional state and that of those around them but have serious difficulties when it comes to persevering in the face of adversity.

We all have different strengths because we are born with them by default. The problem is that as we grow up, we disconnect from some of them and we forget them. Logically, if we don't make good decisions, we will find it harder to be happy. If we're not capable of loving or allowing others to love us, we will not be happy. If we're not able to feel enthusiasm, we will not be happy. Depending on our upbringing and on how life has treated us, we might have developed our different emotional strengths unevenly. However, we need to achieve a good grade in each and every one of them. It's no use having an A+ in some of them and an F in others, which is why it's worth investing some time and effort in increasing and leveling out our competence and mastery of each strength.

But don't worry. The important thing is not what strengths you have and which ones you are missing; the fact is, you can have them all because they can all be learned. Again, taking physical strength as an analogy, I will tell you that you can train each and every one of the emotional strengths in the same way as you can increase your physical strength.

Emotional Strengths Can Be Learned

The most important part of the concept of emotional strength is that the different emotional strengths can be learned, assimilated, and integrated, which is why happiness has stopped being an ethereal concept and moved on to being something that can be worked on in what we call *didactic* (i.e., teachable) units.

We can learn to make decisions. In essence it's not all that complicated; all you need is to learn to analyze the context of the decision; identify the different alternatives available to you; evaluate their evolution in the short, medium, and long term; prioritize them; and make the decision. Of course, you must pay attention to the distorted effect that can be caused by fear, desire, and weakness. See, it's not that difficult, is it? And by using the same strategy, you can learn to analyze people, identify your emotional state, self-motivate, or manage adversity (which is the objective of this book).

Thanks to emotional strength, we are undergoing a revolution in the field of psychology because when we break it down into didactic units, we break the paradigm of dependency on a therapist, and we adopt a new paradigm in which we provide the clients practical tools. We make sure the clients can apply them and end the therapeutic relationship, reassuring them of the confidence and independence that will be afforded through the mastery of what they have learned. In other words, we shift the paradigm of the therapeutic relationship in which the clients must visit their psychotherapists in order to feel well to a new therapeutic process in which we analyze which emotional strengths must be developed. We create a detailed work plan where the "patient" (who no longer needs to be that patient) learns the different emotional strengths needed, assimilates them, and is capable of transferring them to different situations; at that moment the therapeutic relationship ends. They might need to visit the psychotherapist again further down the line, but it will not be for the same issue that has been worked on already.

So I encourage you to connect with your emotional strength because in it you will find the best resource to be able to overcome adversity and heal the wounds in your soul.

You May Need to Develop One or More Strengths

Emotional strength protects and facilitates happiness because it is a mechanism of psychological adaptation. In the same way that the mechanisms of physiological adaptation allow us to survive in a wide range of environments, the mechanisms of psychological adaptation allow us to adapt to a wide spectrum of situations, problems, and adversity. I suggest that we look at some of the emotional strengths so that you can assess how they might have influenced, determined, and even caused the situation in which you find yourself.

I'll start with the ability to understand, identify, and manage the whole emotional spectrum. Some people live disconnected from their emotions, even going so far as to deny them, thus ignoring the critical role they play in regulating a person's own conduct and that of society.

You might need to connect with your emotions, identify them, and give them a suitable name. You might need to learn to identify the emotional state of people around you and how to manage that. You might need to learn to manage the expression of your emotions. When you understand your own emotions and those of people around you, you will be able to identify the moment when your partner begins to disconnect, when your work begins to feel overwhelming, or when the sadness you are feeling is no longer normal and has turned into depression—for which you will need to see a specialist in plenty of time before this terrible illness ends up affecting every area of your life.

You might need to work on your ability to persevere in the face of adversity—another emotional strength. You might be mistaking stubbornness for intelligent perseverance, leading you to ignore the signs around you telling you that you need to make some decisions or change the course of what you are doing. But you might also need to gain in perseverance in order to get one step ahead of the adversity you are struggling against.

Perhaps the source of all your problems lies in your terribly low self-esteem, which is blocking you and causing you to punish yourself. Perhaps you don't feel capable of fighting to achieve your goals, or you adopt a submissive and passive attitude that will lead you directly toward adversity. Again, balanced self-esteem is the best emotional strength because it will allow you to relate to others in the world as equals.

You might need to learn to have good relationships with people. You might relate to others in a passive or an aggressive style, or you might be projecting your fears or be unable to trust because of a past experience that has not been properly processed. And what if the root of your problems lies in the way in which you make decisions? We make plenty of decisions, but we are inefficient when we do so. This emotional strength needs to be reviewed because a vast number of our problems depend on it.

With a good dose of emotional strength you will be able to learn to analyze people better, identify toxic people, and consolidate quality relationships; this will prevent a great deal of rifts and conflict. Thanks to emotional strength you will be able to contextualize what happens to you, choosing what passes into the fragile fortress of self-esteem and separating it from anything that has little importance. And, even better, emotional strength is the set of strengths that will allow you to do all this, strengths that can be easily learned and incorporated in the form of techniques and strategies.

There are many emotional strengths; in the table below I list only the top nineteen. However, I encourage you to review whether the adversity you are experiencing could be in connection to the lack of any of the following emotional strengths.

Emotional Strengths

- Incorporate emotions into your life.

- Correctly interpret your emotional state.

- Give a name to your emotions.

- Learn to identify the emotional state of the people around you.

- Manage your emotions and their expression.

- Persevere in achieving your objectives.

- Manage adversity.

- Balance your self-esteem.

- Don't depend on external motivation.

- Gain in responsibility.

- Choose a positive attitude.

- Choose your own path.

- Seek quality relationships.

- Develop your ability to communicate better.

- Cooperate with other people; develop compassion.

- Manage conflict.

- Live by objectives and make decisions in accordance.

- Ask for help if you need it.

- Enjoy the opportunities that life brings.

The Three Pillars of Emotional Strength

Emotional strength allows you to gain some distance so as to be in a better position to analyze events with a certain amount of perspective. Thus, instead of reacting, we will learn to contextualize in such a way that, when thinking differently—when thinking better—our response will be better and more appropriate in the short, medium, and long term. Finally, when we feel confident and capable, we will be able to take action and ensure that the oft-repeated utterance "I already know the theory, but applying it is the difficult part" becomes obsolete and ancient history. Change is in our hands, and emotional strength will allow us to execute it. What's more, emotional strength is a facilitator and protector of happiness.

But let's analyze in a bit more detail what each phase consists of. You will see that in part 3 of the book I structure each practical case study following the three phases, which I will explain below. It's that simple: there are just three phases.

Take a Step Back

We'll start by taking a step back to be able to see ourselves through new eyes. In some cases, the view from a distance can be revealing. In order to gain that distance we can ask ourselves one simple question: What is the meaning of what I am doing? Ask yourself this question for each and every one of your actions and decisions. Don't carry on with business as usual, don't continue to exist in a state of inertia, and don't keep running away. Stop and gain perspective to be able to choose the correct direction.

I conduct sessions with my clients while walking in the Pyrenees. I tend to use different paths based on the time available and the weather, but in all of them there tends to be a nice walk through the forest that ends up leading us to an area with great views. At the beginning of our walk all we can see is trees, and our gaze is focused on the path we are walking on. Our minds are focused on the path and lack all perspective. Beyond the trees there is a vast panoramic view of the entire valley of La Cerdanya, but we can't see it. The lush forest at the foot of the Cadí mountain doesn't allow us to see beyond the beautiful tall conifers that form it. The valley is always there, but we're not aware of it. Now, when we go higher, the forest gives way to high grasslands, and suddenly the beautiful and majestic view of the entire valley surrounded by stunning mountains appears before us. Well, that is exactly what perspective consists of—elevating yourself above the tree line to have a more general panoramic view that allows you to see things from a different angle.

Think Differently

The second step of the method is somewhat more complex because we have to learn to think differently, to think better. The objective is to learn to think without limitations or distortions, correctly analyzing what happens to us, what we believe happens to us, and what we want to happen to us. We tend to mix fear, desire, and complacency into our own thinking process—distorting it—and we become biased.

If we review our thinking process, we will realize that, quite possibly, we have some overarching notions that govern our lives but that might well be mistaken or inaccurate. We need to review and update our mental and conceptual frameworks to adjust them to reality in a more constructive way.

The world is not the way it is but the way we think it is. To prove this, I propose a little exercise. Imagine for a moment that you can't find your wallet. The observable fact is that you can't find your wallet. You've looked for it in the drawer where you always put it, and it's not there. This is the first time you haven't been able to find it, and you know, in all certainty, that the previous day you used it to pay for some shopping. Several things might come to mind. You might think that the wallet is in the car and that when you go back to get it, you'll find it there. You might also think that your partner took it to buy some things online, as he or she often does. But you might also think it was stolen at the shopping center without you realizing it, that you have lost it, or that you left it behind at the shop where you went to buy some things. The fact is always the same: the wallet is not in the drawer where it should be, but depending on your interpretation, your reality will be different. Based on what you believe, you might either feel a great deal of anxiety or not. You might cancel all your credit cards, report a theft to the police, or go to bed secure in the belief that your wallet is in the car.

In the same way that your belief about your wallet is going to condition your behavior, your beliefs about the large subjects of life—such as love, work, or family—might condition your life, your emotional well-being, and your mental health. Clearly then, the need to learn to think differently is a pressing one. We must contextualize and analyze without preconceived notions, bias, or constraints. If we are capable of reformulating our notions and identifying when we are distorting reality based on fear, desire, complacency, and false beliefs, we will have taken a huge step toward emotional freedom.

Think of your mind as a computer. Isn't it true that every so often you have to update the operating system on your computer?

Well, in the same way, you have to keep updating your notions, thoughts, and beliefs in order to adapt them to reality. The truth is that thinking properly has a lot more implications than you might believe. You might think properly, wonderfully, and in a well-adjusted and balanced way, but you still have to periodically update your beliefs because even if they are well adjusted, the world changes, and if you don't keep up with the times, you will become obsolete and suffer because of it.

Take Action

Finally, we must take action. I know it's hard and that we need courage. Knowledge that is not applied has no use. Taking the first step is the hardest part, but after you take it you won't stop.

Many people won't take action because of their low self-esteem. Despite knowing what it is that they have to do, they are incapable of doing it for themselves. We are often capable of giving advice to other people about their task, and, what's more, we do it well. We are clear on what they have to do and on how and when they should do it, but we are incapable of taking action for ourselves. Do you know why? Because we don't place value in ourselves. We are at the bottom of a priority list; we believe that we are not important and that being happy is not worth the trouble of doing anything to achieve it.

At other times we don't take action because we are afraid. Fear is normal. I am afraid. I have many fears. Fear in itself is not bad because it ensures our survival. In fact, our brain wants us to stay alive, but it doesn't care whether we are happy or not. Being afraid is normal, but thanks to one of your most important emotional strengths, you will be capable of transforming that fear into action. Courage is the emotional strength that will allow you to gain that impulse you need in order to overcome your fears.

To be able to take action all we need is an action plan, a work plan, the plan that will give you power, self-confidence, and direction. So, the best way to take action is to try to follow the plan that you have designed. It's important that you strive to turn good intentions into a plan so that taking action is easier. Again, if something is not applied, it's not useful in any way. There's no point in planning if we don't execute. Taking action is the culmination of a process of change that you are experiencing. Taking action is the necessary and indispensable requirement to be able to heal your emotional wounds.

The Key to Overcoming Adversity

We face adversity in a fundamental way every day, several times a day. If you have emotional strength, you will be able to confidently rise to the challenges of everyday life. Emotional strength will allow you to live with enthusiasm, take life by the horns, and decide your own destiny.

Emotional strength is undoubtedly your best ally. That is why I like to refer to emotional strength as an element that facilitates and protects happiness. When you invest in yourself, when you feed your soul, when you train your emotional strength, you feel different, and you are capable of seeing life with a new perspective. When you develop your emotional strength you feel stronger, and consequently, you value life in a different frame of mind.

Based on your appraisals of what happens to you, as well as your experience and background, you will be able to analyze and tackle adversity in a better way. When you develop your emotional strength, you won't leap to conclusions, you will no longer adopt a fatalistic attitude, and you won't fall into despondency or self-pity. When you know you are strong, you will analyze everything that has happened, and you will make better decisions, which will put you in a better position to cope with and manage life and adversity on a day-to-day basis.

Feel strong! You have everything you need to overcome any challenge or adversity that life brings. What's more, you have already done the hardest part. Until now you have analyzed the events, understood what happened to you, and learned from the experience. The time has come to repair what was broken because it no longer makes sense for it to stay that way.

Don't Isolate Yourself

Don't live through this alone; don't live through it in silence. Don't be ashamed. Sometimes we isolate ourselves to protect ourselves. We believe that if we don't allow anyone in, no one will be able to hurt us, but when we isolate ourselves, we are also depriving ourselves of positive and healing experiences. Isolating yourself is never the solution. When you do, you become weak, and that same weakness causes the sensation that you will not be able to overcome the adversity that is demanding the best version of yourself—all your emotional strength, your resources, and abilities. Don't build a wall to protect yourself because the only thing it will do will be to isolate you.

Don't forget

- You have everything you need to rebuild your life, but it will not be activated until you connect with your emotional strength.

- Emotional strength is the key to be able to overcome adversity and life's challenges.

- Each strength can be learned and developed.

- Every adversity we suffer might be leading to the emotional strengths that we need to develop.

- In order to overcome adversity you need to take a step back and take action.

Sokei could not help smiling; he knew he was not just repairing a broken piece. His task was much more important because what he was doing was restoring the beautiful bowl.

Repair What Is Broken

Repairing or Patching Up?

There is a difference between repairing and patching up. Patching up is a fast, haphazard solution with which we try to regain the functionality of what has been broken without attending to any other criteria. But when you repair something, you know that love and the lesson learned are fused together to create a new piece, a new life that is much stronger and more beautiful than the previous one.

Let's repair what has been broken, but let's do it focusing on what we want, not on what we have suffered or experienced. The time has come to look ahead, to lift our heads high and set an objective. The key here lies in the idea that as we repair ourselves, we start to define our future, our objectives, and our goals, facing our fears with bravery. Repairing what is broken is an exercise of courage because it means accepting that you might break again.

The Fear of Relapse

There is the possibility that the same suffering might repeat itself—the chance is always there—but you know that however many times you break, you will always be able to repair yourself again. You have the gift of rebuilding yourself—the capacity to regenerate, to learn, and to re-emerge from the ashes stronger and wiser, and this is the best of motivations that you can find to gain the confidence you need.

The Fifteen Actions That Will Heal Your Emotional Wound

Below, I propose fifteen actions that you will have to carry out in order to repair yourself. Follow every single step, one by one. Don't skip any because it's important that you erect a building with solid foundations that will allow you to rebuild your reality.

1. Don't Flee from Adversity

Adversity will always be there waiting for you, begging for your attention, asking you to manage it; it will not disappear until you tend to it. We often believe that time heals everything, and we imagine that, at some point, as if by magic, our problems will be solved. You can believe that, of course, but my best advice is that—in the absence of a miracle—you make sure you actively cope with adversity.

Don't deny what is evident, underestimate what has happened, or trivialize the consequences of adversity. The first step in rebuilding yourself is acceptance. Stop running away; turn around and look adversity in the face with the confidence of someone who has decided to put an end to a history of suffering and pain. Stop running away. Stop distracting yourself; don't try to deny what is obvious. The time has come to puff out your chest and manage adversity. We'll go straight to the root of the problem; we'll take into account the emotions associated with adversity, but above all we'll devise a plan of action to learn from what happened and emerge stronger from the setback we have suffered.

2. Don't Isolate Yourself

When faced with a problem we tend to isolate ourselves, which means we lose the perspective we so much need. Speak to your friends and the people you trust because they will be able to offer a new point of view that will expand your horizons.

Adversity is a heavy load that is best shared. You might believe that you're alone, but analyze whether this is really true. I remember the case of someone who was deeply affected by his daughter's illness. His wife, upon learning that their daughter was ill and had the same disease as her husband because it was hereditary, disappeared without a trace, leaving them to fend for themselves. My dear friend fell into a terrible depression, fed in equal measure by the cruel way his wife abandoned him, the guilt of knowing that he had transmitted the illness, and the suffering of his little princess. He felt alone, and he retreated into himself. He focused on his daughter and disconnected from everyone else. He soon reached saturation point but nevertheless continued in his isolation, not wanting to see anyone. He felt lonely, but he actually had a lot of people who were willing and able to help. One day I sent him a message with the link of an association for people who were suffering the same disease he and his daughter were. Reluctantly, he made an appointment at the organization's headquarters. It was, no doubt, the best decision he made during that crisis because at the association he met people with the same problem; he stopped feeling lonely and started to repair his extremely adverse situation.

3. Don't Fall into Helplessness

We sometimes believe there is nothing we can do, and we forget that there is always a way. When we fall into helplessness, our judgment becomes clouded, we find it harder to think creatively, and the potential solutions available to us seem to shrink to a single alternative: to flee.

You might be feeling lost and overwhelmed, but, as when you get lost in the mountains, the one thing you should not do is to sit still waiting for a miracle to happen. There is always a way out, even if it is not obvious, easy, or fast. Never stop searching for it.

When you feel helpless you can tell yourself that you are an explorer, and you can do what explorers do. Take a walk, relaxed, knowing that you have all that you need to deal with adversity. It's only hidden, so remember successful experiences that you have already had. Soon you will find some resources to go on again powerfully.

4. Adversity Brings Change

It might be a sudden change in your circumstances; sometimes it might even be permanent. Come to terms with it, and work on understanding the new situation, the new reality in which you find yourself. Look for information, advice, and the help of a professional. But always update your frame of reference. Don't attempt to continue doing the same thing you were doing before encountering the adverse situation. Your reality has changed, and you need to bring your way of dealing with this new reality up to date. You can't continue to do the same thing, which doesn't mean that you have to renounce your desires. The best option, always, is to adjust your interests, tastes, and priorities to the new situation, taking into account the constraints that have been brought about by the consequences of the adversity.

5. Accept That You Are Facing a Challenge

Challenges must be treated as such. If you are capable of transforming a problem into a challenge, you will be activating all your emotional strength, and you will be putting it at the service of your needs. A challenge is always something positive and stimulating, whereas a problem is something negative that leads us to become blocked. Whatever the situation, you need to respond to the adversity and that response must be correct. It is in your power, so take action.

6. Keep Your Eyes on the Long Term

Many of the problems that we have to face or the adversity that we have to manage entail making decisions that are uncomfortable in the short term but that will no doubt have positive consequences in the medium and long terms. Define how you would like to see yourself in the future; it will be the best of motivations. Visualize yourself in a motivating and inspiring future. What has happened doesn't matter—what you might do in the future is much more important, but to achieve it, first you must heal your wounds. Free yourself of the weight of guilt; unload your backpack, and walk unburdened toward the better version of yourself.

7. Focus Your Energy on the Short Term

The management of adversity requires immediate action. Take the first steps; make the first decisions instead of being paralyzed. It's possible that you are disoriented, but to paraphrase the Cheshire cat in *Alice in Wonderland*, when you don't know where you are going, it doesn't matter which way you go. Take action, make decisions, study the situation, learn, and act. Do something; achieve small triumphs and celebrate them. Be proud of your achievements. Every great journey starts with a first step, so take it sooner rather than later. Just explore and try to do things with no fear of being wrong. To move is better than to be stuck; it doesn't matter where you are going—the key here is not to stay where you are blocked.

8. Change and Accept

As seen earlier, the Serenity Prayer reminds us that we have power over our minds but not over outside events. Realize this, and you will find strength. Ultimately, we need to learn to distinguish between what we can control and what we can't. Face up to reality when it can be changed, but if it can't be, the wisest thing you can do is to accept what happened in order to start building a new chapter.

I remember the case of a person who had an accident that affected the mobility of his hand. For a long time he believed he would recover mobility. He tried all sorts of therapies and went to see doctors, healers, and shamans; he refused to accept that he had lost mobility in his hand, and for that reason he couldn't adapt his life to his new needs. But one fine day he realized that he needed to change his strategy—that it might be possible that one day he would recover some mobility in his hand but that in actual fact the probability of this occurring was low. He realized that he had to start to adapt his life to his new circumstances and accept that it was likely that his hand would remain exactly as it was. At that precise moment, after accepting what couldn't be changed, he focused all his efforts on what could be changed, which resulted in a substantial improvement in his quality of life.

Adaptation Factors

When facing misfortune or adversity, some people develop a series of adaptation factors. When they run out of money, some people steal. When they have suffered, they might cruelly inflict pain on others. When they have been hungry, they might eat excessively to acquire reserves in case there is scarcity again. When they have been jobless, they might work without much thought just to avoid being fired again.

Although these adaptation factors are good on the surface, in reality they are not because they allow only for an immediate adaptation. They don't truly allow us to work on what has happened, they curb growth and resilience, they don't allow us to analyze everything that can be done, and they rush us into action without reflection.

I propose that you analyze what behaviors you are adopting to compensate for your suffering. Review them, and assess whether it makes sense to continue these behaviors.

9. Analyze Your Inner Dialogue

Do this because it's possible that your inner dialogue doesn't inspire you to feel confident in your own abilities. What do you say to yourself? How do you see adversity? There is no reason you should be unable to cope with adversity, but until you believe and internalize that, it is possible that you might be unable to cope. If you send yourself messages that make you feel insecure, then you will not be able to rebuild yourself.

Stop and analyze the way in which you speak to yourself, what inspires you, and the influence it has on the way you think, do, and feel. Think of it as living with an imaginary twin brother or sister who is with you all day, talking to you all the time, and telling you what you are thinking. What does he say to you? Try this little exercise, and you will realize how important the way in which you communicate with yourself is.

10. Transmit Serenity and Peace

If you have people who depend on you, convey a sense of serenity and tranquility because it's possible you might need to spend some time on working to solve adversity. Also, remember that your children, for example, don't have all the information you have, nor do they know what is going on in your head, nor can they predict what will happen. So, in order to manage their anxiety levels, it's best for them to have some information and see that you are serene in working on managing adversity. The best way to transmit serenity is to feel it. Relax. I know it might seem complicated, but try to relax and be calm. There are many resources to relax yourself. You can start by making some time for exercise, being outdoors, taking baths, and having massages; all will help you. But there are many more options like listening to music, meditating, or reading. Try to remember what helps you to relax, and try to explore new ways to relax. The best strategy to achieve this is to know that you are working on repairing yourself and your life.

11. Make Your Own Decisions

Sometimes we give up on things for the sake of other people, and this renunciation involves a passive attitude and an offloading of responsibilities. To resolve adversity absolutely necessitates—whether we like it or not—making decisions, some of them uncomfortable. My best advice is for you to be the one who makes the decisions that will affect your life. In my practice, I have been able to see how, in many cases, adversity was caused by decisions that were not made.

In part 3 I describe a decision-making process in detail, but the main essence is that you review your decision to determine what roles are played by fear, desire, and complacency because these elements might be conditioning the result of your actions.

12. Cultivate Optimism

Don't mistake a positive frame of mind for a naive one; one has nothing to do with the other. Naive people might believe that everything will be resolved magically, whereas optimists know that they can be a part of the solution to the problem and that they are capable of responding to adversity they suffer along the way. Pessimism and dejection might knock on your door, maybe more than once. Pessimism is always on the lookout, waiting for any opportunity to sneak into your life and take control over your thoughts. Invite pessimism to leave, to leave you alone, and to find another place to settle.

Be rational about what is happening; in reality, you don't know what the future will be like. You don't have the gift of predicting it, so don't even try. But if you do, don't opt for a negative and pessimistic view of the future. At any rate, it's always more encouraging to predict an optimistic future.

13. Treat Adversity as an Opportunity to Learn and to Reorient Your Life

Sometimes adversity is the fruit of bad luck, but sometimes it's the consequence of a series of actions, notions, or ideas. Perhaps the time has come to reconsider the way you are living and to make some decisions. In daily life we don't realize that we adopt an endless array of toxic behaviors, we take too many unnecessary risks, and we make a whole lot of bad decisions. If we manage to live in a more conscious way, we will be eliminating a large part of this senselessness. This is exactly where the key lies—in analyzing what sense there is in what you are doing, thinking, and feeling. It's possible that the adversity you are experiencing might have been the first of the signs that you need to review the senseless elements in your life and get the ball rolling in redirecting it.

14. Find an Outlet for Your Emotions

This is necessary for offloading tension and recovering strength. Regenerate yourself because the war against adversity can't be won in a single battle. Create opportunities to experience positive emotions because these will allow you to regenerate and recover the perspective you need. Manage guilt if it appears. Whether you are guilty of what happened or didn't happen is not as important as whether you are willing to manage what happened and to learn from it. Write, talk, or draw, but don't keep what you are feeling to yourself. The battle might be long, so tackle it bit by bit and schedule time for rest and leisure. Seek positive emotions that compensate for the negative emotions you are feeling.

15. Don't Take Any Unnecessary Risks

Be prudent. Sometimes we become blinded in our attempts to come out of adversity, and we take the first option that comes our way. We grasp at straws. When you are suffering, any way out seems fine. But don't be deceived. Remember, you are in a situation of deficiency in which emotions run high. Your capacity to reason might have been affected, which is why it's important that you carefully assess each decision that you make. Reflect and analyze, but, in the same way, when necessary you must believe in yourself and be brave—though not reckless. Sometimes there is no other choice than to take a risk. But be careful to distinguish between when you are rushing things and when you need to take a risk.

These are the fifteen steps that will allow you to repair your wounds and overcome adversity. In part 3 you will be able to see them applied to a range of real-life cases.

A Question of Patience

Collecting all your pieces and repairing yourself after so much suffering will not be a matter of a single day; you are going to have to persevere. The same holds for diets: we cannot lose weight in one day. Nor do we train to run a marathon in one day, and nobody builds a house in one day. Great achievements take time, so check your expectations and develop your patience.

The Structure of Pain Explains the Damage Caused

The actual aggression that you have suffered determines the number of pieces that you will have to repair. Imagine it's 7 a.m., and you have just gotten up. You have made yourself a cup of coffee, and you are on your way to the living room to have breakfast in peace while you read the newspaper. When you are about to put your cup down on the table, you miscalculate, and it falls on the floor, where the parquet flooring protects the cup from breaking. Now imagine the same scene, but this time the cup falls on cold stone floor tiles. Lastly, imagine you trip, and the cup flies several meters, splashing its contents across the sofa, bouncing off the wall at head level, and landing on the stone floor. Despite the initial explanation of the event being the same (I dropped my cup of coffee), the result and consequences are completely different, which is why the kind of repair needed will be different in each case. In the first scenario, it will be enough to mop up the coffee that spilled on the floor; in the second case I will need to mop up the coffee, too, but I will have to add a broken cup to my collection; and in the third case I will have to also add a wall that will need to be repainted and a sofa that will need cleaning.

So listen to the advice that people might offer you, but feel free to ignore it because the structure of what you have experienced might involve you needing to repair yourself in a different way than the person who, with the best of intentions, is giving you advice.

Don't Cover Up the Pain

We seem to think that people who suffer are weak. Society judges the broken people and marks them with a huge X, as if they were incapable of freeing themselves from their suffering. Those who suffer are singled out by a multitude of people who are also suffering but don't want to show it. When you point out others' pain, and you brand it as weakness, it's as if you are convincing yourself of your own greatness, but this is not the case.

Don't hide your pain; don't be ashamed to feel it. You are not weak. On the contrary, you are stronger than those who judge you as faint-hearted. Stop ignoring something that is clamoring for your attention. I know it's easier to distract yourself, and I know you have many resources available to look elsewhere, but you need to stop and avoid covering up your pain. You need to go back to the root and repair what is broken.

We feel incomplete and go around in search of what we are lacking, preoccupied by its absence. How wrong we are! The problem is that we try to alleviate that pain with possessions, achievement, success, and status, but until we accept a paradigm shift, we won't stop suffering. Our nature is not to one day be complete but to keep on making decisions, to connect with our emotional strength, and to enjoy the present moment.

Don't forget

- Don't flee from adversity.

- Don't isolate yourself.

- Don't fall into helplessness.

- Adversity means change.

- Come to terms with the fact that you are facing a challenge.

- Keep your eyes on the long term.

- Focus your energy on the short term.

- Change and accept.

- Analyze your inner dialogue.

- Transmit serenity and peace.

- Make your own decisions.

- Cultivate optimism.

- Treat adversity as an opportunity for learning.

- Find an outlet for your emotions.

- Don't take any unnecessary risks.

Sokei ran his fingers along each and every one of the scars of his bowl, paths of pure gold that showed the value of his repaired creation.

Make Your Scars Beautiful

My body is covered in scars. I've lost count of how many stitches I've received. I can't say what each scar corresponds to, but I'm not ashamed of any of them. Each and every one of my scars is part of a story of accident or neglect. I have learned from each one. Some of them are more than thirty years old, others just a few years.

I remember one of those scars, on my head. Until recently it was a private scar, but now, with my hair gradually thinning, it has come into view. The origin of the scar goes back to a kids' game at summer camp. Every night we played at hunting the flag of the other team. Spread out across the mountain, we had to avoid at all costs being exposed by an opponent's flashlight. All I can remember is I saw a kid from the rival team and literally leapt into the void, ending up lying unconscious on the ground. I don't know how long I was there. The truth is that with that scar I learned that I shouldn't leap with so much impulse without knowing what the terrain was like where I was going to land. That conclusion didn't come on its own; instead, I honed it over time. Every day, for as long as the treatment lasted, I had time to think about it and learn a lesson.

I have another important scar, a large one that spans a third of my back. This one I got when I fell off my bike, not many years ago. I remember my wife treating it as my daughter slept in her cot.

Every day, as she dressed the wound, I analyzed what had happened. In a nutshell, it was because I decided to go out on my bike without wearing my prescription sunglasses, and without them I can't see, simple as that. And one unfortunate day I overestimated my abilities and decided to ride in the mountains without wearing them, and what happened is what you would expect—I fell.

With each and every one of my scars I have learned something. Suffering has never been in vain; I have always taken advantage of it to grow. But I don't only have scars on my body; I also have them on my heart. Psychotherapists like me are people, too; what's more, we are people with a special sensitivity and a certificate. Well, maybe some of us have the certificate but lack the sensitivity. The point is that I—like any other common mortal—have suffered.

I am a sensitive and empathetic person, which is a huge advantage in my profession, but I am fertile ground where suffering takes root at will. I have suffered as a child, a teenager, a young man, and a grownup. I have suffered in my private, family, and professional lives. I have suffered with each and every one of my clients who are suffering, and I have suffered some dramatic turns in my life, perhaps the same ones you have.

But I can say that each and every one of those scars in my soul has healed. It has not been by chance. I myself have been the main author of the cure. I have cleaned, sanitized, disinfected, and healed the wounds. In the same way that you need to be thorough when disinfecting a physical wound if you don't want it to become infected, so it is with emotional wounds.

I have often had to open the wound more, sanitize it deeply, analyze the reason it was hurting, and withstand the necessary burn from the rubbing alcohol, which heals but also stings. On one occasion, I wasn't able to heal myself, and I received the invaluable help of Núria, my partner. She gave me perspective, gently blowing on the sting of the disinfectant she had to apply; she was the one who gave me a hand as my heart gradually scarred over.

Nor do I feel ashamed of the scars on my soul. None of them has been in vain. All of them have taught me something I needed to learn. However, to learn from pain we need a good dose of humility, the proper analysis, a certain amount of distance, and a lot of perspective.

If you tell me that right now you don't have a single scar on your body or soul, I will have to accuse you of the worst of all lies—that of self-deception. You might believe you have cleaned the wound properly, that the infection was inevitable, or that time will heal it just like that. But I invite you to review those false beliefs and not to leave your health and healing to chance.

Perhaps now, having learned what the ancient art of kintsugi consists of, is a good moment to check your scars and wounds. If a wound from the past continues to hurt, it's because it has not yet healed, so I'm sorry, but you still have work to do. Shall we get started with healing old wounds that have yet to scar over?

Perhaps you have suffered a great deal in the past. Maybe, for a long time, pain has been with you day and night. I know what it is to spend a night wide awake from the pain that is oppressing your soul. I know what it is like to have to smile when the lump in your throat refuses to disappear. I know what it is to have to dust yourself off and get back in the ring with the best of attitudes.

There are kinds of pain that sneak into your world and won't allow you to think, sleep, or live. What can we do when experiencing that level of pain?

When everything hurts, the best thing you can do is build. Build. Create. You need a project to manage the pain of the past and even transform it into beautiful memories. When you achieve a certain amount of perspective, when you have managed to gain enough emotional distance, that's the moment when you will be capable of reinterpreting what has happened to you and to make your scars beautiful.

Focus on building a new reality—your own. Abandon the armor that's holding you back, shed your old and dried-out skin, allow the past to be the past, and start to build a new reality where you choose the life you want to live and how you want to see yourself. Building that new reality will require effort, but doing it couldn't be more necessary.

An Extraordinary Person

Not long ago I met Lary León. We were both speaking at the prestigious conference on well-being and happiness organized by the Spanish magazine *Objetivo Bienestar*. I must confess I fell in love with her energy, her vitality, her example, and especially her capacity to build the reality she wanted.

Lary was born with no arms and only one leg. She was not a "normal" person. But is anyone normal? The truth is that the outside world persistently tries to normalize us and often achieves it. But who is normal? People who do normal things? Lary does lots of normal things. She brushes her hair, puts on makeup, writes, and even directs a TV channel for media group Fundación Atresmedia. She gets up in the morning and goes to work. She even eats like anyone else. So, if Lary does normal things, is she a normal person? Of course not! I continue to believe and affirm that despite all the effort she places on classifying herself as normal, Lary is an extraordinary person who has transcended her reality and has been able to create a new reality that was far better than the one awaiting her. She built that new reality when she was a young child. What's more, that new reality allowed her to gain the necessary perspective to reinterpret her old reality. Lary likes to think that she is the reincarnation of a mermaid—that her arms are fins and her leg is the tail.

Have I mentioned that we take life far too seriously? Play with humor because that will help you conserve energy for what really matters. Never lose your sense of humor because it will allow you to maintain the necessary distance to be able to analyze what happens with a certain amount of perspective.

Dear Lary, I give thanks for the day our paths crossed because, like you, I believe that you are in this world to touch and change the lives of everyone you encounter.

You Are No Longer an Abandoned Child

But let's get back to the abandoned child. If this is your case, you need to know that you have the key to help thousands and thousands of children who are growing up in a situation of emotional neglect. You are no longer an abandoned child. Those days are over. What's more, you were never an abandoned child, but a child who had to connect with their emotional strength to be able to grow up in a healthy and balanced way.

Your history is not that of a child but of a hero. You are a clear example of resilience and autonomy, and this is the image of yourself you must hold. You have had a series of experiences that have allowed you to overcome your circumstances and develop your best virtues. It's in adversity when we see who we really are and who we can one day become. Imagine how many people you can help with your testimony.

And what happens if you are a woman who was abused? Build yourself a new reality. You are no longer a weak woman abused by a despicable egomaniac. You are a free woman who has been able to withstand the worst of mistreatments, who has overcome them, and who has emerged stronger from an extremely difficult situation.

What if you are someone who has been affected by an illness or a disability? Well then, you are a person who has been affected by an illness or a disability, neither a patient nor an invalid. You are much more than your illness. However, until you believe it, you won't be able to transcend the reality that is limiting you in order to be able to create a new reality, the one that will allow you to grow and live fully.

There are as many worlds as there are people. Each person creates their own reality. We create our own scenario, and we give meaning to reality based on our fears and interests. But sometimes, some people are determined to force us to live in their world, and we believe it and live there, not knowing we can build our own world.

Don't forget that "the" world doesn't exist. What exists is your world. My world. Her world. Until we are capable of building our world, the world of everyone, we won't be able to understand each other.

When Memories Hurt

Perhaps you have built a new reality in which you can be yourself, the real person you are, rather than the one others have made you believe you are. I know that building it was not without effort for you. At last you have rebuilt your life and healed your pain. Your wound has scarred over and has left you a beautiful reminder of your emotional strength.

Your life transpires seemingly normally until suddenly you receive an input from your past, from that life that was limiting and conditioning you. You're chugging along, and, with some degree of effort, your life feels normal until suddenly a vision of someone or something triggers a memory and causes you to relive the painful reality you experienced. Something might resurface that you believed was buried for good. Sometimes, memories come back to haunt us without asking for permission. A glance, a photograph, a conversation, or a gesture can transport us to that time when we suffered so much. Sometimes a flash of what we experienced revisits us, a cruel and harsh reality that you suffered for a long time. That's all right; take your time to process it, interpret it, and see it back to the door. Don't be scared of it. Don't avoid it. Don't believe that you have had a setback. Our brain perceives things that we're not aware of. Our brain never stops working and often has many processes running in parallel.

At some point you might find yourself face-to-face with the person who made you suffer. Be prepared because it can happen at any time. It's normal to feel nervous about the vision of the abuser who tortured us, but just as we might feel that tension, we know that we have been capable of escaping from their realm of influence and that they can no longer hurt us.

When you feel insecure, look at your scars because they will give you the confidence you need. You have not been working tirelessly on yourself just to allow an old wound to open all over again now. When you come face-to-face with the person who inflicted pain on you, don't hang your head or lower your gaze; don't cross to the other side of the street. Just keep walking with your head held high, with the confidence of someone who has been able to overcome adversity, pick up their own pieces, and put themselves back together. Walk with your back straight and your chest puffed out. Yours is the honor of survival, and nobody can take that away from you. And when you walk past that person, ignore them or greet them. Do whatever you feel like, but do it knowing that you are not doing anything wrong and that, whatever you do, you are no longer the same person that they once knew.

Your breakage has left a trace, no doubt, and some things might still reverberate on occasion. But the fact that you still remember or see certain people should not make you feel weaker.

Make Your Scar Beautiful

Don't feel ashamed of your scar. Don't cover it up. Don't hide it. On the contrary, make it beautiful because in it you have the best proof of your strength. The masters of kintsugi don't hide the scars on the works that come to them for repair. What's more, not only do they not have the slightest interest in hiding them but they highlight them with precious materials such as gold or silver.

A ceramic piece that has broken is living proof of its fragility. A ceramic piece that has been repaired, concealing the way it has been put back together, is a piece that is hiding all its value—the value that resides in its capacity to rebuild itself after adversity. The masters of kintsugi are aware of this, and they want to respect the main value of a reconstructed piece—its scar. Sometimes scars are inevitable, but it's up to you to treat them with respect and make them beautiful.

Our beautiful scars give us the necessary strength to keep on living in the world that we love, in the world we have chosen and built. Sometimes we might feel lost, disillusioned, lacking courage, or simply tired. It's understandable. Building a new reality is not easy, especially when you are exhausted from the pain you have been suffering.

Don't forget that in your scar, in the proof of your strength, you will find the anchoring you so need when in dire circumstances. Find in your beautified scar the impulse you need, the energy that characterizes you, and the courage you have always had.

Transform Your Pain into Education

I am pleased to tell you that, when talking about adversity, not all consequences are negative. You have been hurt. I know that you didn't choose it and that you did nothing to deserve it. It makes no difference; the important part is that you have suffered. You have overcome the pain and have been able to rebuild your life—not without effort. I understand.

Your wound has had some fallout, but not all of it needs to be negative. You have been hurt, and that allows you to be more sensitive and better understand other people who have been hurt. I encourage you to transform your pain into education because you are able to give lessons—a lot of lessons. You broke and you rebuilt yourself; your scars are the best example to follow. You are a true example of survival. Sometimes we look at people who have survived huge dramas and difficulties, and, when comparing ourselves to them, we look tiny.

The "Superhero" Mountaineer

I remember once participating in a conference on psychology and sports performance. As I waited my turn, I listened carefully to the testimony of a mountaineer who had overcome innumerable problems and major adversity. During the dinner after the conference, one of the delegates was chatting animatedly with another: "So-and-so is a superhero; look at how many problems he has overcome—he is a true example of survival."

His claim was partially true, but I have to say I strongly disagreed. So-and-so had freely chosen to expose himself to adversity, being sound of mind. To me, he was not a valid example of survival. I couldn't be clearer. This was for two main reasons. First, his adventure was prepared, planned, and organized voluntarily, which is why it was completely artificial, and it was still a laboratory situation that was more or less under control. So-and-so, having prepared, planned, and equipped himself, faced the adversity that he himself had chosen. In the same way, whenever he wanted, he could have abandoned his struggle without greater consequences than the annoyance of some of his sponsors. The second reason is that this renowned mountaineer, for all his motivational words, was not doing anything other than turning foreseeable consequences into adversity. Getting caught in a snowstorm on the mountain is not adversity; it's something that is more than foreseeable. Likewise, not being able to sleep at over five thousand meters above sea level is not a problem; it's more than foreseeable and expected, an uncomfortable consequence of a scheduled adventure. Thus, if we confuse the uncomfortable consequences of our intentional actions for adversity, we are making a grave mistake.

Stop seeing yourself as small and believing that you cannot contribute anything to those around you. We are all here for a reason. We all have to give meaning to our lives. But let's not forget that life can have more than one meaning, or even several different motivations, at different stages of our life. What is the meaning of your suffering? Well, off the top of my head, there are at least two different ones. To begin with, your suffering has made you stronger but not insensitive. Now you are better prepared to live. You know yourself better, you have grown, and you have more resources. Not only are you stronger but right now you are capable of teaching other people to be strong like you.

We don't need to touch fire to know that we can burn. Likewise, we don't need to go through adversity to gain in strength. Your experience is a valuable resource for those around you in the first place because you can provide them tools to learn to identify what might happen to them even before it happens. You have a lot to give, such as teaching others to identify the warning signs that something is going awry before things become even more complicated. But you can also teach them to manage, face up to, and recover from adversity, acting as a real-life example that demonstrates that you don't need to be a superhero to be able to overcome the greatest of pains.

You know that there is a future and that there is hope. You are a clear and real example. I encourage you to embellish your scars, giving lessons of resilience and the kind of survival that is true, real, and available to us in our day-to-day lives.

Transform Your Pain into Art

Some people claim that art is born from the sublimation of the pain suffered by the artist. We could make a long list of artists who have found in art a way to overcome their pain, from Frida Kahlo to Salvador Dalí. Art, whatever its expression, is an excellent tool to express what words cannot. When we are immersed in a creative process, we gain the necessary distance to be able to adopt a new perspective that allows us to analyze the pain that we are suffering.

The Thursday Workshop

In 2009, Núria, my wife, designed and programmed some "therapeutic workshops" for people affected by Parkinson's. The objective was simply to provide tools to manage the illness.

I remember with special fondness a meeting with my wife where we were working on an issue that we were both worried about: the inability to express emotions felt by some of the participants. On average they were about seventy years old.

Many of the participants were men, so try to imagine a seventy-year-old man attempting to express his innermost emotions in front of a group of about twenty people. Impossible!

But far from giving up on our endeavor and aware of the importance of giving a name to the emotions we are feeling, Núria had a brilliant idea: "I know!" she said. "If they can't talk about their emotions, they should draw them." No sooner said than done. That same day we showed up with a twenty-meter roll of paper, paintbrushes, and paints ready to revolutionize, once again, the famous Thursday workshop. We covered all the walls in paper, laid out plates with different colored paints, and handed out different-sized paintbrushes throughout the room.

The result was truly exciting. The various participants became absorbed in the task and gave an artistic outlet to their pain, their emotions, and their preoccupations. Someone painted a black spiral, someone else painted the sea, and someone else simply mixed colors.

The artistic quality, the proportions, or the beauty of the images didn't matter in the least. What we truly cared about was that it was a pretext to place the different emotions felt by the participants on the table, based on what they had painted.

But what if I'm not an artist? Don't tell me you've even asked yourself this question. Shame on you! You do realize that you are issuing a negative judgment on your capabilities and virtues? What is art? There is nothing looser than the definition of what constitutes art. If you don't believe me, look no further than works of contemporary, classic, or street art. Art is as varied and diverse as the artist can be. Paint, draw, sew, design, or create. I don't care what discipline you choose. Draw without worrying about the proportions or whether it's pretty or ugly. Make abstract art!

Write. Writing is one of the most therapeutic exercises you can undertake, for a number of reasons. To begin with, when you write, you are putting into order all your ideas, preoccupations, and troubles. Writing frees up the soul and the mind. When we put onto paper what we have in our heads and hearts, the offloading effect is immediate.

Build. Go to the beach with a bucket and spade, and start making sand sculptures. Draw and paint mandalas, borrow your children's Legos; start building something, whatever it is. Go to an arts-and-crafts store and buy anything you like. Learn crochet. Design jewelry. Create necklaces and bracelets of glass beads and give them to your friends. Artistically trim the hedge in the garden. Plant a bed in the garden with colorful flowers. Do a puzzle or make a collage. Spend time baking cakes and making desserts, origami, or marquetry. Do some sculpture, design clothes, make your own dresses, or dye T-shirts. Anything will do! Do whatever you feel like, as long as you find it stimulating and fulfilling.

Find an outlet for your pain through artistic expression. Transform your pain into something beautiful. Embellish your scars so that every time you look at them you feel stronger and more confident.

Don't forget

- What matters is not whether you have suffered but that you have been able to overcome.

- A scar reminds us that we have been strong.

- You can learn something from all your scars and transform it into something you can teach other people who are suffering like you did.

- Transform your pain into art.

- Build a new reality.

- Don't be ashamed of your scars.

Part Three

Bīzen-yakī: The Art of Persevering

We are creatures of habit. We are not at ease with our incredible capacity to adapt, to create the circumstances that we want, to live our own dreams, or to regenerate and rebuild ourselves. We would rather live anchored in a habit that we have internalized in the deepest parts of our soul and that has become a routine, an anchor in the middle of a sea of uncertainty, or a lighthouse that warns of the dangers of the unknown sea, a habit that provides us apparent safety when faced with the belief that we are fragile and limited.

We create our reality based on what we think. Our brains—our most precious resource, our best ally—process millions of pieces of data continuously without us being conscious of it, and, based on that data, dictate actions, emotions, decisions, fantasies, dreams, desires, and fears. Our brains make decisions for us, thousands per day, without our consent. These decisions will determine our reality, our lives, and our futures. And we are not even aware of it.

We think based on what we perceive. Our senses capture all the information they want and send it to our brains to be processed and administrated, for our brains to make the best possible decisions. Yes, you read correctly, I said "all the information they want." No, it's not a slip of the pen from me. Our senses capture what they want, or rather what our brains want them to.

Selective attention is a well-researched perception process. We have millions of stimuli in front of us, and because we cannot process them all, our brains provide a hierarchy of priorities to our senses.

First we give preference to everything that has to do with our safety, and after we know that we have a minimum of safety guaranteed, we continue to filter what we perceive based on our interests, priorities, beliefs, fears, and desires. If you have just grown a beard, you will pay selective attention to men with beards; if you are pregnant, you will see more pregnant women in the street; if you want to buy a new car, you will keep seeing the brand you want around town; if you think we've come into this world to suffer, all you will do throughout life is see suffering souls; if you believe you should be a self-sacrificing person, you will keep seeing opportunities for self-sacrifice, and so on—we could fill page after page with a long list of examples.

Our perception is not naive, not at all. It requires a framework of priorities, but based on that it dedicates itself to choosing what fits in best with the idea we have of reality, what our brains will appreciate the most and what they think will be most useful to us. Our perception is a compliant and submissive process that will filter reality to please the big boss, the organ that controls it all—the brain, which rules supreme. Our perception is not neutral, creative, or autonomous. It is no more and no less than an instrument at the service of our brains and their interests.

We also think based on how we feel. Suddenly we feel a chill down our spine, and our brains (again, our brains) decide to transform that chill into fear, and that fear, that feeling that has emerged out of a physical sensation, will provide a frame of reference for our own perception and for our thoughts. What used to be shadows in the night have now become terrible threats; what used to be normal sounds around the house turn into potential dangers; where there used to be nothing but peace, now there is only fear and apprehension.

Everything we feel is born out of a stimulus that causes it, despite the fact that we often don't even know what it was that awakened that emotion that took hold of our peace and quiet. Sometimes it's an internal trigger. All it takes is a slight earache or bout of indigestion to put us in a bad mood. Sometimes it can be a chemical element; a small dose of caffeine will be enough to cause unease and anxiety. Let's not forget that our minds reside in brains that in turn reside in bodies that bathe them with blood and nurture them.

Sometimes it's enough to imagine something in order to awaken the most intense emotion, as happens in the case of jealousy in a partner. In reality, we don't know what our partner might or might not be doing, but imagining them with another person is enough to throw us right off balance. So, as you might have guessed, we also think based on what we imagine. Sometimes our brains mix up what is imagined with what is real. And that happens with other things. We tend to mix up fact with opinion, fantasy with prediction, and fear with a real threat.

Sometimes we are determined to ignore the alarm signals that our brains send us, and we are determined to trick them at all costs, making them believe that what we desire, what we want, what we imagine, or what we fear is what will in fact happen. Whether it is real makes no difference. After we have given our brains a frame of reference, they will start to think in a way that is in agreement with our beliefs, imaginations, or priorities.

We think based on what we believe. If you believe you have been put here to suffer, you will experience suffering. If you think you can't do anything to live better, you'll become stagnated. Your beliefs feed your decisions, your fears, and your desires. Your beliefs limit you. And consider the irony of the situation: your beliefs are born in the most ill-founded way imaginable. Throughout your life you incorporate sentences, beliefs, and scraps of reality that end up configuring your own world, your own reality. In many cases, these beliefs are inherited from our parents and created from conversations between friends where beer is flowing; we get them from commercial movies or novels embellished with large doses of fantasy. In other words, our beliefs have little basis in fact, scant reliability, and a lack of rigor that is less than ideal.

We are what we think, so we must review all our beliefs and everything we take for granted if we want to effect change in our lives.

Your beliefs will determine and condition your actions, perceptions, decisions, priorities, and ultimately your life. Shall we review your beliefs about reality together? I suggest you ask yourself a series of questions: What is it that hurts so much? What is it that weighs you down? And, most importantly, why are you still carrying the weight of the past? We need to hit rock bottom to feel the need to incorporate change into our lives. We don't change until pain becomes unbearable. We suffer and suffer, or we distract and evade ourselves, with the sole purpose of avoiding making decisions or taking action to change.

Many people change only when they can no longer bear the pain. In fact, pain is simply an indicator that something isn't working. Pain tells us that we have to make some kind of change in our lives, because, if we don't, they will become more complicated. In the same way that physical pain tells you that you need to stop and check that joint, rest that muscle, or clean that wound, emotional pain is telling you that you need to stop and analyze what is happening in your life, with the people around you, or with your objectives.

However, too often we try to hide, deny, or ignore the pain. It seems that if we don't pay attention to it, it doesn't exist, and we ignore the facts that pain is necessary in order to live, that it is adaptive, and that it allows us to grow. We would rather take a painkiller than make a decision. We prefer to distract ourselves than to have to come face-to-face with our lives.

At other times we remain anchored in pain, and we are not capable of overcoming it, of moving on, or of learning from it. We don't know how to interpret pain; we don't know its message, and we decide to live with it.

What is your heavy load? Perhaps it hasn't been heavy enough for you to realize you need to leave it behind? Forgive yourself and free yourself from the dead weight that prevents you from flying. I know it's not easy to change the way in which we see the world and relate to it, but nothing good or extraordinary is ever easy. Good things require effort, brave decisions, and focused action.

As you have been able to see, your thoughts can change your life. But don't think it's anything mystical or magical; in the end we ourselves and our thoughts are nothing but biochemistry and electricity. Each neuron we have is interconnected with other neurons, which in turn are connected to different nerves that reach each and every part of our body. Each neuron generates a connection across a synapse that ends up influencing our bodies, our perceptions, our emotions, and our actions.

You might have become accustomed to heaviness, to pain, to feeling broken, to treading barefoot on your own shards, and to endlessly punishing yourself for something you believed you did wrong, but there are other realities, believe me—there are other options. I encourage you to imagine a new life, a life based on easing your pain, a fulfilling life in which you will be stronger. After imagining it you will get to work to achieve it. I know it's no easy task, and for that reason, I'll give you real examples that might be of help to inspire and motivate you to take action. Now you know what you have to do, and you know all the theory and methodology, but I encourage you to shift toward action and put it all into practice. Knowing something is not enough; knowledge alone will not bring any change in our lives. Rather, change will come hand in hand with action—that is, from applied knowledge.

Take Action

I know that taking action isn't always easy, that it requires a good dose of courage, that it's never a good time, that breaking the barrier of fear is difficult—but my best advice is that you move on to action and take the first step. Our mental representation of what might happen is usually worse than what will actually happen. We create movies for ourselves, we imagine a terrifying future, we believe ourselves to be incapable—and all this does nothing but slam the brakes on something as simple as taking the first step.

That's why in this third part of the book I have collected a series of real cases, of stories experienced by thousands—if not millions—of people like you, to inspire you and allow you to take that first step that you need to take so badly. These are people who once suffered but who were able to pick up all the pieces of their broken soul and shattered lives and repair their lives and their dreams. But you'll see that in the various cases it wasn't too complicated. In each chapter you'll find a description of what happened, a detailed analysis of the situation, and a real work plan based on the three steps of the method I describe in my book *Emotional Strength:* gaining perspective, thinking differently, and taking action.

Repairing a Job Loss

Carla's Story: "I gave it my all, and they let me go."

Carla opened the letter, read it, and sat down. Her body was shaking. She couldn't trust her legs to support her. She couldn't trust any part of her body. What had become of her? She leaned her elbows on her knees. She covered her face with her hands. She felt ashamed of herself. She felt ashamed of feeling ashamed. But it was a deep and arid shame that had always lain in wait, stalking her.

Her pride was hurt. Failure hurt. Having made a mistake hurt. The pain hurt. She tried to think about something nice in her life. But she couldn't find anything. All her memories were sad. She had spent years not living. She had given it all for the company, absolutely everything. It had always been the main thing in her life. "We want people who are engaged and committed," she remembered from the CEO's speech at the first conference she attended. The company had been good to her. She began as an intern when she graduated from university, and little by little she climbed up to director of a department for the entire Madrid region.

For years she had prioritized her career above everything. Her husband understood and supported her. She remembered him encouraging her to decide whether it was truly the career that she wanted and whether her total dedication was worth it. She remembered her mother telling her that she was neglecting her family and that she was fortunate to have such an understanding partner. She practically didn't know her children. Her husband, a teacher, had more free time and had been in charge of everything to do with the children. She didn't even know what size clothes her children wore, whether all their vaccines were up to date, or what their dreams or desires were. She remembered her first conference. She remembered her first day at work on that April morning when it was raining. She remembered her first client and her first sale. Everything was wonderful. She remembered that at last she felt appreciated, or perhaps only seemingly appreciated. The distance gave her a slap in the face in the shape of a new appraisal of what had happened. How could she have been so foolish?

Carla needed recognition, power, and status, and those were the bargaining chips used by the company where she worked. There was always a new project to focus on, one that would take up a lot of time. As we know, new projects do require a lot of time, a lot of love. In addition, when they involve elements you haven't yet fully mastered, you need to learn new things and to dedicate even more time to them. Time. If she could just turn back the clock to that moment when her best friend told her she needed to make big changes in her life. She ignored each and every one of the warnings from the people she was closest to. She ignored her sister when she told her to consider the future that awaited her. She ignored many warnings, each and every one of the signs that were telling her she needed to do something, that her empire was crumbling, that her performance was lagging behind because of a vain desire for recognition, for being more, and for being better. But better than whom? "Look at yourself. You kept wanting more, and now you have nothing. You have less than nothing. You've been a foolish and immature child," she told herself. She tore up the letter in a fit of rage. How dare they get rid of her after she gave them everything? How could they do it by letter without giving her any explanation in person? She opened her hand without being aware of it, and the letter fell to the ground, and with it fell Carla's mood, energy, future, confidence, and self-esteem.

Carla had given everything for her company, the same one that was now letting her go because of a simple financial matter. "Nothing personal," they said. It was all a matter of indicators and bottom lines. "Nothing personal," they said, despite asking her for absolute engagement and personal commitment. She felt utterly betrayed.

Carla's hope fell to the ground silently, unobtrusively, dispiritedly, and broke into sixteen pieces—sixteen large pieces—one for every year she had worked in that high-profile, successful company.

Take a Step Back

So you've lost your job, right? Then let's take this step by step. If you like, we'll start by objectively analyzing the reasons for your dismissal.

Let's start at the beginning. Let's imagine that they fired you for a reason such as low performance. I encourage you to do an exercise of self-criticism and analysis. It's more important than it might seem. Have you been fired for low performance for good reason? Don't be outraged. I often work with companies, and I see hundreds, if not thousands or millions, of workers dragging their feet at work, trying to hide their complete lack of motivation for the job they are doing or their job position. You may have also seen this as a customer or as a coworker.

Are you one of those people who while away the hours and do the bare minimum required? If that is the case, don't worry. Don't punish yourself because of it. Life has given you a great opportunity. It has put you in front of a mirror so that you can take a look at yourself and avoid spending the rest of your days feeling bitter and hating having to get up every day of your life until you retire. Someone once said that retirement is an invention of people who hate their jobs. How old are you? For how many years have you been hating your job? Look, it's best for you to close this dark chapter in your life and open a new one. Learn from what has happened to you. Be honest with yourself. Don't be dramatic. If your performance was low, it's likely that it was because you should have left your job a long time ago.

Do you realize what a big favor life has done you? Or do you want to end up as a completely bitter old person hating yourself for not being capable of turning your professional life around? I understand that you are terrified of looking for a new job. I understand that you are disenchanted with work, and you believe that it's impossible to enjoy working; after all, you must have spent years not enjoying your job. I understand that giving up on a substantial severance pay check takes a good amount of courage, but believe me, nothing is worth as much as your health and happiness. Often it's possible to reach an economic agreement that is beneficial to both parties. If you are stressed about going to work, and you believe the situation with your current company can't be corrected, ask for the bill and negotiate a dignified exit. No monetary payout is as valuable as leaping out of bed in the mornings because you can't wait to go and work on a project that makes you feel excited and motivated.

In addition, your dismissal might well have been wrongful, bringing you a payout that will allow you to think about a new professional project—so you will be responsible for taking advantage of the favor that life has done you by learning from your mistakes and seeking or creating a job that you feel passionate about.

But let's get back to the subject at hand. Perhaps losing your job had nothing to do with you or with your performance but with a purely financial matter. This kind of dismissal is nothing personal; it's just business. Don't allow your self-esteem to feel attacked by something temporary and unrelated to your performance; don't let it block you and leave you sunk in a deep depression that will take a lot of effort to get out of. In Carla's case, her job loss was the result of a pure and simple reduction in costs. She had been working at the company for some sixteen years, which incurred a salary far higher than someone recently hired would be paid.

Now, we have to analyze this job loss properly because, if we don't, it might end up having a much higher than expected emotional cost. Let's take it bit by bit. Losing our jobs hurts because it's a change that we didn't choose (except if it's a dismissal because of low performance, as we have discussed above), and that makes us feel bad; it takes us out of our comfort zone and puts us in a precarious position. In addition, losing a job means a change to an uncertain future, which is in reality an advantage—the problem is that we tend to mistake it for a change for the worse. But don't make that mistake; a job loss is an uncertain change. You never truly know whether the life that awaits you after you lose a job is going to be better or worse than the life you have led until now.

Let's analyze the job loss in a balanced way. Is it inconvenient? Of course; there is no point in denying it, but from there to thinking it's a catastrophe is a huge leap. Again, let's analyze the event with some perspective. You've lost your job, and you possibly have a severance payout that will allow you a few months of security in terms of paying bills. Keep calm! Personally, like millions of people all over the world, I haven't had a stable income for sixteen years and no paycheck whatsoever.

I know that the unknown is scary. I know that leaping into the void without a safety net makes you panic. Who wouldn't? But the conceptual error here is that you are leaping into the abyss without a safety net. You are just entering into a terrain that is thus far unknown to you. But let's not get ahead of the facts; further along, when we take action, I will provide you some strategies to defeat this understandable but exaggerated fear.

Another reason you might have lost your job, which can make you especially angry, is that you have been usurped. Let me explain the case of a person I worked with for a few years as a consultant. This person used to hire my services as a workshop facilitator and consultant. We already know that the more you spend time with someone, the more affection you develop, and, being of an easy nature, I became fond of her. One day she introduced me to the person who was to be her right-hand woman. She had selected her herself. When she asked my opinion, I said sincerely and with affection that she had not gotten safely past my scanner, that she was a dangerous person, and that it would end badly. And guess what? My friend got mad at me. I didn't get it. She had hired me as her star consultant to analyze the most difficult cases, and when I put myself at her service, with nothing but affection for her, she ignored my diagnosis. It's not hard to imagine what happened: she told her "right-hand woman" my diagnosis. Her right-hand woman started to gain power. They stopped working with me, and, a few years later, on the day when I was inaugurating my center for emotional well-being in Barcelona, she came to see me to tell me that she had been fired and that the new head of the department was her right-hand woman. Sad and inevitable.

So it's possible you might have lost your job because you've been usurped. My dear, candid soul, don't forget that you are working at a pyramid organization where resources are scarce and valuable; in other words, where there is always a pushy person willing to do your job better. It's sad but true, but it's not enough to just work; we have to dedicate some time toward protecting ourselves, building relationships, and proving that we are working. Do you know who will usurp you? The person you least expect. So, without succumbing to paranoia, but without being naive, I invite you to activate a system of alert and fortification that protects you and allows you to focus on what matters, on working and enjoying your contributions.

I have also met people who have lost their job out of someone else's fear. Yes, suddenly they felt afraid, they felt threatened, and they hatched a plan to do away with the source of their fear—you. You might not have done anything to cause fear in that person, but it might have been enough for your superior to have complimented you in their presence, compared you with him or her, or cited you as a person who is engaged, hardworking, and committed. That's enough to make a conspirator suffer and possibly speak ill of you. It's a shame, but instead of channeling their own fear constructively, making more of an effort, or learning from you, what they will do is eliminate their source of anxiety in order to dissipate any threat on the horizon. I would like to be able to warn you and tell you to be careful not to run into anyone like that, but it does not depend on you. Most of the atrocities I've seen, the cruelest conspiracies that my clients have suffered, have been born out of fear that was sometimes paranoid and unfounded. My advice is that you don't pay attention to or worry about those kinds of conspirators or about people who form an opinion about you based on the web of lies created by that toxic person.

You don't have to do anything in particular for someone to decide they've got something against you. The fact is, if you are a good and responsible worker, of course you have a better chance of success. There is a Japanese proverb that says that the nail that stands out is the one that gets hit by the hammer. If you make someone's mediocrity obvious, they won't think twice about starting a vendetta against you, creating a lobby of archenemies, and developing the kind of toxic strategies that Machiavelli, if he came back to life, would write another book about. Here again, there is little you can do because you are not an expert in search-and-destroy strategies; also, you are probably focusing on working and producing, honoring your commitments, and developing your mission with excellence, which is wholly incompatible with setting up a system of defense against paranoid attacks.

Finally, there is one last scenario for losing your job—bad luck. Sometimes bad luck conspires to ruin your day and change your life. Sometimes you lose your job through bad luck, by chance; several names go into a hat and yours gets pulled out. It's that simple, that cruel, and that fortuitous. Three people with specific salaries have to be let go, or the bosses want to send a message to the rest of the team, or they have decided to sell the company and the new company decides to make do without a part of the workforce. That's all there is to it. Don't link it to your self-esteem or your performance or just ask yourself why. There is no reason; you won't find it. Your job loss was a product of chance. Until now we have talked about the different reasons you might have lost your job: for bad performance, for financial reasons, because you've been usurped, because of fear, and because of bad luck. Of all these reasons, only the first one has to do with you; the rest of them, little or nothing at all. So do yourself a favor and dissociate your job loss from your self-esteem.

Don't forget

- Analyze the reason for your dismissal free of guilt and shame.

- Learn from what happened to avoid repeating the same situation.

- Dust yourself off and start again, this time wiser and with more resources.

- Dissociate your job loss from your self-esteem and self-image.

Think Differently

If you have had the same experience Carla did, I encourage you to review your expectations around work. Yes, I know that work dignifies us and that holding a respected position at a reputable company makes you appear successful, but that has nothing to do with your self-image. In fact, therein lies the problem—in social status.

Social status, that apparent mark of social recognition, can end up making us do whatever it takes to avoid losing our job. We sell our soul to the devil for a company car. We forget about our life for a paycheck. We mortgage our dreams for seeming financial security. We numb and bury our talents and virtues in order to fit into the environment in which we are working. And when we are woken from that dream with a slap in the face in the shape of a job loss, we realize that we have been nothing more than a bargaining chip in a commercial relationship where we earned money in exchange for our work—no more and no less than that.

Carla mistook what she needed to be with what she was in reality, but life is the way it is, not the way you want it to be. She mistook stubbornness for the necessary intelligent perseverance to make a professional career grow. She mistook obsession for engagement and commitment, and mistaking a desire for reality is dangerous. She had enough clues to recalibrate her perception, but she refused to come to terms with reality until it was too late. She had a clear objective, but she wasn't aware of it. She wanted to triumph, to prove to herself that she could become an important and admirable person because of her professional position, and she did things that she thought would go well, but she did it without control and without planning. She wanted to do better than her father, her successful family, and the ghosts that haunted her.

The time had come to say "enough is enough"—enough of self-pity. There's only so much crying you can do after a betrayal. As I've observed before, people don't tend to die from falling into a river; they die from not getting out of it. We can cry because of a betrayal, but we can't remain anchored to a great disappointment. We must move on. "Onward and upward!" as a good friend of mine always says.

I know it's not easy. The decisions that we don't make don't hurt us. In contrast, difficult decisions, such as coming to terms with reality and rebuilding ourselves, are painful because they mean having to come to terms with many more implications. We must know how to say "enough is enough" and know what we are doing without losing perspective, without losing sight of our objective. It's all a question of expectations. If you are aware of the fact that a job is a mere commercial relationship, when you lose your job you can cope better with the blow, your self-esteem suffers a lot less, and you are in a better position to return to the job market.

But watch out. Let's be clear. While we are working, we have to concentrate and perform at our best with the sense of responsibility that is expected with a commercial contract in which you receive remuneration in exchange for your talent. But you can't focus your entire life and energy on work because you'll no longer be living in a balanced way. It's not good for you or the company you work for. Adjust your expectations, and live a balanced life, if you want to be happy and not receive a huge blow on the day you lose your job. Don't allow what happened to Carla happen to you. There is always a new project, always a new stress, and always something else to do. You are always under the threat that at any moment you might cease to form a part of that select group of the most valued workers, your boss's circle of trust—the same boss who has been playing on your guilt and fear, always playing on your ambition.

A healthy person is someone who works, learns, has fun, grows, laughs, and dances all in a balanced way without sacrificing a fully lived life, without entering into a spiral of obsession, and without losing sight of who they are—always keeping it all in perspective and context. Carla was lucky with her partner, but that's not always the case. I've seen many broken relationships and grandparents burned out from having to look after their grandchildren during their own children's marathon workdays, as well as children—the most defenseless of victims—in a situation of emotional neglect, lost, and without a guide or a role model.

There are moments that require an additional effort at work. There are moments when we have to dedicate more time and energy to our job; but be careful because devoting more time is not synonymous with working more, and be careful, too, because all effort has a beginning and an end. If you've been forcing yourself for a long time you might need to stop, take a step back, analyze the situation, and make decisions on how to grow the work team, restructure the workload, assess your ability to self-organize, analyze your performance, and revise project deadlines.

In contrast, there are people who have poor expectations from work, who believe it's impossible to enjoy their passion, and who think that going to work is nothing more than a succession of problems day after day until the much-anticipated day of retirement. Work is a necessary formality in order to earn money, which you will then spend on luxuries to make up for the negative emotions caused by going to work. Look at how toxic that cycle is: you have a job you don't enjoy that makes you sad or stresses you out, and to compensate for those negative emotions you spend a large part of your salary on products or experiences to make it up to yourself.

Work should not be a punishment—far from it. But a job you don't like is more than punishment; it's torture! I remember a conversation with a young man about thirty years old who was completely depressed, in this case in a reactive manner as a consequence of the torture it meant to him to go to work every day on a job that he was not the least bit interested in. He had started working at the factory to occupy the position that his father had left him when he retired, a common practice in many factories in Spain. Anyway, this young man had other aspirations, but, of course, why would you let such a great opportunity pass? Wouldn't you like to start work with a permanent contract, considering the times we're living in? So he didn't let it pass him by, and after three years of working there he came to visit me in my practice in La Cerdanya, seeking my help with his depression. My advice was clear. No pills, no therapy; the solution to his problem was to find another job. A short time afterward he opened a dance academy (one of his two passions), which he combined with his job at the factory (to avoid leaping into a financial abyss), and, after a few years, he opened a bicycle shop and workshop (his other passion). These days he is more than happy, feels radiant, and gets out of bed in the morning feeling in love with life, exultant, and with a hunger to conquer the world.

His story allows me to introduce the concept that the proper expectation, a well-adjusted one and the one that I propose you adopt, is that you can enjoy your job. For seventeen years I haven't taken any job offer; instead, I create my own job opportunities. Nobody asked me to write articles about psychology for newspapers or journals. I never saw an ad in the paper asking for a psychologist to write periodically about psychology and contemporary issues; instead, I offered to create a section on the psychology of daily life. I currently write a weekly article for the newspaper *El Periódico*, a monthly one for the magazine *Psicología Práctica*, and another for *Objetivo Bienestar*. I didn't answer any ad because it did not exist.

For almost two decades I have been creating my own work. When I was young I showed up in the middle of Pallars, in the Catalan Pyrenees, and I asked for work as a rafting guide. One fine day I phoned the director of the television show *A Punto con La 2*, and today I have a weekly slot on it. One day I decided to write a book, and I found a publisher to publish it for me. Today you are reading my second book. If I can enjoy my work, you can, too, trust me. I don't possess any special virtues that you don't have. I have done nothing but think and work, work and think, make decisions, be proactive, and take risks; and the risks haven't even been that big. All in all, I have stuck to my idea that life is short, and we must live it and enjoy it, including when it comes to our work.

Don't resign yourself to going to work at a place you don't feel passionate about, that doesn't awaken the best in you, and that doesn't motivate you. You are a compendium of virtues, and you can work as whatever you like, and if the job position doesn't exist, create it for yourself. Think differently. Think that being able to work is a blessing and that many people cannot work: people affected by illness, people who are outside the job market, and people who would give anything to be able to work again. But don't leave everything aside for a job, as Carla did. And don't drag yourself like a zombie every day to a place you hate to do something you don't enjoy. Find your opportunity, and, if it doesn't exist, create it proactively. How? I'll explain that right away.

Don't forget

- Review your expectations regarding work.

- Dissociate your self-esteem from your professional achievements; you are a lot more than your work successes.

- Life is the way it is, not the way you would like it to be.

- Readjust and recalibrate your perception constantly to avoid more major shifts down the line.

- Live your life and your work to the full. A healthy life is a balanced life.

Take Action

Let's go; come with me to the store cupboard. We're going to look for fine gold. You are broken, and we need to repair you. Today you are stronger. Don't hide your scars because they are proof of your courage, your growth, and your fragility turned into hardness. Life is a long-distance race where you will fall at some point or another. There's nothing wrong with falling. There's nothing wrong with breaking. You might fall again and break at some other time. It doesn't matter. However many times you fall, you'll always be able to get back up again, all the stronger and wiser for it.

Reflection without action is not useful in any way. Similarly, action without planning is an investment in unfocused energy, leading to fortuitous results. If you find yourself in a situation like Carla's, here you will find an action plan that can help and orient you. We have already analyzed the reasons that have brought you to this point; now is the time to examine the resources available to you to move onward and reconnect with your emotional strength. Above all, what you need to do is learn from what happened, free of guilt and shame, to be able to get up again stronger in order to heal your life and your future.

Reconnect with Your Essence

We'll start by repairing your self-image. When we suffer, our self-esteem becomes distorted, which is a serious risk when attending a job interview or starting a new project. When under the influence of an intense emotion, we cannot make good decisions because the fear of suffering again limits the real expectations available to us; fear paralyzes and constrains everything. You cannot present yourself in front of another person if you are hurting or resentful, whether it is looking for a job or seeking financing or clients for your new project. So the first step is to raise a smile again; eliminate any shadow of anger, resentment, or fear; and recover the more charming version of yourself.

Be careful—you might believe you don't feel that bad or even that you have things under control, but resentment has an effect similar to drugs. You think you have everything under control, but you don't. At the beginning of 2016 I underwent a gastroscopy, and I was sedated with propofol. I don't have many memories of the moment when I awoke, but I do remember that I wanted to drive back home to La Cerdanya from where I was in Barcelona, some one hundred and fifty kilometers away. I thought I was fine, but my wife, the nurse who was looking after me, the supermarket employee I bought water from, and every living being I crossed paths with simply laughed at the string of nonsense I was babbling.

If you don't have things under control, you cannot turn up in that broken state. You need to repair yourself first. I suggest that you take some time—a morning, an afternoon—and go for a stroll. Think about different people you like—public figures, friends, or acquaintances. Make a list of their names, and write next to them what you like about them. Do it because it's likely that here you have a part of your aspirational desire, and it can be a good point of departure. Next, make a list of the people you don't like at all, and write next to them the reason you don't like them. Here, again, you have an initial guide to identify undesirable aspects. When you have completed both lists, I encourage you to do an exercise of introspection and try to define yourself using adjectives, words, or phrases. With a little bit from here and a little bit from there, you'll be able to start to connect with your true essence.

Perhaps you made a mistake. It's all right to make a mistake. We don't have to seek out mistakes, but if a mistake is made, it'll be fine. What would be truly terrible would be to continue anchored to that mistake, especially if, as in Carla's case, you are someone who is capable of working with quality, commitment, and engagement. You are not a failure for losing your job. Let's look at it with perspective. However, if you don't want to repeat the same mistake again, you need to rebuild yourself on a good foundation, which is what happens when you properly adjust your self-image, without overrating yourself and without underrating yourself.

You have numerous talents and plenty of areas you need to work on, just like the rest of us mortals. If you are capable of learning from what happened, taking a step back, thinking in a wiser way, and taking action, then a few years from now you will remember this episode as a simple crisis from which you emerged stronger.

You don't have to do anything other than reconnect with your essence, with the essence you have never lost. You might believe you don't have it, but you're mistaken. You have it—of course you have it—and, what's more, you don't need to experience what has happened to you as a failure but as an opportunity for learning. You have only made a few bad choices, nothing out of the ordinary. If you are capable of learning from what happened, you won't repeat the same mistake again.

Share Your Essence with Other People

So you have connected with your essence. Great! Now's the time to share it with others. Reconnect with your circle of social influence, and, if you don't have one, look for one and create one. What cannot be seen does not exist, so you need to gain visibility and allow yourself to be seen. Invest in your professional development, enroll in a course, connect with other professionals, and attend work meetings. Look for things you want to be a part of, and put yourself forward as a suitable candidate. Perhaps what you are looking for does not exist, but don't worry because you can always propose it yourself in a proactive way.

Prepare a cover letter that outlines your talents and all your potential, look for email contacts, and introduce yourself to the right people with a proposal. When a job offer is published, the selector who acts as the first filter will likely be a person in human resources (HR) or an assistant in the department. They start to look at resumes from different candidates, but when they believe they already have a sufficient number of potential candidates, they ignore the rest of the resumes, and perhaps yours is in that pile; that is, they haven't even looked at it.

I propose something a lot more risky but more effective. What kind of job do you want—sales? Well, look for the name and email address of the head of the sales department at the company you want to work for, and send them an email directly, explaining who you are, why you are motivated to work for their company, and what you can bring to the table that no one else can. In these three statements you have the secret to a good cover letter.

Transform Your Dream into a Project

Now, you might decide to create your own project and know that the energy and vision that you are going to invest in it will have more direct consequences for you. That's fantastic! You can now get to work. Start by studying the subjects you don't know so much about. A company, no matter how small, needs a leader with knowledge in finance, marketing, management, operations, and many other areas.

Train in business management, and at the same time create a business plan, your business plan. A good business plan is what sets apart successful from unsuccessful businesses. In this kind of plan we see reflected even the tiniest strategic and operative details, in such a way that it will be easier to start your own business, and at the same time it will provide you a guide for making decisions.

Work, think, work, readjust, make decisions—and your project will turn into a beautiful reality. There is no other secret than that. Of course, you do need to be careful with the distorting effect that the following three factors might have.

The first factor is fear, once again. Fear blocks us, remember? Don't be afraid (but that's easy to say, isn't it?). To paraphrase Franklin D. Roosevelt, the only thing you should be afraid of is fear. I would like to confess something to you. I am a fearful person. Yes. I admit it without shame. People who know me superficially would not believe it because I've scaled huge rock faces; climbed mountains several thousand meters high; run along the top of breathtaking ridges; delved into the depths of the earth; and navigated a river in the middle of a flood, chased by an enormous fir tree ripped out by the wind, barely a few meters away from me. But those who know me well know that I'm a scaredy-cat, although they also know that my courage is greater than my fear. You might be wondering where my courage comes from.

I will gladly explain. In fact, I strongly believe that in this world we need more people with courage. My confidence comes from my emotional strength. I know that if I make a detailed analysis of what is happening, I will be able to make a sensible assessment of risk. But that is not enough. I know that just like you, I have a backpack full of resources and techniques that are guaranteed to help me cope with that fear. What's more, I know that if I don't have any techniques to tackle a specific situation, I am capable of creating new ones. There's no reason I shouldn't be able to respond to most of the situations I will encounter in my life, exactly in the same way in which you are also capable. Knowledge will set you free, so make an effort to learn, study, read, travel. Do whatever you want, but learn, and only then will you be free. When you feel afraid, approach your fear, study it, and find the unknown quantity within.

Now that we have identified one archenemy, let's go for the next one: desire. Carla mixed desire with reality, which led her to the great disappointment she experienced. Desire is a bad adviser because it makes us believe that it's more likely that what we desire will happen, when in reality that isn't the case. When we mix desire with reality, we activate a selective mechanism that filters the stimuli that we perceive in such a way that we discard what we don't need or what confronts us with the reality we want to avoid. This process of selective attention causes us to magnify any indication, no matter how small, that justifies our decontextualized idea. In this way we become blinded in thinking that we're right—that we're doing fine—and we ignore external signs that might help us recalibrate our perception. And we continue without altering our course until we crash into our unrealistic expectation, which is impossible to achieve.

We have one last archenemy of success in your project of rebuilding your essence: the opinions of others. Opinions are free, but they are not reliable. People can have any opinion they want, but that doesn't mean their opinion is correct, that it is true, or that you need to follow their advice literally. Watch out—I am talking about both positive and negative opinions. If they are positive but have no foundation, we cling to them as a bastion, as a buttress that supports our deluded idea. When we feel supported, we will feel stronger, and we will disconnect further from reality. Remember, you need to analyze things constantly, all the time. However, if opinions are negative and again have no basis, it is likely that we will fall—that we'll become discouraged and start making strange decisions based on data that are not trustworthy or are out of context. So be careful with the opinions that you hear, especially if they come from people to whom you give certain credibility or with whom you have an emotional bond because you will believe them without questioning whether they are correct or whether their ideas are false.

The moment of truth has arrived, the moment when you need to stand face-to-face with frustration. We need to manage frustration because, if we don't, it becomes ossified and ends up turning into resentment. Your future depends on its correct management. You will never be the same person again. If you don't manage it properly, you'll end up discouraged, bitter, belittled, broken, and unsettled; if you manage it properly, you will emerge stronger from this situation with new knowledge, with renewed emotional strength that will provide you greater security, more self-possession, and better resources. Now you know what you should do and how to do it. Take action. Heal yourself. If you don't do it, who do you expect to do it for you?

Do you know what Carla did? She decided to put herself back together after losing her job, and these days she has a new career that she finds fulfilling. She decided to turn her passion into her work. Carla loves cooking, something that she had relegated to New Year's Eve and to the odd party or special occasion. So she set to work on a business plan, and in less than a year she had started her own catering company.

Where Do I Start?

- Reconnect with your essence.

- Share your essence with other people.

- Transform your dream into a project.

How Do I Achieve It?

- Analyze what happened to you.

- Transform your negative emotions (shame, self-pity, resentment, pride, etc.) in a constructive way without rejecting them or settling into them.

- Don't blame yourself for making a mistake. You have a right to make mistakes, but you also have the obligation to learn from a mistake and avoid repeating it.

- Don't mistake desire for reality. Continue to recalibrate yourself to ensure you still have your feet on the ground.

- Don't start to look for a job without having first reflected: What do you want to work in? How would you like to see yourself?

- Transform your desires into objectives, create an action plan, and then decide whether it is viable.

- Listen to the opinions of others and assess them, but don't incorporate them without submitting them to a detailed examination.

- Attend to the signs and indications telling you that you need to readjust your plans.

- Trust yourself and your capabilities.

- Build little by little. Don't rush things; take your time. It's better to do things slowly and well than quickly and badly.

Repairing Your Self-Esteem

Carlos's Story: A Sharp, Deep Pain

Another contemptuous glance, and Carlos's heart felt a stab of pain. He managed to hold back the tears just until he got back to his bedroom refuge. He couldn't understand why he was incapable of holding back the tears. He wasn't crying from rage but from sadness, a black and intense sadness.

Physical abuse leaves a visible mark, an unequivocal sign that in other people's eyes justifies the toughest of decisions. But what does it matter what everyone else might think? The most demanding, most severe, and least understanding of gazes tends to be our own. Physical pain is temporary. No blow hurts forever. Our bodies are wise and know how to heal themselves quickly after pain.

But there is a kind of abuse that is far worse, a silent and treacherous kind that is cunning and shrewd, a sophisticated pain that hurts endlessly, long after the physical blow has healed: a dull and deep pain that dries up your soul, a pain that is not the result of physical abuse but of contempt, neglect, a hateful glance, a rejection of your innermost being. That is doubtless the worst kind of pain. That was the pain that Carlos felt. He knew the pain of insults and of a lack of understanding. He also knew the pain of comparison, a comparison in which he always fared badly. Everyone was better than him; any achievement, even when tiny or meaningless, was more important than his own.

Carlos went to his little desk at home, searched in his school bag, and pulled out a book that he'd taken out of the library. The library had been such a good find! Carlos devoured book after book. He was thirsty for knowledge; he wanted to know about other realities, he wanted to understand, learn, and grow; but above all, he wanted to stop feeling the pain that kept him awake at night, his throat dry. "Yes, that's it, hole yourself up to read a load of nonsense; that'll sort a lot of things," he heard as he shut the door to his room. His parents were charming to everyone but him. Well, not to everyone, just to people who made them feel like good people or victims.

Carlos hated victimism and lies. He hated his mother's manipulation and criticisms and the way she tore into his brothers and sisters. He hated the lack of dialogue, the absolute lack of respect, and the dictatorial regime imposed by his mother. He didn't understand why his father stole at work and bragged about it. "Stealing isn't right." "If it's from your boss, it is," he received as an answer, along with, "Son, you're an idiot."

Suddenly the door to his room opened. "Hey, crybaby, you've upset Mom again," his sister yelled. "You're a selfish little brat." Carlos listened to a string of unfair insults. But then, are there ever any fair insults? "I need to get out of here," he thought. He took the book and went for a walk, aimlessly, with no fixed destination. Any place would do, or at least would be better than home. Or, better put, the house he had happened to be born in and lived in.

He cried. His soul was in pain. He allowed himself to cry, but he knew he had to do something to understand and overcome his pain, his sadness. He looked for a song that would comfort him. He looked for something fun, a cheerful and stimulating dance. He wanted to combat his sadness. The MP3 player suggested Czárdás, an ancient traditional dance. He sat on a bench and closed his eyes. He imagined a Hungarian violinist playing his old violin, producing a sad melody, as sad as his feelings were. Carlos imagined himself playing the violin.

What a great resource imagination is, to be able to escape from a world that we don't like! He closed his eyes and played next to the violinist. He found an outlet for all his sadness in a mournful melody, but little by little he surprised himself because his own melody had been transformed. The sparing and gloomy rhythm of the opening bars had turned into a cheerful and fresh tempo. He cheered up to the rhythm of his new melody, the melody of someone who knows that pain is not eternal if you do something to avoid it. That evening as the sun set, as Carlos broke into dance in the middle of the street, his eyes starry with hope, he decided that he would not leave any aspect of his life to chance.

Take a Step Back

The case of Carlos is that of an abused child, but what I explain here is just as valid if you have been abused by your parents or your partner or another person at home, school, or work. You have suffered, that's clear, and what's worse, you have suffered doubly because as well as putting up with the person who abused you, you have had to suffer in silence to avoid the stigma from people around you.

Nobody understands your pain. Nobody understands that a single glance can cause a huge amount of pain. But what people don't realize is that a glance is simply an instrument, a resource to give an outlet to the hate or contempt that the person feels for you when they should love you or at least respect you. You were simply an unknowing child, a child who wanted to be loved by your parents, like any other child in this world, and it's difficult to understand the reason for so much hate, the motives behind that senseless rejection, the origin of so much suffering.

You were abused during childhood. You were unlucky. It's purely a matter of bad luck. Depending on the family you were born into and the toxic motivations of your parents and siblings, their emotional states, or their psychological imbalances, you might have won the cruel lottery of senseless abuse (as if any abuse makes sense).

But let's take this step by step. You were the victim of abuse. I know you feel shame—perhaps you even feel guilty about it—but you are definitely not the only person who has suffered this. If every person who has been abused carried around a red helium balloon, I can assure you we wouldn't see the sunlight.

Abuse is withstood in silence. No one will understand that your charming parents were charming only on the outside. Some people might even deny what happened or justify the abuse they received, as if there was any act or omission that could justify it.

Let's think about this with perspective: until now you have been the passive victim of an abuser, but now, in this moment, you can take a step forward and free yourself from the chains that join you to a heartless and cruel person. Take charge of your life, and bring this dark chapter to a close. Pick up all the chains, remove them, and leave them on the ground. Don't continue to carry them. You need to bring what happened to a close in order to heal yourself. Don't continue to suffer for it. Don't continue to carry the past with you. I know that finding a reason would help you to understand, but often there is no answer that could explain the senselessness of pain.

If you suffered abuse as a child, you need to know that the only reason to explain it is chance. A child is always the victim, always a victim of the family they were born into without even choosing it, a victim of the emotional states of their parents, a victim of the school they went to, or a victim of the jealousy and the perverse cruelty of other children.

Now, things change when we are talking about a relationship within a couple. I often meet people who actively choose to be with a toxic partner who abuses them. Sometimes we mistake love for admiration, protection, or even status. Be careful because the price you will pay is going to be high.

Carlos had to listen to how he was to blame for all the ills of his mother, father, family, and the world. Yes, that is one of the worst after-effects of psychological abuse, the feeling of guilt. The ruthless abuser doesn't care in the slightest about your suffering and also knows that, by blaming you, they are multiplying the devastating effect of their toxicity. Yes, you are guilty, and the abusers (whether your mother, father, partner, or boss) are within their rights to abuse you. But there is another reason abusers play on the guilt of their victims, which is that if they want to sleep at night, their conscience must be clear, and your guilt will give them that peace. So let's start by eliminating that feeling of guilt, lifting the heavy load that has been placed on your shoulders and prevents you from walking freely toward your own destiny. What are you guilty of, exactly? Nothing. But even though this premise is easy to posit, eradicating the terrible and parasitic feelings of guilt is a lot harder.

Abusers are able to change the self-image of their victims; what's more, they won't stop until they have made sure that the DNA of their victims spins around guilt. Do you know how they achieve this? By changing your style of causal attribution—that is, the way in which you interpret what happens to you and the people around you. The abusers define their victims as the origin of all evils, whether directly or indirectly. If your abusive mother drops the iron while she is in the dining room and you are in your room, it's your fault because you made her nervous and made her hands shake. If she is diagnosed with cancer, it's also your fault because your annoyances are killing her. If she gets a varicose vein, more of the same. Everything, absolutely every bad thing that happens to the abusers is the fault of their victims; they manage to construct the most outlandish arguments when there is no argument to be made.

Another of the changes that abusers seek in their victims is to create insecurity. They know exactly how to achieve it: by underestimating their achievements and teaching them the ideas that they don't know anything, that they aren't capable, and that they can't do things on their own. In the following pages you'll find the keys to move on to action, but I will say now that the axis of change resides in you changing your self-image and providing yourself the chance to get to know yourself and let go of old ideas.

Abusers might also isolate you from your environment. They might have set up a stage for you—one that is convenient to them—a stage with two actors, you and them. You are the supporting actor; you are at their service, you are basically scum, and they are doing you a favor by being with you. If you have no other reference point, that ends up being your reality. Here the key lies in the reference points. This is the reason they isolate you—so that you don't know any other realities. They will isolate you little by little, subtly, and discreetly. Your abusers won't like your friends, your activities, or your interests. They will absorb you with their aches and pains and needs, and before you realize it, you will have already fallen into their trap.

I am sorry that you were the victim of psychological abuse. I am deeply sorry if it was your partner, but allow me to be sad and angry with you if those who abused you were your parents. Don't worry, we are on this journey together. You have already taken the first step; you have gained perspective and seen that what happened to you has been the fruit of bad luck, that you are not to blame for anything, and that you need to learn again to live and relate to others. You have been lost in a forest, but the time has come to start climbing the last hill, the one that will allow you to position yourself on top of the mountain, giving you the perspective you need. What's more, you are not alone—you are with me.

I can see it. I can see you next to me on the Moixeró, one of my favorite Catalan mountains. We are sitting together, enjoying the fresh air on our faces, watching the valley open up to us, and identifying the mountains we have conquered and the paths that we will not tread again.

Don't forget

- You have gained perspective. Now you know that your past does not determine your present or your future.

- You know that you are a person who is full of virtues that are waiting to bloom.

- Your testimony and example will be of help to thousands of people. Don't feel ashamed, don't feel guilty, and don't feel alone.

- Now you have seen things as they are, not as you have been led to believe they are. Now is the time to start thinking differently.

Think Differently

Let's begin by busting a few myths. The concept of family is over-rated. There, I said it! If I don't get that off my chest, I might get a hernia. It's possible that you are the most fortunate person in the world, and that you have a wonderful family. In that case, congratulations! However, for every happy family, I assure you there are hundreds that are unhappy.

It is also my duty to point out that there are "wonderful" families because they have to be wonderful or else. In this kind of family, self-trickery and the stubborn defense of something that is more a desire than a reality are the rule. If you ever meet someone who belongs to this kind of family, don't try to convince them otherwise or show them the truth. When the news is bad, people tend to shoot the messenger.

We are born where we are born out of pure chance. We don't choose our parents or our family context. Our parents and siblings might be delightful or they might be serial killers. It doesn't depend on us in the slightest. The ideal, of course, is that you get on well with your family, but often not only is it not possible but the price you would have to pay to achieve it is too high.

I would dare to go as far as to say that most of my clients have or have had problems originating directly or indirectly from their families. It's not research, and it's not science, but I can assure you that family relationships cause a lot of suffering, as well as devastating negative consequences that persist for many years. We cannot put up with something just because the person doing it is our father, mother, or brother. We cannot tolerate everything. We cannot tolerate physical or psychological abuse or gratuitous suffering.

Of course I am in favor of family life, but only if it is beneficial to all members. I am much a family man, but I don't have blood ties with everyone in my family. We don't need blood ties to love specific people as if they were siblings or children of our own. In the same way, having blood ties doesn't have to mean feeling an emotional bond.

What Kind of Family Did You Grow Up In?

1. A good family: the kind in which every member is respected, where there is quality communication, where every family member is trusted, and in which everyone collaborates in favor of the common good. A good family fosters the autonomy of its members in such a way that it doesn't generate dependency or promote it.

2. A good family on the face of it: this is the worst-case scenario you could find, keeping up appearances in such a way that it appears as an ideal family or even a role model in the eyes of everyone except you. This kind of family shares all the characteristics of a toxic family deep down and those of a good family on the surface.

3. A toxic family: some people mistake family relationships for relationships of domination and submission, in which the children are there to satisfy the needs, egos, or psychopathic deviancy of their parents. At other times, the abuse comes from the siblings themselves, promoted by envy and abnormal motivations.

4. A temporarily toxic family: sometimes, because of specific circumstances (for example, a job loss, separation, or illness), we lose balance and respect at the heart of a family. If we don't want this situation to become chronic, the sooner we recover the balance, the better. This kind of circumstance creates a lot of problems among siblings because some have been brought up in a healthy environment and others in a toxic environment, in such a way that among them there tends to be a lack of understanding and a lack of empathy.

Objective: To Increase Your Confidence

Let's start with you, by repairing your self-image and your self-esteem. The image you have of yourself is completely false and distorted because it is the one that was built by your abuser. I will also be clear with my advice: break away from this image and give yourself the opportunity to get to know yourself again.

But let's take it step by step. Let's review your concept of social relations. Again, I am going to be clear: you are not at the service of anyone. A healthy relationship finds its foundations in mutual respect and the possibility of expressing the needs of both parties.

The first step is to strengthen your self-esteem—to recover faith in yourself. But what does it mean to have faith in ourselves? It has nothing to do with religious faith or the belief that a divine being, god, or other entity will provide us help or protection. Rather, I understand it as an ability that allows you to trust in yourself despite not having any evidence to back you up. Throughout our lives we will have to face challenges that will require us to give the best of ourselves without even knowing whether we will be capable of doing it. Often, when faced with a problem, objective, or goal, we turn back and dive into our past in search of something that allows us to grow our confidence or guide us in our desire to overcome it, but sometimes we don't find anything. There is always a first time, there is always something new to overcome, and there are always situations we don't have full control over or that we have never experienced. When this happens and we don't manage to find any idea or resource in the database of our experience, we remain blocked and disoriented.

Now, there is an emotional strength that will allow you to move on despite not having any support to help guide you: faith in yourself, or the certainty that you can face up to the challenges that life has brought you. Why would you not be capable of doing it? Here what matters is the judgment you make regarding your potential, and reality is not as important as you might believe. If you believe you can't learn new skills and abilities, trust me, you won't learn them. But if you believe you can learn a new skill, such as a new language, within a few months you will be building phrases in French, Spanish, or, as in the case of a friend of mine, Japanese.

Faith in yourself is based on your capacity and ability to respond, which is without a doubt much richer and fuller than you can imagine. You have a lot more resources than you think or than you are aware of. What's more, many of the resources you have will not be put into practice until you need them, which is why, in reality, what matters is not your history of achievements but your potential to cope and achieve results. When you find yourself faced with something unknown, you don't know whether you will be capable of overcoming it, but neither do you know that you will not be able to overcome it. So don't be biased in your answer when in reality it's often impossible to predict whether we will overcome adversity until we have started to work on it.

When you believe there is no reason you should not be capable of coping with any challenge that life brings, your motivation, confidence, and vitality will be activated without you even being aware of it. When faced with a challenge or adversity, the best version of yourself will become activated, mobilizing resources creatively and focusing on the solution to the problem. When you have faith in yourself and your capabilities, your chest puffs out with courage, and you feel full of strength to cope with difficult, new, and unknown situations. The truth is, we don't know what we're capable of until we achieve it.

When nothing gives you total certainty in your capacity to tackle an obstacle, when you look back and cannot find any resources to help you cope with adversity, in that moment look inside yourself and assume and believe that with a work plan and a good dose of faith in yourself and in your ability to make decisions, you will be capable of overcoming the greatest of challenges. A person who has suffered abuse has to learn how to face numerous new situations, so you must have faith in yourself and your capabilities, which have been deliberately eclipsed by your abuser. So, in reality, if you feel like you are in that situation, you are a compendium of virtues to be discovered. Despite being made to believe that you lack the capacity, the truth is that you have everything you need to be happy. I know it can seem like a difficult, practically impossible task, but it's really not that complex. Confidence is a necessary and basic emotional strength needed to live fully and freely in our everyday lives.

Would you like to know what the secret is for gaining confidence? Reviewing the way in which you appraise what happens to you. Have you ever checked how you appraise what happens to you? There is a plethora of motivational messages that invite you to gain confidence, but they don't tell you how to do it. Right now I will explain how based on research conducted by renowned psychologists, so be prepared to analyze your appraisals of what happens to you!

We appraise everything our senses perceive. Every sensory input into our field of perception is appraised subconsciously with the objective of analyzing whether it represents a threat or danger to us. There are two possible appraisals: that what happens to us is irrelevant or that it is a threat. If we appraise it as irrelevant, that's perfect, but if the conclusion of our analysis process is that what we have perceived is a threat, our brains will send alarm signals to our bodies that will prepare us to flee from or fight against that threat. So, with our bodies prepared for action, our minds conduct a second appraisal with the objective of distinguishing whether we have the resources to cope with that threat or not. Again there are only two possible answers. If we decide we have resources to be able to cope with it, our bodies will relax, and it will be as though nothing happened. However, if we conclude that we lack the resources and that we don't know how to cope, our brain will activate an alarm bell in the form of anxiety and stress. Psychologist Richard Lazarus's findings in his theory of appraisal (explained above)[1] are interesting and important here because they allow us to understand the mechanism through which we feel fear and to know the strategies available to us to gain confidence. In the case at hand, if a significant person in our life—who in our case has abused us—has made us believe that we are not capable of coping with different challenges and situations, our second appraisal will always situate us in a position of disadvantage and will cause anxiety and fear. But the wonderful part of this whole process is that we carry out another appraisal still, a third one in which we ask ourselves what we should do to deal with the threat that our senses have perceived. Now we have all the actors of the movie on the set. If we say good-bye to the fearful guard who analyzes every event, and we instead employ a new one with more experience of the world, we will carry out better primary appraisals. If we fire the second actor, the one who says that we can't and that we don't know how to and who sees everything that happens to us as a threat, and instead we hire a new actor who is more motivating and capable of transforming problems into challenges, our secondary appraisals will be more correct. And finally, if we fire the third actor, the one who has little creativity, and we hire a new actor capable of finding resources, imagining, and creating, our confidence will increase because we will be aware that we have the resources to cope with adversity, and that if we don't have them, we will know where to go to find them.

My advice is:

Think differently. Continuing with the movie analogy, I advise that you abandon the stage set of the movie you have been living in until now and that you start writing the script for your next film, the film in which you are the main protagonist.

Take Action

The time has come to get started on the biggest work you will create in your life, the most important house you will ever own, the home of your soul. Let's rebuild your life with strong materials of confidence, self-esteem, and courage. I want you to be a free and confident person, and to achieve that, we need to work hard.

Begin by getting to know yourself. You have no idea what you are like or what you are capable of achieving. During the most vulnerable years of your life, people made you believe that you weren't capable, that you couldn't do things, that you didn't know how to, and that you were worthless. They ignored you, overlooked your achievements, and punished you, and all that has wreaked havoc on your self-image.

Look for silence and try to reconnect with your essence. Discover yourself, and explore yourself. It's no easy task, I know, but that's no reason to avoid it. Observe yourself without judgment, and get to know yourself a little better each day, the same way you would with a new friend, car, or house.

Stop being afraid, stop worrying, and stop running away without looking back. Forget about fear, stop reacting, and start analyzing. That is the key: to analyze instead of reacting. Life is a dynamic process, which is good news because you can grow, learn, change, and above all gain confidence.

Contextualize what happens to you without rushing in your appraisals. Now you know how appraisals work according to Lazarus's theory as outlined above. Now you are capable of identifying when you are carrying out partial appraisals based on fear or a negative self-image that do nothing but activate your alarm systems and generate anxiety for you. The first step toward gaining confidence is understanding, the second is detection, and the third is management. Engage in rational thinking to avoid the tunnel-vision effect that a closed and imperceptive mind has tried to contaminate your soul with. Simplify reality, and eliminate the fear factor. I propose an exercise of imagination. Imagine you are at a meeting expounding your point of view on a project, and that suddenly your boss takes out a piece of paper and starts taking notes. You don't actually know what they are writing, but if you feel afraid, you will believe they are taking notes on the things they didn't like, when you don't really know. Perhaps they loved it. Or perhaps they have simply remembered a task they still have to do. So when you don't know something for sure, don't rule out any of the options, either negative or positive. This, precisely, is what tunnel vision consists of.

You have many more virtues than the ones you imagine. You are capable of many more things than you believe. You have suffered in silence the malign abuse from someone who should have loved you, cared for you, and nurtured you, and you have overcome it. Do you think there could be anything worse?

Recalibrate your concept of the words *danger* and *threat*. Traveling is not dangerous, taking the subway is not dangerous, loving someone is not dangerous, skipping class to enjoy a sunny day is not dangerous, being nervous giving a presentation is not dangerous, and your peers looking at you is not dangerous. You might believe that people are dangerous and decide to isolate yourself. You might believe that loving is dangerous and decide to live in solitude. You might believe that living is dangerous and fall into depression. I cannot deny that, of course, there is an element of danger in all the things I have just listed, but far from avoiding it, what we have to do is learn to manage that danger, that threat. Danger is like salt. Salt, in itself, is neither good nor bad; it depends on how you consume it. If you start eating a kilo of salt by the spoonful, it's possible you'll die. But rather than deciding to stop eating salt altogether to avoid the risk of death, I encourage you to learn to identify the appropriate dose of salt altogether for each occasion.

I'll give you a personal example. Throughout my life I have played several sports, and some of them have carried an elevated risk, such as rock or ice climbing at high altitudes. The climbing in itself entails a risk, but depending on how I manage it, I can increase or decrease that risk; that is, climbing can be more or less dangerous depending on how I manage some parameters, such as the choice of path, my level of physical preparation, the state of the equipment, my roping partner, or the weather forecast. I can tell you that I have experienced some of the best moments in my life in the mountains, and I have never wanted to give it up. I can also tell you that I haven't had any serious accidents from pursuing these sports despite on many occasions being dependent on a rope of a smaller thickness than my little finger. Throughout my life I have had two paths to choose from: renouncing my love of the mountains out of fear or learning to appraise and properly manage the risk that I am taking. Learn to distinguish between something that means a threat and something that is of uncertain evolution or that seems unknown. These things are not the same, and your happiness will depend on their correct identification. Sometimes, when I start on a new path in the Pyrenees or the Alps, I carry out this appraisal; I often take uncertain or unknown paths but rarely dangerous ones. Something uncertain is something whose evolution we are not clear about. Uncertainty is a part of life, of our daily experience. We can't always lead a serene and calm life. It is uncertain how life will turn out, which is more of a blessing than a problem. Mother Nature, aware of the uncertainty of life, has provided us all the necessary tools to cope with it: the capacity for analysis and the capacity to make decisions.

We often walk on uncertain paths. I encourage you to try to obtain information before undertaking them if possible, but under no circumstances should you avoid a path out of fear of uncertainty. When you are on an uncertain path, activate your alert system, analyze what is happening, and start making decisions—but you should never, believe me, avoid them out of fear.

Sometimes we confuse danger with the unknown. Big mistake! If you are facing something unknown, with an uncertain path, look for a map, a GPS, or a compass, but you need to know that when faced with the unknown, the best thing you can do is study it, analyze it, and get to know it. So, again, my best advice is that you don't avoid doing something because it is unknown.

Remember, review your appraisal according to what you have learned from Lazarus above because your happiness will depend on it. And if you really want to feel confident, there's nothing better than having a good repertoire of coping strategies—that is, a good database to guide you and orient you toward your goals.

Consider the fact that you've been isolated from your environment with the objective of not allowing you to know other realities. So now the moment has come to connect with many people, to get to know new realities, and to analyze new coping strategies. Enrich your repertoire of coping strategies; the best way to do this is undoubtedly by seeing the world. Travel, read, meet people of different profiles and from different cultures. Learn with an attitude that is inquisitive, confident, and open. There's no great secret here other than your attitude: the attitude of thirst for knowledge and endless learning—the learning that will provide you the confidence you need.

Your Capacity for Analysis Is Your Best Resource

Sometimes people who have suffered isolate themselves and no longer want to connect with others, but that's not the solution. The solution entails learning to analyze people, to be able to tell who you need to stay away from or who you need to adopt a prudent and cautious attitude toward, as opposed to those who really deserve you sharing your life with them. In contrast, some people, especially when it comes to their partners, still continue to look for a relationship profile that is similar to the one they had with their abusers, though seemingly less extreme. When learning to analyze people, you can identify when you are repeating mistakes and implement a solution.

Exercise Responsibility

Teachers, tutors, leaders of after-school activities, and coaches can change the lives of abused children. How? By offering them new alternatives, allowing them to enter into contact with healthier ways of living, offering them other relationship models, fostering their self-esteem and confidence, and giving them the love and the care that they need.

If you have an abused student, give them a scholarship to study abroad, to attend summer camp, or so that they can play a sport or do some after-school activity every day. If you are a teacher and you need to take action, I appeal to your responsibility as an educator and as an adult. You can also think differently; don't forget that you have the key to remove a child from the toxic environment they are suffering in.

Where Do I Start?

- You have nothing to be ashamed of. If you don't fit in with the family you have, don't feel bad about it. If you can't live with someone who beats women; abuses other people; steals; or is simply sexist, homophobic, a liar, or a manipulator, you have nothing to be ashamed of.

- Don't feel guilty. Be careful with guilt caused by your family and the guilt that family representatives try to generate in you. And be careful, too, with the guilt those people make you feel when they position themselves in favor of one of the parties (the family) without interesting themselves in the other because they are not interested in the slightest in your reality or opinion.

- You might not love your family. That's all right; we cannot love people who harm us repeatedly.

- You are not the exception. Don't feel like a freak. Most people suffer directly or indirectly because of their families. Someday there will be research carried out that will demonstrate that the origin of many mental health problems lies not in huge traumas but in the family.

- You have nothing to justify. You don't need to give explanations. It's possible that they will not understand you. If someone asks you, judges you, or insists, you can recommend they read this chapter of *Kintsugi*.

- Close a chapter to be able to open another. Drop the dead weight; stop carrying the things that limit you. You are where you are because of simple chance; you have been born into the family you have out of pure chance. Start to write your own destiny.

- Don't turn your back on forming your own family. You have experienced a huge life lesson, and you can be the origin of a beautiful and wonderful family where respect and love reign supreme.

How Do I Do It?

- Reprogram your inner dialogue. Replace the image you have of yourself as a helpless kitten with that of a lion full of courage. What I propose is not an affirmation without basis but an affirmation based on the confidence that is given to you by everything you have experienced and overcome.

- Get out of the circle of influence of your abuser if you are still with him or her. If you cannot do it, find allies and support from outside who will help you compensate for the situation, avoid losing perspective, and learn new roles.

- Learn to set limits on people. Sometimes we mistake kindness for submissiveness. Throughout life you will find different types of people—some of them wonderful people full of respect—but also toxic people who are irreverent and disrespectful, for whom you should mark out boundaries.

Repairing Your Life

Daniel's Story: When the Soul Breaks

Some people believe we do not have a soul, but they are mistaken. However, not everyone has a soul. Some people, as they are growing up, lose it. Only people without a soul can be capable of breaking the soul of another person. Yes, there are people who have a soul. Not just a few, believe me.

The soul is something ethereal, something that can be seen only if you have the right gaze. People with souls are easily recognizable for their sensitivity; they live connected to their surroundings, and they care about what happens to the people around them, whether they know them or not. They have a special gaze. It's hard to describe, but when someone with a soul looks at you, you can feel their soul.

The worst thing that can happen to these people is that they get their soul broken. Yes, souls can be broken. Like Daniel's soul. Some people believe that men don't have a soul—that only children and women are sensitive enough to have a soul—but they are wrong. Daniel had a huge and compassionate soul that through his candid gaze went around looking for other souls to connect with.

Daniel thought he had connected with a soul; he believed that he would live happily ever after with his family full of souls and kindness.

But one day, one terrible day, death snatched away his dearest soul, that of his daughter, his princess and soccer player, his clown and mascot, his beloved daughter, and his most precious treasure. "To hell with cancer!"—all his empty soul could do was repeat these words over and over. "To hell with cancer!" Daniel always held the hope that his beloved princess might overcome the illness. He found himself praying, running, crying, fighting, and seeking help from one place to another. He tried everything, but it was no use. When his precious daughter died, he noticed how his soul exploded. So much accumulated sadness for such a long time, so much useless hope, so much pain, and so much incomprehension. Yes, his soul exploded like a supernova waiting for his daughter to go to one of those stars that shine so bright in the night. "But who would believe such bullshit!" he surprised himself by yelling.

Daniel was left empty, exhausted. So much suffering wasn't human—it was unbearable—it wasn't possible. Tatiana, his wife, put her hand on his shoulder. "Daniel, we need help," she managed to whisper. "My soul is broken, Tatiana," replied Daniel, "and there's nobody who can heal a broken soul."

Take a Step Back

I've worked with practically all the faces and disguises that pain uses. I've suffered with my clients and helped them in their lowest moments, and together we have fought to recover their hope and strength. Believe me when I say that I know pain and suffering well. I've known it firsthand in my own life. Nobody escapes its twisted ways, not even me. Pain is universal. But no pain is as terrible and cruel as that of losing a beloved child.

Healing the soul of such a parent is difficult, for many reasons. The main one is that there is no form of reasoning that can provide solace from those choked and stifled tears. The senselessness of it all immerses you in the most toxic and devastating lack of hope you can imagine. When there is no reason, suffering becomes gratuitous and cruel.

Healing a broken soul is an arduous task because the wound always remains fresh. Wherever you look, there is always something that reminds you of your princess; whatever you do, you could have done it with her. So much still to teach them, so much yet to live. When faced with the death of a child it becomes more necessary than ever to take a step back and gain perspective; otherwise you will feel dead inside. Death is with us every day, it's the law of life, and it's of one and the same substance as our existence, but that doesn't make it any easier to cope with, especially when it is unexpected.

There is never a good time for death, least of all that of a child. What I am going to explain to you will be of use to manage the grief of the death of a loved one, whether it's a child, a friend you loved as a child, your partner, or even your faithful pet. As we know, love knows no gender, race, or species. Don't forget that pain is different for each person and that the death of a dog you have spent more than a decade with can be painful.

But let's get back to the task of this section: gaining perspective. We need to take a step back from pain, or at least find moments of peace. You didn't choose it, but life has changed you forever. What used to be normal yesterday, today no longer is, and this is the point of departure for the entire healing process. I know it's easy to say and hard to do.

Accepting death is a complex process that we call bereavement. Its initial phase can last months and is characterized by a torrent of intense and varying emotions. During the bereavement process, our emotional state is fragile, erratic, and unstable. We oscillate between sadness and anger, we are incapable of thinking clearly, and our incomprehension and search for answers torture us day and night. Little by little, the storm waters abate as we begin to assess the events from a certain distance. But it's not always that way, and if we don't manage that grief, we might end up embittered forever, depressed, or resentful for the rest of our life, which is unfair to us, to the people around us, and to the person who died.

Our dear son, partner, or loved one didn't have the choice to continue living, so the best homage we can offer is to live for them. A professor of mine lost his wife and children in the notorious flash floods in the Biescas campsite in northern Spain in 1996, and I remember seeing him wander around the city, beside himself. He looked like he was dead inside. In that time I wasn't able to understand the magnitude of what happened, but I would have liked to tell him that he needed to live again, that he had an obligation to live life fully, that his family had not been able to choose to live, and that the best memorial and homage he could pay to them would be not to allow the life ahead of him to pass him by.

I remember, too, reading an interview with the French actor Carole Bouquet in which she explained that when her husband died she had two options: to feel dead inside or to live, and she chose to live. It wasn't a fast or instant decision; it didn't come naturally, but it happened after a grieving process of several months.

My advice is:

If you are immersed in sadness because you have lost a loved one, you must know that you are facing the worst of challenges. But despite how hard your loss is to bear, the best thing you can do is live again, I insist, for you, for your loved ones, and for the beloved person you have lost.

Think Differently

I recently watched a film with my daughter called *The Book of Life*, produced by Mexican director Guillermo del Toro. It's a film that talks about life and death and presents death in a fun way. The culture around death in Mexico is interesting. I don't want to give any spoilers in case you decide to watch the film—which I highly recommend—but it deals with the idea of an existence of two parallel worlds: the world of the people we remember, where there is a party that never ends, and that of forgotten people, where sadness is the norm. The action of the film takes place on November 2, the Day of the Dead, the day when you can feel the presence of your departed loved ones. Perhaps herein lies the key, in the way you remember your loved ones and the way you hold them in your heart.

After we have gained a certain amount of perspective, the time has come to think differently. We are faced with one of those problems where you cannot go to the root, and yet you have to manage its consequences, the associated emotions. We can't bring back the person we have lost, but that doesn't mean that we must sit idly by. In fact, there are a few things we can do, but until we think differently, we won't find the energy we need to take action.

Life is one of the most difficult things to repair. The past acts as a dead weight that won't let us move forward. We carry with us a history that is not just our own, and our heavy backpack digs into our shoulders and heart.

A change of attitude is needed. Take your time. You are suffering because you are grieving. But you should know that at some point or other in your life you will have to take a step forward and start living again, and you will have to do it for yourself, for your loved ones, and for the person you have lost. It's important to take that step because your recovery depends upon it. You deserve to live, and you deserve to activate the impulse that will allow you to reconnect with life.

Consider the possibility of contributing toward preventing more people from suffering in situations similar to your own. You can donate toward the research on the illness that took your child, you can devote your time to collaborating with an association to prevent anyone from having to go through the same experience as your child, you can share your experiences with other people, you can transform your pain into art, or you can do many other things, but the first thing you must do is make the decision to do something. By doing one of those actions or creative processes, you might find the motivation that allows you to take that first step. The death of a loved one paralyzes our body and soul, and leaves us in a state of stupor and lethargy. And unless we overcome it, we won't be able to look after ourselves.

My advice is:

Sometimes we reject help and wish to continue anchored in pain. When we feel a desire to live again, to have hope, or to feel happiness, we might think we have become a heartless being who didn't love the person who died. We pressure ourselves, and we feel pressured by the ideas we have about what people around us will think.

Take Action

Let's start by repairing your life, which has changed completely. You have just lost someone who was a part of your life, which is why you cannot carry on business as usual, or continue with life organized in the same way as before.

Little by little the pain will subside, the sadness will wane, and the anger will start to dissipate. Gradually, your emotional state will start to moderate itself, and you will recover your ability to think straight. When this happens, you need to take advantage of a window of tranquility to design a new life. What happened is painful, but the memory of what happened is painful, too. When you walk past that empty room, every time you see that unused bed or that photograph, your suffering revisits you. You need to change your life, adapt your environment to your new reality, and find a distraction because we can no longer influence the root of the problem. We can't bring back our loved one, so we need to manage our emotions and the consequences of adversity.

Whenever one of my clients has suffered because of bereavement, I have advised them to change their place of residence. The act of moving house has a significant symbolic component because what is actually being done is rebuilding a life.

We all have dreams we want to achieve, plans that we leave until we retire, businesses we want to start, and adventures we would like to experience. Life has hit us hard, but it has also told us that our lives are finite and that we should not leave until tomorrow what we can do today. So you need to start working on achieving your dreams because this is the best homage you can pay to your loved one. He or she did not have the chance; you should not allow yours and theirs to pass you by.

A Dream Cut Short

Some people, after the death of a loved one, invest all of their strength and energy into fulfilling the dream of their loved one. In theory this might seem like a bad idea because there are in fact many strands implicit in this strategy, such as the feeling of guilt for not doing it sooner, the perpetual state of remembrance of the person who passed away, and the denial of our own needs. But it's not for me to deny the numerous positive effects this strategy can have because it provides existential motivation, a "why" and a "what for," a reason to keep on living, and that is what you need after losing a loved one.

But there is yet another positive benefit. On many occasions, achieving the dream of our loved one acts as a compensatory action, like the closure of a chapter. While you are working on achieving the dream, your own motivation is the best distracter (let's remember we can't go to the root of the problem). After we have fulfilled the dream, having experienced new adventures, we can then consider the chapter closed, which is so necessary for being able to start building again.

When we rebuild our lives, we are not for a moment forgetting the person we loved. When you put away their photos, when you move house, and when you change your bed, don't see it as improper or as a betrayal but as an action that is necessary to mitigate the pain and to be able to keep on living. Adapt your environment to your new reality, adjusting it to your new needs, to a life that has changed for you, and to the absence of someone who will never return. Allow their memory to depart, allow yourself to live, and allow yourself to remember your loved one; to do so you don't need their constant presence because that won't help you.

Don't Give More Importance to Death Than to Life

I have seen many people who, grieving over the child who passed away, have forgotten about their living children; or people who, mourning their deceased partner, have forgotten about their children. Other people, weeping for their son, have forgotten about their partner, and lamenting their loved one's absence, have forgotten about themselves. Dear reader, this cannot be. You have a responsibility as a parent, partner, and even as a caregiver toward yourself—a responsibility you cannot evade.

Life goes on, unstoppable. When our souls are broken because we have lost a loved one, we believe that life is cruel. Everything continues to be exactly the same; nothing has changed. The sun continues to rise for everyone, cities continue with their frenzied pace, the seasons follow on one after another, and everything continues to be the same for everyone—except for you. But in reality things aren't like that; life is not cruel but noble and balanced, and we know that we must move on and that we cannot forget about the rest of the creatures in this world who are still alive and who need to live.

Don't forget about yourself or the people around you. Don't prioritize death over life. I know it's not at all easy, but you must try. I know it is easier said than done, but you must try. There is no special technique because it is only a behavioral stance, a declaration of intent that must guide your thoughts, emotions, and actions. Choose to live; opt for doing so with your loved ones, and don't forget that this dynamic attitude does not mean that you have forgotten the beloved person you have lost.

Channel Your Pain

One of the best ways to channel the pain we feel is to transform it into experience and advice for other people. Allow me to explain the case of a wonderful little girl who died of a rare disease. The pain her parents experienced was dreadful; I stress again here that there is nothing worse than the death of a child. After a reasonable period of mourning, the parents decided to channel all their pain in a constructive manner and undertook their personal battle against that terrible and rare disease.

They are fighting in two different ways: on the one hand, in a concrete and visible way—raising funds for research and offering their experience to the medical world through an association of people affected by that disease and the parents of sick children; on the other hand, on a more abstract level, if you like, through campaigning work with social and medical organizations, contributing to reducing the pain of other children and parents by carrying out all the creative actions they can think of.

Sometimes we can't contribute to resolving the root of our problem, but we can contribute to resolving the root of the problem for other people. This strategy is based on transforming pain into something constructive. Building is a wonderful action, and, when we see the result, it acts as a constant reminder of the beauty and greatness of what has been built. Often, the beautiful building erected on pain turns into an homage, a kind of monument to the memory of the beloved—but far from being a sad memory, it's a positive memory, a constructive contribution—a memory that the death of your loved one has served to create a better world, and thus it ceases to be an empty, meaningless death.

Manage Your Memories

When we lose a loved one, our thought processes become disturbed. The process of death itself is a never-ending source of emotional blows that can be intense and painful. If our loved one passed away after an illness, we might have spent their last days watching them suffer and deteriorate; if they died because of a sudden accident, we might have no end of negative emotions such as guilt over that conversation we weren't able to have, the reproach that came out of our mouth, or that time when we had an argument. But in any case, however it has been, even in the sweetest of deaths, the whole process of dying, then the funeral, produces a series of images, words, and emotions that will remain ingrained in our memory, accompanied by pain, confusion, and suffering.

It's not right that those memories should eclipse the countless beautiful memories we have of that wonderful person. We laughed, played, danced, and lived with our loved one. It's not right or fair for you to hold on to a sad memory, so I encourage you to choose an evocative memory that does justice to what you lived and not to what you suffered. In order to make a good choice of evocative memory, you must take an initial step. I encourage you to make a photo album of beautiful moments you experienced together. Look back and go over all those good times. Every time you see a photograph or a video of a nice moment, without being aware of it you will feel a part of that same happiness just through the evocation you are experiencing; the memory of a situation is capable of evoking similar emotions to those experienced in that moment, albeit of a lower intensity.

Make that album. Look at your photos and videos. As you put together this album of memories, you will feel happy and sad, and you will laugh and cry. And that's fine—that mix of opposing emotions is normal and expected. Don't be afraid; allow yourself to cry and to smile. Creating that compilation album is a kind of vital review that will help you to relive beautiful moments and provide a counterpoint to the intense memories associated with the suffering that comes with the end of a life. When you complete it, put it away in a nice, accessible place but not in constant view. Don't keep it next to your bed or in the middle of the dining room. It can be put away in a cupboard or drawer. It must be easy to access—you can look at it as many times as you like—but it shouldn't constantly catch your attention.

You have traveled back in time to a better place. You have relived emotions and memories. Now the time has come to choose one memory among them all—the most beautiful one, the most joyful, the most evocative, or the most representative—that will be your "lead" memory. I have a friend who, when he meets someone or adds a new name to his contacts, takes a photo of them to identify them, and he is happy to make them sit for the photo as many times as necessary until there is a lovely, uplifting image that triggers a positive emotion for him every times he sees it. So I encourage you to do the same as my friend. The lead memory of the loved one who passed away must not be sad or negative; it cannot be in a hospital, at a wake, or with their face disfigured by pain. Your lead memory must be beautiful and sweet, one of the best moments experienced; going over all those beautiful memories will help you find it.

You must not remember your loved one suffering. Instead, you must remember their beauty, their smile, and their vitality, not their tears. Your lead memory of them will be the last thing you have left of them, so choose a nice one that will be with you everywhere you go. As in the film *The Book of Life*, a nice memory will allow you to keep them close to your heart.

When Our Parents Die

We parents have a huge responsibility toward our children. Having a child is one of the greatest acts of love and responsibility. Because our children didn't ask us to bring them into this world, we have an obligation to look after them and give them all the tools they need to be independent, free, and strong. Yes, I said independent. We often confuse being parents with being overprotective. There is nothing worse than creating dependency in our children.

Some parents feel reinforced in their role if they do everything and give everything for their children; they feel needed and important, and they feel that their role as parents has a purpose. However, such parents aren't doing their children any favors. Grown people, when their parents die, cannot be left helpless. In my case, I am consciously bringing up my daughter to be independent so that the day when her mother or I are not here she doesn't feel helpless, lost, and broken.

Our task in raising our children will end when they are independent, strong, balanced, and free. And that means providing them the necessary tools so that they feel confident and able to cope with loss.

Temporary Disconnection

Another strategy that I propose when managing the loss of a loved one is temporary disconnection. When our suffering is out of control, unrestrained, like a wild stampede, our minds become exhausted as a result of all the intense and confusing emotions. This intense emotional overactivity needs to be calmed in order for us to be able to start thinking with a certain amount of perspective. Sometimes all we can do is let life go on for a few days or weeks. If this happens, and if, after trying different strategies, things do not start to shift, consider the possibility of disconnecting temporarily, changing your surroundings, staying with a friend or relative for a few weeks, moving to the countryside, or going to a different city—basically removing yourself and finding distraction in a completely new environment. Maybe you can visit a spa, a monastery, your parents' country cottage, your sibling's house by the beach, or a friend's mountain cabin—it doesn't matter. The main thing is that you remove yourself, change your environment, and surround yourself with people who love you and will help you to alleviate your pain little by little.

You will see that your mind, which is intelligent, will increasingly regain control—thinking, analyzing, and rationalizing. Little by little you will be capable of seeing things again with clarity, contextualizing and building a new life according to your new situation.

Watch Out for Blame

Sometimes we need to find someone to blame so we can explain the pain, a scapegoat that allows us to find an emotional pivot. There are many couples who have lost a child and have transformed their pain into anger against their partner, into rage, hate, and blame.

Be careful with that transferral of the object of pain because you might be ruining the life of someone who is suffering just like you. When faced with a misfortune such as the death of a child, it makes little sense to blame your partner.

Tread lightly with blame because it will lead you to hate, and hate will hold you fast to suffering. Center your energy on finding support instead of finding people to blame.

What's on Your Own Bucket List?

When the storm of grief starts to abate, start thinking about yourself. Look at yourself in the mirror. You have suffered. You are trying to heal. The hurricane of emotions has started to recede. Little by little, sadness is drifting away from you. The time has come to ask yourself the toughest and most healing of questions: What's on your bucket list? Don't live in this world without squeezing the last drops out of life.

Don't resign yourself to surviving, to being an emotional zombie, traipsing from work to home and from home to work. You have an obligation to live, and living is not the same as surviving. What's on your bucket list? What do you need to do? What places do you want to see? You are broken, but you have been able to heal. Now you are stronger, more beautiful, and more majestic. Look at yourself in the mirror. You deserve to live. You deserve to be happy. Happiness isn't one facet with sadness on the opposite side. We can be sad and happy at the same time. We can be in a state of happiness at the core but see a child suffer and feel sad. In the same way, we can be sad about the death of our loved one but incorporate moments of happiness.

Do it; don't resign yourself to suffering. Think about yourself and what you deserve. You don't have to atone for anything, you don't have a debt to repay, and you don't have to do anything apart from live and take advantage of the opportunity that life has given you. Look at yourself in the mirror; don't let death take you by surprise when there are things you still want to do.

Watch Out for Compensatory Behaviors

When we need to heal after the death of a loved one, we are in a vulnerable position. Death has torn away a piece of our soul, leaving us with an emptiness that we need to fill. I want you to fill it with gold, following the ancient art of the masters of kintsugi, but some people try to fill that void with toxic, compensatory behaviors.

Some people try to fill the void with alcohol or drugs, others with daredevil acts that challenge death in a game of chance—goading a kind of accidental suicide—whether it's speeding in a car or other risky pursuits. There are some who surrender themselves in a desperate plea to death, invoking it to end their suffering. There are some who punish others, who torture animals, or who torture themselves. On the surface, these can seem like strategies for easing the pain, but, believe me, they won't do you any good. When we lose a child, the love of our life, or even a beloved pet, we can also momentarily lose all sense of reason.

If someone close to you is suffering bereavement and has adopted unhealthy compensatory behaviors, I encourage you to try to help them with kindness and show them that this sort of behavior is toxic. Try to provide them the perspective they have lost. You can be a light-house in the darkest of storms.

Allow Yourself to Cry

We don't have anything to spare, biologically speaking. Nature and evolution are the best designers that exist. Thousands of years of evolution have managed to give us everything we need and have gotten rid of anything superfluous.

Sadness and tears are not only not negative, but they are good and necessary. We live in a time in which happiness is upheld and sadness demonized and punished. Sadness (though not depression) is a part of the basic set of emotions that allow us to survive. Sadness and its ultimate expression, tears, have an adaptive function. Sadness allows us to retreat and to focus on ourselves in order to think and heal. Like-wise, tears have an important double function: on the one hand they allow us to give an outlet to the emotional tension accumulated in our nervous system and in that way offload the emotional exhaustion, and on the other hand they communicate to the people closest to us that we need help.

So allow yourself to cry. Don't hold back the tears. Crying is going to help you. If your body is asking you for it, cry. Cry as much as you need to because after crying you'll feel better. Cry without feeling guilty, without shame, with abandon, until you don't have a single tear left. Cry as often as you need to, and when you have cried every last tear, dry your eyes and connect with yourself once again, willing to truly live life, knowing yourself to be stronger and more capable.

Don't Isolate Yourself

When you are suffering, you don't want to hear from anyone. Until a certain point in time, this is understandable. We believe we can bear pain better in solitude, but the truth is that this is not the case. We do need moments of quiet, of calm reflection, and of silence. But we know that people who spend time in which they receive social support have a faster and better recovery from bereavement.

Find the balance between solitude and company. Connect with the good people around you. Accept what they offer you. Join a family meal or friends as long as it is pleasant; allow yourself to be cared for by the people who love you; and, above all, don't isolate yourself. Don't isolate yourself from the world or from people. You don't need to have a huge social circle. In these cases, less and good is better than more and bad. Allow yourself to be cared for, let love in, and accept people's displays of care and support. Pick up the phone, open that email, and reach out to your friends and loved ones. Grief is a heavy load that is best carried when the weight is shared between several people.

Coping with Flashbacks

It's possible that the death of a loved one awakens a certain amount of post-traumatic stress. If that's the case, the memories will crop up in the least expected moments—during the day in the form of flashbacks or during the night in the form of nightmares. When a sense of unease takes over your life, and anxiety decides to reach for your hand, you need to take action because it's not only sadness that is torturing you; anxiety has also decided to hop on the bandwagon.

Bring healthy practices into your daily life. Your nervous system is overstimulated, out of control, and stressed. Take action by providing your nervous system calm surroundings. Stop consuming caffeine and stimulants, decrease your activity level, practice some kind of gentle sport, have a hot shower, sleep, rest, go for a walk, and meditate. Seek active and passive relaxation.

A flashback is an extraordinarily vivid image of what happened, specifically a moment with a high emotional charge. These kinds of images barge in without seeking permission at any moment in your life. When this happens, invite them to leave. Take control, and don't allow them to be the trigger of a flood of sad and painful memories. Actively distract yourself and seek your lead memory image, the one you decided to associate with your loved one. Search for it in your mind, in your memories. Change the screen in front of your eyes in the same way that we do with our phone: swipe your finger across the screen and swap the pain for the beauty of a memory.

Don't Let Yourself Go

The grieving process is a complex and often badly managed reaction. The pain of loss is so intense that for some people their thinking and their lives revolve only around loss. This focus causes each and every one of the interests we had before the bereavement—including interest in looking after ourselves and living—to be gradually lost. Every day seems the same, every hour seems empty, and this attitude of giving up on life and letting oneself go usually leads to complications in the management of the trauma.

We let ourselves go when we don't care what we eat or don't even care whether we eat or not. We let ourselves go when we wander the streets without paying attention to what is happening around us, what route we have taken, and which people have crossed our paths. The defeatism becomes visible when we stop taking care of our personal hygiene, appearance, and the way we dress. People who let themselves go speak to you with glazed-over eyes; they might act like they are listening, even nod their heads, but you can see how their minds are a million miles away.

Letting oneself go is neither easy nor hard; it's not only for cowards or for the weak. Sometimes letting oneself go is the consequence of unbearable pain, the only possible choice when facing a world that is crumbling around us.

But, dear reader, don't let yourself go. And don't let friends or loved ones let themselves go after the death of a loved one either. When we let ourselves go, we begin a downward spiral, we create limiting beliefs, and we end up dying inside or living as souls in torment. If you notice someone letting themselves go, reach out to them and do what you can to avoid letting them fall into oblivion. The response tends to be good because this lack of self-care is born from the lack of alternatives. It doesn't matter whether they actually have alternatives or not; what matters is whether the person who is letting themselves go believes they have them. In any case, reach out to them because, in that place of emptiness and despair, when someone offers a hand, a light, a smile, it's as if suddenly the person who is suffering regains perspective and connects with life again.

Compensate for Your Suffering

When our souls break, when a loved one dies, we are clear about one thing: the pain will be with us for a long, long time. Recovering from the death of a child is complicated, and it will be impossible to avoid that pain for the rest of your life. Every time you visit a new place, when you see your loved one's favorite bike on the street or when you see parents and children playing happily, you will be seized by a feeling of sadness, whether the tears roll down your cheek or in your heart. Those will be the moments when your scar will hurt, when you will look at it with sadness, and when you should see a beautiful scar. The pain of the loss of a loved one will be with us for the rest of our lives, with greater or lesser intensity. When the anniversary of their death draws near, it will hurt more; when we get distracted, a little less. Even if they are not a constant presence, there are so many occasions to think about the person we lost that it seems nearly impossible to believe that we will not continue to suffer for the rest of our lives. We must be prepared for it, prevent it, and manage it. The best strategy is to compensate for our suffering but in a healthy, balanced, and kind way. The suffering is compensated with life, living, enjoying positive emotions and pleasant sensations. Our scales must always be balanced. Our bodies can easily tolerate a momentary lack of balance, or even a sharp pain, but they cannot repair large and powerful imbalances sustained over time.

Incorporate a compensation plan into your daily life. Create a list of actions, thoughts, or memories that generate a positive emotion that allows you to compensate for the suffering. It might be taking a walk, enjoying a memory, or even writing a letter or some reflections. You can compensate for your suffering with a vacation, a good read, or a chat with friends. Compensate for the pain with an emotional painkiller that will allow you to mitigate your suffering and distract yourself.

Actively reconstruct your emotional balance. Fight to reestablish that necessary balance in order to continue living, to continue looking after yourself, and to continue to be connected. Compensate for the pain actively, free of guilt and shame, and remember this is absolutely not an insensitive or frivolous position to take.

Our lives are guided by the process of necessity and compensation. Motivation is what keeps life going and is always born from a lack of balance that must be compensated. When we feel hungry, we need to compensate for that sensation, that need. When we feel thirsty, we activate a compensation mechanism that consists of drinking. And so, in the same way, we compensate for tiredness, pain, or any of the emotional needs we have.

Our Needs

Our needs have an adaptive role. Our bodies communicate with us through needs. The need to eat, drink, and sleep keeps us alive. The need for affection, achievement, and recognition allows us to achieve objectives that are important to us and to the people around us.

The body's homeostatic mechanism is governed by need. When there is an imbalance, our bodies or our minds send out a signal in the form of a need, which is why we can say that needs have a clear adaptive function.

In general we often believe that needs are bad. But, far from this unjust and thoughtless demonization of needs, we should realize they are not only good but they are also necessary, if you will forgive the self-evident nature of that statement. The problem appears when needs are out of focus (for example, because of excessive sadness), and they turn into a disorder that conditions our life.

What happens is that often we don't know how to translate the messages that our bodies are sending, and we satisfy that imbalance with needs that depart from its demands. In this way, the need to have an extramarital love affair is in reality nothing more than the need to stop and analyze the life we are living as a couple and to reconsider a few things. The need to acquire possessions might be showing us that we need to reconsider our lifestyle. The need to eat compulsively might be showing us that we have elevated anxiety levels and that we must reconsider our priorities. The need for recognition or protection is giving us a clear message about our self-esteem.

In addition, it's also clear that there is an extensive and complex needs industry that bases its activities on the creation of need in order to sell products. This is not a conspiracy theory but just a statement of fact. We only have to watch television for a few minutes to see that there are endless products manufactured to cover certain needs that we don't really have, or rather, that we should tend to but in a different way. Thus, a new car will be able to give you the security you need, an expensive handbag will communicate your status and your power, and a vacation in paradise will allow you to impress your colleagues at the office.

Dear reader, don't deny your needs; don't avoid them. Try to tend to them and understand them. Analyze them, discover the message that your body is sending, and don't think twice about covering your needs in the best way.

Needs, like pain, are good and adaptive. Pain prevents us from continuing to do something that is damaging us, just as going to the doctor may prevent further complications. Something similar happens with needs, whatever their type, but often we don't know how to understand, manage, and respond to them. Some people claim to eliminate needs from their life, but far from this being a viable option, it shows a vital lack of coherence that is covered up with bizarre justifications, trying to buttress a building that is impossible to hold up. We need love, we need comfort, and we need acknowledgment in the same way that we need food. The problem is not the needs we have but that we have not been taught how to understand and manage them.

Where Do I Start?

- Start by crying and allowing the sadness that you feel to be expressed.

- Accept that your life has changed, and adapt it little by little to your new situation.

- Don't give more importance to death than to life.

- Give your pain a constructive outlet.

- Manage your memories.

- Do what you have always wanted to do.

- Practice self-care; don't let yourself go.

- Compensate for your suffering; regenerate yourself. In the same way that in a long-distance race you need to be hydrated and nourished, you need to regenerate yourself because grief is a long-distance route.

How Do I Do It?

When a loved one dies, sadness takes over and relegates the rest of our world to the background, including ourselves and our needs. If we adopt the following practical steps, we can better cope with the death of a loved one:

- Sleep well because the body and brain regenerate themselves during sleep. Sleep as much as you need but no more than nine hours; have a nap if you need to.

- Eat well. Don't stop eating, and when you eat, choose healthy foods. Eat a balanced diet, eat fruit and vegetables, and eliminate toxic foods and habits. Eat in a balanced way, without seeking an escape in food. Don't stop making your own food, don't eat just anything, and don't eat compulsively. Eat because food is the best guarantee of balance that we have.

- Distract yourself. Thinking a lot about the absence of a loved one doesn't mean that you love them more or that you miss them more. Visit friends and family, go to the theater, go for a walk, read, travel, and do whatever you like, but distract yourself because this will allow you to recharge your batteries, finding the energy you'll need to cope with the difficult process of grieving.

- Physical activity is a precursor to a good mood because it releases endorphins, distracts us, and allows us to connect with our natural environment. Do some sort of physical activity (walk, run, cycle, or swim), and whenever you get the chance, do it in a natural, pleasant, and inspiring environment.

- Talking is good for the heart because it lessens the weight it is carrying, and it gives shape to the sadness that invades us. Don't keep what you feel inside to yourself. Speak up, share it with someone else, and, when you share it, you'll see how it slowly takes on a gentler and more developed shape.

Repairing Love

Broken Hearts

Maria

She never imagined that her love would break her into a thousand pieces. She found out by chance, as often happens. They had guests over at their house. She went to the downstairs bathroom, but it was in use. So she went to the upstairs bathroom, and there she overheard her husband speaking on the phone. She couldn't believe it. She didn't want to believe it.

She went into the room next to the bathroom and caught him red-handed. He went into the sort of rage that any liar shows when trying to distract and play for time. She snatched the phone off him and saw who he was talking to; she saw messages and photos. She was brokenhearted. Her husband threw a relationship of ten years onto the shattered pieces of her disappointment, breaking her into a thousand pieces. Maria bent down and picked them up. Disappointment became mixed with sadness, rage, and guilt, the kind of guilt experienced by someone who has been a victim of emotional abuse.

Robert

He fell head over heels with his first love, always the most beautiful and intense. He knew that he was giving himself unreservedly to someone with more experience in matters of love. He knew it, and he gave himself unconditionally. Can first love come with conditions? He gave himself stripped of any shield or protective armor. He gave his soul and his body to someone who swore eternal love.

He knew that first love was the most beautiful but also the one that hurt the most when it broke. And it did break. And with it his soul, his life, his dreams, and his poetry were shattered. He had known it and, despite everything, had not been able to avoid it. "I will never again suffer for love," he swore as he picked up the pieces of his wretched heart.

Isaac

He glanced at her from across the table. He decided to have one more drink. "How could I have fallen in love with someone like that? What has happened to us? We had such a lust for life, and we kissed with such passion; now I can't look at her without feeling intense pain and rage. Were we really the perfect couple?" The merlot fogged his memory. "Maybe we never should have married." He wasn't sure if they had ever truly shared anything. On the surface they had, but the passage of time had done nothing but demonstrate that that midsummer night in Menorca would mark them for the rest of their lives and not in a good way.

"How could I marry someone I met while I was drunk at a party?" Now everything seemed so clear—or so confusing. Love is wayward. He wanted to love her. But they never should have started what now he could not finish.

His strength failed him. What about the children? He needed an impetus. He poured himself another drink. He felt more and more in a fog. He got up, feeling dizzy. He saw the picture of the children on the mantelpiece. "Maybe I'll tell her tomorrow," he thought. "I'm off to bed, darling," he said to his wife, and along the way his dignity shattered into a thousand pieces.

Natalia

She wanted him to love her. She desired him so much. She didn't care what he asked. She mistook love for submissiveness. She wanted to feel loved. He saw that she wanted love, and he allowed himself to be bought. She bought eagerly. He didn't have a "no" for any of her requests.

Nothing costs as much as loneliness. She liked seeing him happy, and making him happy was easy—nothing that her healthy bank account couldn't cope with. Everything was going really well. Their relationship was fantastic—on the surface, at least—until one day, after spending a few days at some friends' house, she realized what true love was, the kind of love that is needed to start a family, to raise children, to overcome the adversities of life, and to grow old together.

That night she couldn't sleep. That night she realized that she couldn't buy love. But why would she have to buy it? Would she never be able to find it? That night she realized that it was better to be to all appearances alone than to all appearances in a relationship. That night she burst into tears, tore up his photo, and broke off the relationship. What hurt the most was not having been able to do it sooner. Natalia picked up the pieces of her shame, which were scattered through dreams, and she cried herself to sleep, exhausted from suffering so much.

Take a Step Back

What about you? Are you sure that what you have discovered is bad news? The end of a relationship is hard work, a disappointment, and a terrible kind of pain. But I think you'll agree with me that, if you look at it with a certain amount of perspective, there is no reason it should be all bad news. In the first place, when love comes to an end, whether it's the result of an infidelity, through running its course, or because it never existed, a situation becomes evident that you perhaps intuited but that you didn't want to confirm. In fact, in many situations similar to the ones I have described above, the person who has been deceived, the worn-out person, or the one with a broken heart feared something or expected something. And the truth is that we often consciously allow ourselves to be deceived because, if we don't, we would have to accept and come to terms with some painful and uncomfortable consequences. After almost twenty years of working with and seeing innumerable relationship problems, I can confirm that when a relationship ends, what hurts the most is the fact of having deceived yourself, having denied the reality that you were perceiving.

All right, your partner has left you—she cheated on you; he was unfaithful to you or ignored you—which is tough, I stress that, but if you look for the silver lining, you now have evidence that you need a change in your life. We don't tend to change until the pain is too hard to bear—until the suffering runs too deep. It's possible that for a long time you have been aware on some level that your relationship wasn't working, and there was nothing you could do to turn it around. But the time has finally come!

Now you are clear about it. The end has come sooner. The denouement has come to your doorstep. I understand your pain and bewilderment, but I have to say that practically 100 percent of people I have helped overcome an infidelity or a failed relationship have become a lot happier in their lives after the initial pain.

There is no reason the end of a relationship should be a negative change; in fact, it's a change of uncertain nature. We cannot say that it's a change for the worse because we don't know what destiny has in store for us. It's true that initially everything looks grim. Emotions take hold of reason like a violent and cruel tornado. Overcoming a breakup is no easy task, especially if it involves a separation after living under the same roof. There's a long list of problems and negotiations we would have never imagined, such as having to look for a new house, dividing up possessions, and formalizing custody of children. However, what I have just described are not negative consequences of a separation, just uncomfortable consequences. Don't confuse them. Don't mistake something uncomfortable for something negative or a change for the worse. As I say, nearly 100 percent of the people I have helped overcome a separation, after the initial discomfort and necessary reorganization, have learned to enjoy life again with a great deal of passion, in a way that they had not done for years.

However, we cannot say that a separation will necessarily be a change for the better because, if we don't do anything, nothing will happen. Maybe chance will smile at you, but I suggest that while you are waiting for the joy of good fortune, you go and look for that "good luck" yourself. You know, in reality, you have no idea what your future will be like, but what you can be sure of is that it's in your power to bring about a positive turn in your life. In the different cases outlined earlier, which are as real as they are common, after a few troubled months the different protagonists enjoyed life intensely, asking themselves over and over why on earth they had not realized sooner that the people they were sharing their lives with didn't love them at all.

In the same way, I'll tell you that in practically all cases I have to work hard for my clients to relearn how to love so as not to give up on something as important as sharing their lives with other people. But I'm getting ahead of myself because I'm so eager to explain to you how you can overcome a failed relationship. Come on, let's think differently!

My advice is:

It's always better to end a chapter than to crawl on with it at any price. When faced with the earliest signs that the relationship is not going well, assess whether it can be turned around. If there's any chance of turning the situation around, go ahead—but always with a deadline. But if the relationship is doomed, don't prolong the agony of the inevitable; swiftly bring that period to a close.

Think Differently

"How can I be sure that my partner still loves me? How can I prove it?" Often one half of the couple experiences insecurity and fear. Maybe this fear is justified because of a change in attitude of their partner, or maybe not. But in any case, when fear shows up, insecurity takes over our minds and souls, tormenting us and doing away with our ability to enjoy our relationship as a couple.

"I share increasingly little with my husband." "Can I get my wife back?" "Can we feel passion as a couple again?" "How can I love my partner again?" "Can we overcome an infidelity?" "For years we've been focusing on the children and work, and we've neglected each other. Is it possible to recover what has been lost?" I've often been asked these questions by couples who have been together for between ten and twenty years. During that time, both halves of the couple have lived in parallel, together but disconnected. They often seem more like roommates than a couple once burning with passion and imagining a future full of exciting plans.

How did they get to this point? One day you cancel dinner with your partner because of work. Another day you have no time for each other because one of the kids is ill. Another day you're too tired to share an intimate moment. Another day you have to get up early for work, and you're in a bad mood. Then it's the holidays, and you need to disconnect from it all and have time to yourself. It's Christmas by now, and you don't feel like going to your in-laws' because you would rather go on a short trip away; an argument ensues. Now it's the festive period again, but because of work, we have only one week off at the same time. Suddenly years have gone by, a whole decade. And suddenly the kids are all grown up and I don't recognize myself or the person who lives with me. And then the doubts appear, the crises, the fear, the impulsive decisions, the arguments, the disenchantment, and so forth.

Give Yourselves the Chance to Get to Know Each Other Again

Over the years I have changed, and so has my partner; we are both strangers, which is a problem and at the same time an opportunity. It's a problem because I can't continue to do the same thing that I was doing five, ten, fifteen, or twenty years ago. But it's also a wonderful opportunity to get to know each other again: to talk to each other again; to explore our bodies, souls, fears, and desires again; to talk about the future; and to close one chapter and open another.

I have seen how many couples have decided to break off their relationships without giving themselves the chance to get to know each other again—couples who simply needed to rebuild a bridge of communication between the two of them—couples who just needed to spend a few hours together alone, flirting, talking, and dreaming.

The Legend of the Red Thread of Fate

There is an ancient legend in China and Japan that says souls who are predestined to come together on this Earth are tied together with an invisible red thread so that they can find each other and not lose each other. The red thread might strain, stretch, or become tangled, but it never breaks.

There are times when an ideal couple—a couple with a high level of connection indicators, a couple who can be happy—strains their thread for different reasons. Sometimes it's because of illness, stress, pressure from other family members, children, or any number of scenarios that present us challenges and problems. These couples, the ones who are truly joined together by the red thread, should dedicate some time to rebuild their relationship before deciding to abandon it.

"Why has love gone away?" Whenever I am asked this question, I reply with a question: "What have you based your relationship on as a couple? On the body? On physical attraction? On passion? On fun? Was there ever truly love in the relationship?" Life presents us different scenarios as individuals and as couples, which can create tension and distance between the two people.

And Suddenly Life Got Complicated

I have met people who haven't been able to handle an experience or a problem, which ends up affecting the relationship as a couple. Throughout our lives we come across situations and events that hugely distort our emotional states, thoughts, and behavior, and they tend to have a high emotional impact. They can even cause changes in our personalities. They tend to be situations like job loss, pregnancy, diagnosis of an illness, accidents, change of place of residency, and so on.

Any situation that generates stress, anxiety, or uncertainty of whatever kind will have certain negative effects for the individual and for the couple. When stress materializes, we become more irritable, more intolerant, and less understanding. We communicate less, and the content of our communication tends to be more negative and to be in the form of reproaches. We lose the spark and everything that makes us fun and interesting. In addition, this change creeps up on us slowly, without us realizing it. Suddenly we have nothing to do with the person we used to be. Our partner doesn't understand us, or as happens in other cases, our partner has made a huge effort to be tolerant and understanding, which starts to take its toll. Depending on how we manage these traumatic situations, they will have one or another impact on our relationship as a couple. However, the first step is always the same. The point of departure consists of realizing the emotional state you are in, which is not always easy.

Sometimes this situation can be turned around; sometimes it can't.

Getting to know each other again can be a stimulating, interesting, and fun adventure. Don't make a decision from a place of exhaustion. You can't end a relationship without analyzing what has happened. If you devote some time to analyzing the context of your relationship as a couple—how you have gotten to this point, why the possibility of a separation came up, and whether there is any real possibility of succeeding as a couple—you will be in the right place to make an informed, correct decision, whether that is to stay together or to break up. In order to be able to make this right decision, I propose that you take action. Start by analyzing your situation, looking for alternatives, and foreseeing the consequences in the short, medium, and long term for each and every one of the different alternatives; likewise, prioritize and decide on the better alternatives.

But let's start at the beginning, relearning how to love. Throughout my clinical practice I have been able to observe that, for many people, separating from a toxic and harmful partner has left a deep mark on them, but in reality it has been a blessing. On many occasions, the quality of this mark has been negative and has influenced the course of their subsequent relationships. The blame and shame have obscured what in reality was liberation.

Most couple separations are a result of the fact that a false positive has seeped into the relationship. When we believe that something is working, or someone is right for us, and it's not the case, we're faced with a false positive. If we start a relationship as a couple with a false positive, it's only a matter of time before we have a frustrating and negative experience, which can become painful and will influence all our future relationships.

I've known people who have decided not to have a partner again, not to trust anyone again. This kind of decision tends to be motivated by suffering. When we have a painful experience, certain defense mechanisms appear that put up high walls to protect our hearts. I've met people who, after being in one or several tempestuous relationships, have decided to show a passive and submissive attitude toward their new partner. That attitude provides them tranquility and stability but only on the surface and in the short term. In the medium and long terms, passiveness turns into frustration and implosive or explosive aggressiveness.

There are people who because of past experiences adopt a resigned attitude when entering a new relationship. Resignation cancels out willpower and can even have the opposite of the desired effect because the other person can become tired of carrying the weight of the relationship. In addition, in the medium term resignation evolves in the shape of reproaches or disconnection by saturation. In the worst cases, resignation is applied at the moment of choosing a new partner, so no criteria are applied and any old candidate is accepted, whether suitable or not.

I've seen people who have concluded that they must adopt a dominant role as a result of their past experiences. These kinds of behaviors, again, are highly toxic and cause suffering in the medium and long terms. Domination completely nullifies the submissive person, creating dependency and anxiety.

There are also people who believe that to love is to manipulate, to be cruel, or to inflict a punishment. Perhaps these people have needs that can be met only by means of a toxic couple relationship.

Whatever the case, the best approach to be able to enjoy a full and satisfying life as a couple is to learn how to love. Perhaps we have reached this point because of past negative experiences or conclusions extracted from negative experiences that are partial, out of context, and based on generalizations, but now the time has come to relearn how to love and, of course, to relearn how to love yourself.

My advice is:

When faced with a painful, negative, emotional experience, our cognitive process (that is, our thinking) is affected in such a way that it loses analytical capacity, reducing our ability to think clearly, put things into context, and extract valid and trustworthy conclusions. In many cases, or dare I say in most of them, the origin of these relationship problems can be located in the conclusions we draw from our earliest experiences related to love and romantic relationships.

Take Action

The time has come to take action, to get to work on ourselves—our hearts and our concepts of love. It's clear, crystal clear, that at some point or other your heart has been broken. All right then, pick up the pieces—yes, the ones you have been keeping in the darkest corner of your past. Pick them up because we have work to do. We have to repair your heart so that it beats strongly again—so that it is thrilled by a kiss, moved by a caress, optimistic about love.

Review Your Past Experiences

We look at the past from the present. From here you can enjoy the perspective afforded you by time and distance. If you like, we will use it to analyze what happened. Allow me to share an example that illustrates a common situation.

The case of a client who had a bad first relationship experience comes to my mind. Nothing out of the ordinary happened; she just experienced a disappointment soon after the start of the relationship. And from that she concluded that she had been hurt, and she took refuge in armor that no one could get past. Without her realizing or being aware of it, this armor was responsible for the failure of the next four relationships. The same ending was always repeated. She wasn't able to relax and go with the flow—she wasn't herself in all her splendor—she was always tense and defensive. Her partners could never get close; doubts arose, and they would end up calling it a day. My work with her was complex and difficult; in fact, until she took a step back, she was not able to see that she was the one who was causing the end of her relationships.

I suggest that you choose a past relationship that didn't end the way you wanted. Now gain a bit of perspective and analyze what happened. Don't worry, I will come with you and guide you throughout the whole process. I'm sure that with the benefit of distance you will see that there are aspects of that past relationship that were not good and others that were. It's about analyzing, free of prejudice, what happened in order to be able to draw better conclusions. When we are suffering, we need to rapidly eliminate the tension we feel, which is why we run away, which in turn carries a high emotional cost.

I remember, too, a client I spent hours and endless sessions with talking about a difficult relationship. The woman he was in a relationship with was with him out of an interest that went beyond love. He, madly in love, sought consultation for an anxiety disorder. After carrying out the diagnosis process, I was able to see that his anxiety was reactive and that the origin of the anxiety was the relationship—well, not exactly his partner, but the contradictions that existed because of the dissonant inputs between his perception and reality. That is, he was experiencing a conflict between the reality as perceived by his senses and the feelings that emanated from his heart. He continually saw things that he didn't like, that were out of tune with how things should be, or that contradicted how a loving attitude from his partner should be. He could see it, and he could feel it, but he didn't want to accept it. His friends, his family, and even his partner's friends warned him and tried to show him reality.

I helped him to analyze the situation, to find evidence, to study the dissonances he was feeling, and to give credit to his perceptions, and he decided to abandon the process. He disappeared from the consultation room and didn't walk back through the door until five or six months later. At last he had gathered the necessary courage to believe his own perceptions and to leave his partner. But along the way he paid a dear price. A few months of the relationship cost him an addiction to alcohol and marijuana—which he used to self-medicate his anxiety—and broken self-esteem. He realized that he had been manipulated and that he had been unable to see it, despite the feedback and signs he had received. In reality, the only thing that had happened was that he had tried to force reality to fit in with his desires, deceiving himself. He made a decision and tried to stick with it despite the clear signs that were indicating a lack of adjustment in his thoughts and beliefs.

When we worked together again, he was able to gain the necessary perspective to properly analyze what had happened, draw the right conclusion, and learn from his mistakes to ensure he would not jeopardize his future relationships. We started the process again, but under one condition: we had to begin by analyzing what had happened in the past and its consequences in order to be able to close one chapter and start another, free of prejudice and errors.

Analyze the Critical Events

What were your past experiences like? Why were they like that? Now is the time to analyze them from afar. Analyze the reasons things went well or did not, and try to draw some conclusions. Without thinking too hard (we'll filter this later), make a list of factors that caused conflict or influenced the course of the relationship.

I invite you to analyze each and every one of your relationships. You can even make a summary table for each partner. I've met many people who tended to repeat patterns in the different relationships they had. In this case, we tend to select the same kind of partner, with the same characteristics, repeating the same behaviors, with similar outcomes.

Your analysis must be detailed, and it must contain the elements outlined below. Please do answer these questions with perspective and a sense of distance—minimizing your involvement—and sincerely, without being afraid of the answers you might find.

The first question you must answer is: What was the reason the relationship went wrong? It's likely that there is no single reason. Perhaps it was an accumulation of reasons and events that led to the end of the relationship. Try to pick them apart and analyze them, without resentment, without pain—like someone watching an old film, as a spectator.

Now that you have analyzed the reasons the relationship didn't work, you need to take a step further. Which of the reasons for the breakup or the bad experience are attributable to your partner? Try to think about concrete things and then abstract them: "We always argued about where to spend Christmas, which was really just a display of selfish and disrespectful behavior." There are things that we accept as normal when we shouldn't. Trying to dominate someone else's will through manipulation or coercion should not be normal. If we take the last example, we can analyze different communication styles, which reveal the couple's different attitudes. We are often manipulated, coerced, or bribed into meeting the desires and needs of our partners, as in the example of deciding where to spend Christmas. A healthier behavior could be to put the cards on the table and have a conversation about it—a conversation, not an argument.

After we have evaluated the responsibility of the other person, the time has come to analyze which of the reasons we have specified on the list are attributable to ourselves. Maybe you won't find anything, but I believe it's worth making an effort to analyze things. You shouldn't punish yourself, or self-flagellate, but neither should you deceive yourself with your conclusions.

Now we are going to analyze everything that went well and that we did like. Sometimes we contaminate our perception with a halo effect in accordance with the quality of our experience. It's possible that, if the relationship went badly, you will contaminate the memories, tingeing them with negativity. Try to notice whether the halo effect appears. Don't generalize; analyze in detail. It's possible that you might find something interesting. Don't deny everything; look for the enjoyable moments—the sweet memories—if there were any. If you are capable of discriminating without issuing a judgment and without contaminating what happened with negativity, you will be able to analyze in more detail and with greater efficiency.

What Can You Learn from This Experience?

Let's see what you can learn from what happened. What conclusions are you left with? This process that I have just told you about is the same one I use in consultations as we walk, pedal, or ski around the Pyrenees. I would like to give you a concrete example that I think might help you.

Sara had a bad experience with her partner. After two years together, her partner decided to end the relationship in order to start a new one with a different person. When carrying out the exercise of analysis, Sara realized that the relationship had gone badly because the degree of involvement from both partners was different. He wanted to move the relationship on faster, and she displayed a certain amount of coldness and fear of commitment. Over time he was disenchanted with her; he found it increasingly hard to put up with her coldness and her scant displays of affection. Sara decided that her partner was responsible for communicating better and making his needs explicit. Other things happened, too, but to simplify, by way of example, we will stick to the communication problems with her partner at the time. As she continued to complete the exercise, Sara realized that she was partly responsible for the failure of the relationship. She admitted that she had been cold and distant, that she didn't manage to get close to her partner, and that she was running away from making plans for the future with him. What she considered to be normal back then, she now perceives as inadequate. She needed a few years, some distance, and a bit of maturity in order to analyze the relationship. But, above all, what she needed was to analyze what happened without distorting her thoughts or reality. As long as we are distorting things, we will not be in a position to decide what aspects we need to change and improve before starting a new relationship.

Did you identify with Sara's example? The time has come to analyze how you have cognitively processed these past experiences with the objective of identifying whether there are any "cognitive distortions" or defense mechanisms.

Learn to Recognize Your Cognitive Distortions

There are many ways in which we deceive ourselves more or less consciously; in psychology, we catalog them as cognitive distortions. I have selected a few of the most common ones. Perhaps you are applying one or more of them, but don't worry, this is common. With this exercise I would like you to acquire the knowledge and skills necessary to be able to identify and work through them.

There are people who tend to polarize their thinking. They think in terms of all or nothing. Either I give myself wholly without asking for anything in return, or I don't let people in. Either I have a stable relationship, or I never go on a date with anyone ever again. In romantic relationships, as in the rest of life's situations, nothing is black and white; it's all just a continuum of shades to be discovered.

In some cases we tend to overgeneralize what happened in a relationship. Based on an isolated fact, we draw a generalized conclusion that is normally false: "All boys are insensitive," "All girls are too sensitive," "No one can be trusted," "Everyone is bad," "Everyone wants to take advantage of you," and so forth. This kind of thinking cancels out any initiative and doesn't allow us to learn or analyze what has gone wrong or right in the relationship. It's about notions that aren't true or real, though what matters, as in other cognitive distortions, is not reality but how I interpret it—because ultimately, my thoughts will guide my interpretation of reality, my emotions, and my acts.

There are people who apply a negative filter to their experience in such a way that they focus only on the negative and harmful aspects. We can't start a new relationship from this perspective because we will be anticipating the future in negative terms, focusing on all the bad things that could happen.

There are more distortions, many more, but with these we have covered the most frequent situations that take place in relationships between couples. Distorted thinking gives us a certain amount of peace and short-term resources, but in the medium and long terms it damages us. We can't build a conclusion on a foundation that isn't solid.

Another concept I would like to highlight is that of the self-fulfilling prophecy. In psychology we observe this phenomenon when someone, whether consciously or not, ends up causing what they believe will happen. For example, if you believe you are going to have a bad time when you go to a party, it's likely that will be the case. Why? Because you will be less receptive, you will have a hostile attitude, people won't approach you, and those who do won't have a positive interaction, without you realizing it. If, on the contrary, you believe you will have a really good time, it's likely that this will happen. You will probably actively seek the chance to enjoy yourself and have a good time, you'll be receptive, and you'll fit in well with the communication needs of other people.

Until now I have listed a series of phenomena, mechanisms, and relationship styles that can be a negative influence in a relationship between a couple. It's important that you understand them and are able to identify them because we are often not aware that we are under the influence of one of these processes. The first step consists of analyzing whether it happens to you and whether you can identify with any of these situations. Acknowledging and coming to terms with this is difficult, but it is the only way in which we can initiate change.

Don't Repeat the Same Mistake

At times we are not aware that we are repeating a pattern. I know people who have left abusive partners and repeated the same situation with a new abusive partner, and again four times in a row with four different partners. It's not that that person is not learning from the experience but that they might have a filter that only sees someone who meets certain criteria as a potential partner. In this way, only abusers pass that filter and are deemed as potential candidates. From there on, the selection consists of choosing the best option among the candidates—that is, the least abusive one.

On other occasions it's as though we are doing charity work, in which case the relationship is destined to fail. "He'll change eventually," "I'll help her," or "I'll change him" are phrases that show early signs of a failure foretold. If you remember, in the first exercise we dedicated some time to reflecting on the importance of starting a relationship from a place of acceptance, both of what we are like and what our partners are like.

Where Do I Start?

- Start by making a decision—the firm
  decision to love again intensely.

- Learn from what you have experienced, but
  leave the ghosts of the past behind.

- Don't rush things in your relationships. Time
  is the best ally to get to know a person.

- Don't try to get something from a relationship that you are lacking.
  First become strong in yourself and then look for someone
  with whom to share life, not someone who drags you down.

How Do I Do It?

- Analyze how we interpret what has happened
  to us and our negative experiences.

- You need to relearn to love following experiences that
  took place with a false positive, or with an error.

- It's as important to learn to identify the potential
  candidates, as well as to draw the right conclusions
  from a relationship that is ending.

- Identify whether you are suffering any of the most
  frequent attitudes that happen after a relationship that has
  gone wrong: passiveness, aggressiveness, disconnection,
  power struggles, despondency, and so on.

- Remember how hard it is to become aware of, and
  then come to terms with, the fact that you are
  distorting reality to suit your interests.

Repairing Hope

Chloe's Story: Falling into the Void

Chloe walked slowly, her gaze vacant, looking for a shred of hope without finding it. She was dragging her feet; she was tired. Her life was exhausting. She was tired of suffering so much, of worrying about everything, of letting everyone down. At last she was clear about one thing in her life. The fence separating her from the void below hit her at waist height. Life hurt, failure hurt, hopelessness hurt, the fact that she had failed everyone hurt. She took a swig from the bottle of gin that hung from her hand. She could no longer bear all this suffering.

She slid her legs to the other side of the fence—first the right, then the left. Before her was the abyss. How ironic. She had always lived in a void, facing a bottomless sadness that no one could understand. Chloe had it all; any woman would envy her. She was beautiful and intelligent; she had a partner who loved her and wonderful children; she lived in a dream home; she had the ideal job; and, despite it all, she was unhappy.

She felt the fresh breeze all over her body. She felt cold. Who wants to wrap up warm to die? She had been looking for warmth and shelter for a long time. For too long, Chloe had not been able to enjoy anything; she couldn't relax, she couldn't even sleep. She took another sip. She threw the bottle into the emptiness like someone who sends a scout out to check the terrain. The emptiness; that emptiness she felt. How ironic! In the end, emptiness had won.

She had tried. Every morning she tried. Getting out of bed is a tremendous feat when you have spent the whole night turning things over in your head and crying. She struggled to give a meaning to her life—the life that held her trapped in a cage of sorrow and loneliness. For the first time she became aware that her sorrow was at last going to end, her suffering and that of the people around her. She was so often stigmatized as weak, fragile, immature, capricious, and demanding. Her parents never understood her; neither did her husband. No one understood her sorrow, her chronic dissatisfaction, her lack of hope and energy, her existential emptiness.

There she was, alone and facing the void; it couldn't be that bad. For a long time she had felt alone, and she had always felt guilty about it. She had always been made to feel guilty. "I can't count on you for anything." "You always have to ruin our day." "You aren't capable of enjoying anything." "You go around all day like a zombie, with vacant eyes."

And there she was, faced with the void, with a hope, with the end of a life that she never truly lived, the end of a suffered life. The deep sorrow she was feeling was going to come to an end. She closed her eyes. She looked for a nice memory, something sweet. But she couldn't find anything. She hung her head. Her hair covered her face. Nobody had helped her. Everybody had judged her for her depression. "Make more of an effort," her husband yelled at her. "You're too sentimental," her father yelled at her. "You never play with us," her children yelled at her.

She looked up and opened her eyes. The sun was coming out. She was looking without seeing. Her eyes were tired and sad. There was no hope left in her. The wind played with her hair. She looked to her right, hoping to find something, looking for something, hoping that the world would give her a new chance. But all she could see was pain and suffering. She let herself fall. She leapt into the void. She was more than familiar with that sensation of emptiness, of not knowing who you are or what you are supposed to be like. She leapt into the void. And she felt the pain of giving up, the pain of failing, the pain of being different, the pain of not even being able to live—a task that anyone is able to do. She felt an intense pain on her arm, and she let herself fall.

She was suspended in the air, not wanting to open her eyes. She heard some distant voices. She was shocked. She had not been taught how to live—how to respect herself—not even how to love herself. Life flashed before her eyes like a horror movie. Neither had she been taught how to die. "I've got her!" yelled one of the young hikers. "Help me," he yelled at his companion, who was running over. "What the hell are you doing?" he yelled at the girl as he held her firmly. More yelling. "Everyone yells at me," she thought. She was exhausted. She had no more strength to speak. She closed her eyes again. She burst into silent tears.

Her chest collapsed; she had a lump in her throat. It was difficult to breathe. She had no strength even to cry. She shut her eyes tight. Nobody wants to lose their life, but when life is no longer life, there is nothing to lose. She heard distant voices again. She was no longer cold. She was lying in bed. She tried to open her eyes. Everything was blurry. She could feel her empty and broken heart, full of fragments of memories, hopes, and fears.

"Darling." She heard that voice again. It was sweet and calm. It transmitted the peace she had been seeking for so long. "Your life has broken, but you can rebuild it again, and when you do, you will see that you are stronger than you ever believed. It doesn't matter what happened; what truly matters is everything that will happen from now on. We're going to pick up all those pieces and give them a shape again, without feeling ashamed of our past, without hiding our scars—because they show that we have been stronger."

Take a Step Back

Chloe has a huge problem—a disorder that affects a large part of the population and that is being underdiagnosed; a problem that takes years to fully manifest, which is why people don't seek treatment from a psychotherapist or psychiatrist until it is too late; a problem that puts you on the ropes until you can no longer bear it; and a problem that has a name: depression.

Am I Depressed?

If you feel sad and empty most of the day, every day; if you are incapable of enjoying things and you feel unsatisfied; if you have lost or gained weight; if you are sleeping less or more than usual; if you are experiencing physical agitation or slowness; if you feel fatigued and you have less energy; if you have inappropriate and unjustified feelings of guilt or worthlessness; if you have trouble thinking, concentrating, or making decisions; and if you have recurrent thoughts about death or suicide, it is likely you are depressed. These are the symptoms of depression, a terrible illness. They are symptoms that, unlike those of a broken leg, go by unnoticed, are judged by society, and subject the afflicted person to unimaginable suffering.

That's right, depression is an illness. Never underestimate the impact that depression can have. Only people who have been through it are aware of what it means—of the slow apocalypse that it is to suffer it. Depression is a terrible illness that takes over your life little by little, without you realizing it. I often meet people who arrive at the consulting room saying that they have separated from their partners and, as a consequence, have become depressed, when the reality is that they have been depressed for five or six years, their partners were not able to live with it any longer, and they ended up separating.

Yes, depression is the slow death of our whole being. People believe that depressed people spend all day crying, but what they don't know is that most depressed people go unnoticed. Depressed people are fighting a terrible battle in silence, have to muster a tremendous amount of energy just to be able to get up every morning, suffer constantly, and struggle to survive. As if that were not enough, depressed people also grapple with loneliness, being misunderstood, and the criticism of people around them. In some cases they are dismissed as conformists and in others as self-pitying. At other times they are told that they should try harder, that they should make more of an effort, that they have let themselves go, or that they should get over it and be stronger.

What people don't realize is that being sad is not the same as being depressed, in the same way that having slightly high blood sugar is not the same as being diabetic. When your blood sugar is a bit high, you just need to adjust your diet slightly; but if you are diabetic, you will have to inject insulin several times a day, and your health will be in great danger every time you break the delicate balance resulting from the spikes that insulin and sugar create in your body.

What people don't understand either, if they have not been through depression, is that depressed people don't choose to be depressed; they don't want to be ill, and they don't enjoy the pity of those around them. Depressed people don't want to arouse another's pity, much less draw attention to themselves; what's more, they hate being fussed over—all they want is to go unnoticed and to be left alone.

Depression is such a severe illness that it ends up affecting most of our cognitive processes. Depressed people think less and, worse still, are incapable of making decisions, and suffer delusions about their capabilities, their self-esteem, and their future. At the same time, they have to fight against the illness while being misunderstood and stigmatized by the people around them. Depressed people lose hope and all enthusiasm for life and the future.

Depressed people lose their capacity for self-control and the ability to self-motivate, which is why it takes them between four and six years to seek treatment, if they ever do. During that time, their family life has been affected, their partners have reached the limit of their patience, their work productivity is way below what would be desirable, their physical appearance has been affected, and their health has been damaged.

In this scenario, the easiest thing is to decide that life has no meaning. Without the understanding of the people around them, with a dark vision of the future, and with the feeling that it is impossible to turn the current situation around, there are few paths left to follow. With no future, tired of suffering, feeling a profound loneliness, and living in emptiness, people with depression have few options left. I have never met anyone who wanted to stop living. No one wants to stop feeling the sweet warmth of spring, the sound of the sea, or the hug of a child. No one wants to consciously renounce seeing the sun each morning, enjoying a stroll, feeling the touch of clean sheets, the warmth of a stove in the middle of winter, or the kiss of a loved one. But if you can't enjoy the small pleasures in life, if no matter what you do you are incapable of experiencing a positive emotion, if a terrible depression has taken over your life, then you stop living, you stop feeling excited about getting up every morning, and you start to question whether you want to continue that way for the rest of your life. Life, for depressed people, loses meaning and becomes so torturous, dark, and deep that they no longer see the light at the end of the tunnel.

Look around—you know more depressed people than you might think. You can see them in your neighborhood, on television, on the street, at the supermarket, and at work. You can offer support by encouraging them to avoid waiting years before seeking treatment from a specialist, by avoiding complicating their difficult existence, and by offering your warm and nonjudgmental understanding. Depressed people are not usually aware that they are depressed. They will drag themselves along through life despite the tremendous efforts made to avoid that kind of existence. So, please, don't add more pressure. If you believe that thanks to this chapter you have identified depressed people who are not aware that they are depressed, let them know. Give them this chapter to read. Be concerned about them. Offer them your hand and help them climb out of the bottomless pit.

And if, after reading this chapter, you believe that you are depressed yourself, you need to get to work. There are different kinds of depression that require different kinds of treatment. What you are not allowed to do is cross your arms and do nothing. Seek treatment as soon as possible from a specialist in depression or, better still, a team of specialists in depression because it's possible that you might need an interdisciplinary approach in order to win the battle against this cruel illness.

And if what I have just explained is all Greek to you, don't worry; try to understand the serious consequences of this cruel disease and show compassion toward depressed people, but above all don't judge them as weak because struggling to get up every morning requires an amount of willpower that most of us don't have.

Now you know what you are facing—what kind of monster is torturing you. Let's go and get it.

Don't forget

- Depression is an illness of the nervous system with severe consequences at every level.

- Many depressed people go unnoticed.

- Depressed people are not seeking attention or pity; they just want to be able to live again.

- Nobody voluntarily chooses to be depressed.

- Depression affects the body and the cognitive functions.

- Depressed people often have no awareness of depression until they are several years into it.

Think Differently

Let's think differently, guided by two simple examples. In the first place, let's imagine that you have the flu, one of those galloping bouts that knock you out and confine you to bed. Try to imagine yourself in that situation. It's not just a common cold but the flu with a capital F. That's right, the kind that causes intense pain in the ribs, that renders you unable to stand up, that feels like there's a bass drum in your head. Are you there now? If you have ever suffered the flu like that, then you know that whatever you do, you can't influence its origin, so the only thing you can do is alleviate its symptoms. Why would you not take action to mitigate the symptoms? Dear reader, science has developed with the objective of making our existence easier—are you not going to make use of it? Even if you can't cure it, you must do something about its symptoms because these have negative consequences that can make everything worse and complicate your health beyond the simple, but brutal, flu you are suffering.

Let's move on to the second example. Sometimes we suffer from something that does have a cure, making the suffering senseless. Imagine you have a fridge that isn't working properly, which causes some foods to spoil, which in turn have given you gastritis. It's possible that you haven't identified the origin of your digestive problems and that you have resigned yourself to silently suffering gastritis periodically. But this would be wrong: if you do nothing, the situation will simply get worse! However, it's also possible that you have tried different strategies to heal yourself. You might have changed your diet, gone to the doctor, and even installed a water filter system. But unfortunately, all your efforts have been to no avail because they have had not the slightest effect on the source of your problem. Well, the same thing happens with depression. Sometimes we believe we are doing something that will help us, but we are not only not tackling the root of the problem, we are getting further away from it. What did you think of these two examples? Is it not true that you know you must do something to cure your gastritis, to mitigate the symptoms of the flu, and to avoid complicating the illness process you are suffering? And you are in no doubt at all about that? Well, in the same way, we are going to focus on treating this depression. No matter what kind of depression it is, we're going to stop fiddling around and focus on treating it as if it were the flu or gastritis.

Depression is nothing more than an illness—a terrible one, without doubt. It is often underestimated and trivialized, but at the end of the day, it is just an illness. Don't resign yourself to suffering it a second longer. Don't punish yourself over a simple but devastating illness; don't be ashamed of the symptoms of your depression. Think differently: we have the flu, which requires proper management, and gastritis, for which we need a cure.

Take Action

You might have been depressed for many years, with consequent repercussions at the social, family, and professional levels. We can't waste any time, so let's get to work with a clear objective in mind: for you to regain hope.

Before starting, however, allow me to highlight something truly important: don't rule out the need to see a specialist so they can assess whether you are depressed and what effect it's having on your life.

Throughout this chapter, I am going to provide you some strategies that will be of great help, but this is not a substitute, ever, for the necessary diagnosis and therapy with a qualified professional. I am taking it as a given that you will do so, but in the meantime we can't sit idly by. What's more, there are a lot of things we can do. There are a lot of things we must do. Shall we get started?

Explain (Selectively) Your Experience

Let's start by assessing whether it's worth even speaking to some of the people around us. I encourage you to analyze this calmly because, if possible, it's always better to try to reduce the pressure exercised by key people in our lives who don't understand our emotional state. Sometimes, talking to your parents, partner, or boss is beneficial because it allows them to become aware that you are suffering as a result of something you haven't chosen. Sometimes, just sometimes, some people are capable of switching gears and will stop pressuring you. However, it's important for you to consider whether it's worth sharing and with whom. Not everyone will understand, so, if you already know that, you don't need to explain it to them, and you can save that time and energy to invest it in a more productive way.

And what is it that you need to explain? Well, I would advise you to structure your discourse into two parts; first, a straightforward informative part, and second, a part to make sure they will be sensitive to your situation. In the first part, which is important, tell your interlocutors that you believe it's possible you might be depressed and that you want to clear up any doubts about it. You might show them the section in this chapter called "Take a Step Back" and explain to them that, when you read it, you recognized yourself in the description of the symptoms and that you want to verify whether you are really suffering depression. But meanwhile you have decided to take action and take a few steps, among them to share your intentions and questions with the people you care about. Explain to them how you feel and, most importantly, how your interlocutor makes you feel. At this point you will reach the second part of your message, in which it's important to make your interlocutors sensitive to your situation. Share with them what you need and what you would like to have happen, especially when it comes to their attitude, while being aware that they might or might not understand.

If the result of the talk is positive, that's great and should be celebrated. But if it's negative, which might also happen, you mustn't worry. I understand that it comes as a disappointment because you were expecting your interlocutors to show a certain amount of empathy, but don't forget that if you are talking with those people it's because up until now they have been pressuring you or they have shown they didn't understand your situation or your needs, so perhaps they are people who rushed their judgments and need to develop empathy and increase their capacity for compassion. You have made an effort, and that is already the best reward. Just by trying, you have had the courage to do a lot more than many people ever do, which in itself is of great intrinsic value to you.

Redecorate Your Life

What do you say we redecorate your life together? You live in a dark, damp, and cold little house with no windows, so the time has come to renovate or even move into a new house.

Feeling sad is not incompatible with feeling joy at specific times, as we have already said, so we need to actively seek positive emotions that allow us to compensate for how we feel. Here, the principles of practicality and compensation apply. You might live in a tiny house, but it's pretty. Open the windows, paint the walls, decorate the interior, change a few items of furniture, and you'll notice it will cease to be the same old house it used to be.

I suggest you create a list of all the things you enjoy and that enable you to change your emotional state. You might have to do this in the company of someone—a friend, your partner, or your children—who can refresh your memory or open your mind regarding the things you enjoy. Everything counts, from a sandwich (if it's one you like, of course) to a romantic weekend away. Include small and big things, small gestures, acts of kindness, gifts, experiences, and little pleasures. After you have completed the list, write down each item on the list on a slip of paper, fold the pieces of paper, and place them in a special box. It can be a shoebox with a hole or a jar, as long as you keep it handy. At least once a day, put your hand in the box; take out a piece of paper; and, whatever it says, force yourself to do that thing then and there or to schedule it as soon as possible. Don't postpone it; don't put it off until tomorrow or next month. Enrich your life with small doses of pleasure. Remember that you are suffering from depression and that it's difficult for you to be able to keep self-generating moments of joy unless they have been scheduled. This way, with fun and spontaneous planning, you will make up for your lack of interest in having positive experiences.

Redecorate your life, paint the walls, let the light and warmth in, and enrich your daily life—that's right, your daily life. In most cases you'll notice that the sum of small actions will result in a big change.

Take the First Step

I'm sure you have had invitations to do nice things. Think about it—that friend who is always saying you should play badminton together, that dinner you've been meaning to arrange, that school mom who suggested you go to a language class together—but you are probably anticipating a negative outcome from the proposals you receive. You would like to play badminton, but your skin is pasty white, you don't fit into your sports clothes, you see yourself losing a lot of the points, and you think you will feel tired and sore the next day. Of course you would like to go out to dinner, but you think you'll be the most gaunt-looking one in the group, that everyone will look great except you, that you'll be out too late and hungover the next day, and that you'll spend money that you could invest in another way. Yes, you would like to brush up on your language skills, but you're anticipating the disaster of embarrassment in class; you imagine the whole class laughing at you and your total inability to remember a single word. These are all delusional, negative thoughts. These things could potentially happen, of course, but realistically there is no reason they should. Your mind, which is depressed, gets into negative resonance and tinges everything with negativity.

I know that it's hard to do, but I can assure you that after you have taken the first step, when you have agreed to go and you have gone, you'll see what a nice time you had, you will have enriched your daily life, you will have broken the monotony of your mood, and you might even want to do the same again!

Dear reader, take that first step. I know it's hard, but it will bring nothing but benefits, I assure you!

Keep Any Delusional Negative Thoughts at Bay

Be careful with delusional negative thoughts because they are true masters of disguise. "Nobody loves me" is a delusional negative thought through and through! Take note of the fact that it checks all the boxes of a proper delusional thought, appearing true even when it is not. Of course there is someone who loves you, but if you refuse to see it and tell yourself that nobody loves you, you'll end up believing it and feeling the sadness caused by such a cruel thought.

"I'll never be able to dig myself out of this hole." There we go, another delusional thought! It might not be easy or quick. You might have to make a lot of changes and work hard on yourself and on restructuring your life, but the truth is that you can and will overcome this. But, of course, if you believe that whatever you do, nothing will come to any good, then again, this unjustified delusional thought is causing you pointless suffering.

"I should be able to make more of an effort." There's another one! You do make an effort; you try hard, and you know it. Getting up in the morning is a Herculean task, defeating sadness is an epic battle, and putting on a smile to pick up your children from school is a marathon achievement. You'd better believe it: you are making a tremendous effort. If you think the opposite, all you are doing is self-flagellating and blaming yourself. Did you know that one of the symptoms of depression is a lack of life energy? There you go—now you know it. A depressed person has to invest a lot more energy than a nondepressed person in order to achieve the same objective.

"My life is a mess." Come in, delusional thoughts, make yourself at home! Your life is not a mess—it's wonderful. You are wonderful, but a cruel illness has decided to join you and affect your life. So again, this unjustified delusional thought is causing you pointless suffering. Your life is great, but depression is capable of making you see everything through dark-tinted glasses that will change your view of each and every one of the things you do.

Remember: delusional thoughts must be kept at bay. To do this, you just need to identify them or get the help of someone who can provide you the perspective you need. Contextualize them as delusional thoughts and ignore them by applying reality, the reality that shows you with clear facts what your mind wants to hide from you.

Get Back a Sense of Excitement

Excitement is the salt of life, the filter that makes all your photos look good, and a breath of fresh air that comforts your soul. It's a pencil case full of new colors. It's the perfume of a freshly blooming rose, the song of a nightingale, and the cool sea lapping at your feet. Excitement has the shape of a smile—the smile of a happy and energetic child. It is the driving force of life, the propellant of happiness, and the best stimulus for living intensely. When we stop being excited, we stop living in order to simply survive.

Excitement is a vital attitude, a kind of choice that will enrich your life. If you invest excitement in everything you do, you will be happy, and you will enjoy life. Live life with excitement! Add a generous dose of excitement to your life in order to be happy.

Excitement is an impulse that is born from cognition, desire, and hope. Without excitement we wouldn't be able to achieve our objectives. However, in order to feel excited about something, sometimes we need to want to feel it. Living life with excitement requires willpower and a desire, the desire to enjoy each and every one of the things life offers.

However, excitement is also an additional energy that spices up your objectives and your way of living. When willpower fails, excitement pushes on. Excitement is the main motivator available to us, and it acts as a drive that provides additional energy precisely when you need it most: to begin a new chapter and to stand firm when facing challenges.

Things rarely go according to plan at the first attempt. You might have been depressed for many years. The more important the undertaking and the more ambitious our objectives, the more effort will be required of us. You will never be able to reach a great achievement, an extraordinary achievement, if you do not bring with you a large dose of excitement. I like to imagine excitement as those extra energy deposits that can usually be found in racing car video games. Do you know what I mean? There is often an option to buy a turbo that gives your vehicle greater speed. Sometimes the race is neck and neck. The finish line is near. All your competitors are on their last legs, but you suddenly use that turbo you were saving and voilà! Your car speeds up and positions itself ahead of the rest. Well, that is exactly what excitement is: extra energy that allows you to go faster for a period, make an effort, gain momentum, and get closer to your objectives. Excitement will be the best anchoring point that you could hope for in order to overcome that devastating depression.

Every day, throughout your life, you have to keep feeding your sense of excitement. Imagine you have a bank account and that each time you do something that makes your pulse race, it gets topped up with a generous amount of excitement. In contrast, each time you are disappointed or down, your level of excitement is reduced. In actual fact, the truly important thing is your ability to create excitement for yourself. And do you know what the secret is to be able to self-generate good doses of excitement? The key is making your own decisions and choosing the path you want to follow.

You have made the right decision; you are on the right track. Feel it and feed your excitement, the excitement that will give you the energy you need to overcome and forget that chapter of your life.

Lift Your Head High

Nobody is embarrassed because they have the flu, because they are diabetic, or because they broke an arm. Nobody feels guilty about breaking an arm. Nobody feels they are to blame for twisting their ankle, for having a headache, or for suffering an ear infection. Why then do we feel ashamed that we are depressed? Psychological disorders never come on their own; they come with large doses of shame and guilt that influence and make the symptoms of depression even worse. So lift your head high—you have done nothing wrong. You are not weak. You didn't choose to be depressed. You have done nothing to end up depressed. Don't feel bad, and don't allow others to make you feel bad.

When someone tells you that they were depressed, too, and that they managed to overcome their depression, remember it's likely that isn't the case because anyone who has suffered that much can't avoid offering a hand to someone who is going through the same thing as them. Say goodbye to anyone who doesn't understand you. Don't try to justify yourself. Anyone who doesn't understand your point of view won't understand your explanation either. Remember that you need to focus on your battle against the illness, concentrate all your energies, and avoid anything that might distract you and waste your resources or that might steal a minute of your time because you will need all those resources for yourself.

Take Care of Yourself; You Are Important

You might well have forgotten about yourself and your needs, but it's important that you practice self-care and pamper yourself. When depression takes hold of our minds, one of the first things we do is forget about ourselves and even submit ourselves to self-abuse, a kind of subconscious punishment.

You have already experienced plenty of neglect along the river of life! Look after yourself, and pamper yourself. Have a nice bath, spruce up, enjoy a shower, get a massage, go to a spa, buy yourself some face creams, change your wardrobe, sunbathe, tone your body, sleep, and eat well. I am completely serious! You must love yourself, respect yourself, and practice self-care. You have only one body, so treat it the way it deserves.

Not only must you care for and pamper your body but also your soul, mind, heart, spirit, or whatever you want to call it. Analyze your inner dialogue. What are you saying to yourself? What messages do you send yourself, in what tone? Analyze what you say to yourself and what you don't say to yourself. Depression involves deterioration of our self-image and self-esteem. Many of my patients afflicted with depression literally insult themselves; they treat themselves as useless beings and look down on themselves all the time.

Analyze your inner dialogue because you need to be kind to yourself. Treat yourself well, and be understanding of your needs. Don't abuse yourself; don't punish yourself. Learn to live with yourself with peace, respect, and harmony.

Develop the Ability to Self-Motivate

Motivation is one of the main emotional strengths affected by depression. When you are depressed, you find it hard to do anything because motivation drops to ground level. When experiencing this symptom, the best strategy is to do some planning from a place of calm. What I mean is, with depression, as with a toothache, we can observe certain cycles of recovery and relapse. My best advice is that you take advantage of a recovery cycle to do some realistic planning in which you contemplate all of the aspects you wish to work on, such as taking on a project, meeting up with friends, playing more sports, cooking more, spending your money better, and so on. This planning needs to be conservative and realistic because after you have done it, you will have to follow it. When motivation fails, you can turn to your plan.

I have always maintained that a plan is a guide that you can skip if you need to, except when it's a therapeutic tool to generate the impulse you need because that impulse can't be provided by your own motivation.

If You're Contemplating Disappearing from the Face of the Earth

If at any time you have considered that death would put an end to your suffering, that no one will miss you, that you will be doing a favor for the people around you, or that life is not worth living, I need to tell you that you are utterly mistaken. I know you are suffering, that everything looks grim, and that you believe it will always be like this. I can't feel what you do—I can only imagine it—but I know that one fine day it will all have passed. One day, sooner or later, you'll look back and see that you were able to overcome a terrible illness.

Little by little you'll see yourself regaining confidence. Little by little you'll recover all your cognitive functions. In the same way that a person who has broken a leg needs a process of recovery, as soon as you start working on yourself you'll be able to see how you are climbing out of the hole, moving forward through the tunnel, and starting to feel better.

I know you believe that death is a way out to end your pain. That amount of suffering is too much to withstand, I agree with you. But death is not the only way out. There are other ways, and they are not as complex as they might seem.

Don't give up on life because the pain you are feeling is temporary, and always, always, after the darkest night, the sun rises again. Always, always, after the most relentless storm, calm returns. There is always an alternative and a way.

Where Do I Start?

- Start by seeking help from a qualified specialist to find out if you are depressed and how this is affecting your life.

- Next, explain to yourself what you are experiencing from the perspective of an illness, and consider whether you need to inform anyone.

- Schedule activities that generate positive emotions, and stick to that plan.

- Identify and manage negative, delusional thoughts.

- Enrich your life, and give it a motivational boost that is capable of awakening excitement, the additional energy that you need.

How Do I Do It?

- Stay away from shame and guilt, as well as the people who cause you to experience these emotions. The last thing you need is someone at your side who doesn't understand you, who judges you, and who brings you more negative emotions.

- Think about the battle against depression as a battle against any illness. We have to attack both the symptoms and the root of the problem if we want to get rid of it.

- Practice self-care, pamper yourself, stop being at the bottom of your list of priorities, and put yourself at the top.

- Check your inner dialogue, and give it a touch of optimism and, above all, self-respect. You are without question your own worst judge.

- When motivation fails you, turn to the plan you created from a place of calm.

Repairing Joy

Elsa's Story: When the Body Does Not Respond

"But you're not a builder or plasterer; you can still pick up a pen." The words of the medical assessor echoed in her head. She glanced at the clock. It was 3:00 in the morning. The pain caused by the weight of the blanket had woken her up, as it did every night, and, after she was awake, her mind started racing with negative thoughts, mixing sadness with rage and pain, a dry and muffled pain that weighed on her body and soul.

She didn't want to receive payment, a diagnosis, or a sick note; all she wanted was to stop feeling pain, to regain the energy she had always had, and to feel strong and active. She didn't want to run a marathon or climb mountains; she would be content if she could just play with her children. She wanted to be able to pick up the shopping bags, vacuum the carpet without needing two days to recover, dance with her partner, and go for a walk in the woods with her dog.

A tear ran down her cheek. Her legs were aching. She got up and took a painkiller and a sleeping pill. "Tomorrow I want to get up early," she said to herself as she wiped a tear. She fell asleep, exhausted again.

"Mommy, are you going to pick me up from school today?" Elsa woke up with a start. What time was it—6:30 a.m.? "Damn! I only wanted to close my eyes for a while. What a disaster of a day, like every day! What kind of a life is this?" she said to herself. She got up that morning, made breakfast for her kids, and did their hair. She was unable to take them to school. Her legs were still aching. She said good-bye to her children from the door and went back to bed. "I'll close my eyes for a second and get ready to pick them up," she said. But she spent all day in bed.

"Sweetie, make yourself a sandwich for your afternoon snack and start doing your homework, Mommy's coming."

"Don't worry, Mommy, you should rest. I'll make a ham sandwich, okay?" her son said as he left the room.

She tried to get out of bed, but she couldn't. She had spent all day sleeping, but she was completely exhausted. "I'm not asking for that much," she muttered. "All I want to know is what is wrong with me and how to cope with it." She switched on the tablet and searched again: autoimmune specialists, rheumatologists. She closed it again. She got up and went to the fridge. She poured herself an energy drink and combed her hair. She couldn't leave her children by themselves. The mirror reflected an Elsa who was tired, sad, emaciated, and trapped in a body that would not respond to her. She dried a tear and went to the dining room with her arms in pain from the effort of doing her hair.

Along the way she smiled. Elsa was a positive person, capable of transforming adversity into a challenge, and capable of self-motivating time and again, despite the fact that it was becoming increasingly harder for her.

Take a Step Back

Elsa was a joyful person, full of vitality and capable of huge efforts. She had been a natural-born sportswoman and played any sport you could think of, she worked with determination and a huge smile, and she always found a way to devote part of her time to social tasks. All in all, she was an extraordinary, sensitive, intelligent, and courageous person. Despite the fact that she didn't see herself as such, she lived life intensely, not questioning how she was or what she should be doing.

But at some point Elsa gradually started to lose her energy. It was increasingly harder to play any sport; travel; meet with friends; or even, after a long battle motivated by her sense of duty, go to work. The previous few years of Elsa's life had been completely the opposite of her identity, her energy, and her priorities. She could barely enjoy a couple of good hours a day. She couldn't sleep at night, and during the day she couldn't do anything strenuous; she struggled constantly between states of fatigue and pain.

Elsa felt trapped in a body that didn't represent her and that had cost her dearly on every level. For Elsa to stop suffering she needed to connect with her identity, continue to maintain her essence, and adapt to the new circumstances in which she found herself. She was still the same extraordinary person as before, if not more so, but she didn't see herself that way.

Dear Elsas of the world, don't ever forget that you are extraordinary people, and you continue to be, in essence, the same people you always were. But now you have to ration out your extraordinary virtues carefully and, in particular, protect your precious identity and preserve it from the fatigue and pain that always lie in wait.

The issue of identity is highly complex. One aspect is who we are, another is who we believe we are, another is who we believe others believe we are, and, finally, who others actually believe we are. What a mess! When faced with such complexity the only possible option is take a step back and look at things with perspective, so I'll get straight to the point.

You are the way you are. What's more, don't worry about how you are or how you are seen, much less about how you look. I'll tell you why. You are not an expert in psychology; neither are the people around you, which is why their judgment is nothing more than just that—an opinion—and an opinion is not a fact. Don't continually analyze yourself; don't judge yourself; and, most importantly, don't pay heed to the judgments or opinions of other people because down that road you will find nothing but suffering.

Elsa asked herself over and over what her father would say. Nobody understood why she spent all day holed up at home, least of all her father. But do you know what? You don't need the understanding of the people around you. I won't say that having it isn't helpful, of course, but the fact that others don't understand you shouldn't weigh down on you because few people are able to deeply empathize.

The Desire to Be Accepted

Taking advantage of people's desire to be accepted is one of the oldest strategies for controlling and regulating members of a community. Consider that you are born where you are born out of pure chance and that it's possible that you don't fit into that place.

So, if you don't fit into a specific environment, gather your bits and pieces and get out of there because you have feet, not roots. Don't stay where you aren't respected. Find your place in the world. You are unique for many reasons, but there is sure to be a place where you fit in. Don't sacrifice who are you are in order to be accepted; don't give up your identity for a superficial sense of being loved. Those who don't respect you don't love you, those who don't understand you won't accept you, and those who don't accept you have no place at your side.

We had our work cut out. We had Elsa suffering to justify what she could and could not do, her life and her pain before a large tribunal of interrogators made up of all the important people in her life, and presiding over it all her decontextualized, disproportionately hyperdemanding self. Elsa was always asking herself why she had no energy, why even the weight of her hair hurt, why she couldn't lead a normal life, and why she wasn't capable of winning the battle against pain. But that's not the issue; what really matters is how you feel, not what you should feel. So, you'll need your life to keep in step with your needs—but what's wrong with that? Who do you need to give explanations to? Stop judging yourself continually and accept your identity—accept yourself just as you are—and don't stop growing.

But please, please, stop judging yourself and torturing yourself with "shoulds," and "have tos," and focus on enjoying the good moments that the present brings.

You have suffered a dramatic change in your life, moreover a change that you did not choose and that will have an uncertain evolution in some aspects and a negative one in many others. But the most important part is not allowing your identity to be affected. If Elsa started seeing herself as worthless and wretched (as she did), in addition to the negative consequences of the illness, she would have to deal with a negative self-image that is horribly unjust and false.

You Are Much More Than Your Circumstances

Your identity is one thing, and your circumstances are another thing entirely. You are not an invalid; you are someone afflicted or conditioned by an illness. Never forget that you are above all a person. You are a human being, a wonder of nature, a compendium of virtues, a vessel full of plans, a bunch of opportunities, and an infinite number of possibilities.

You are a person, special and unique. Don't confuse what you are with what you are experiencing. Be careful—there is only one thing worse than confusing your identity with your circumstances, and that is that you believe others see you in a specific way, in a way you don't want to see yourself.

I never tire of repeating to my daughter over and over that it shouldn't matter to her in the slightest what others say about her. Any person can form an opinion of you, of course, but that opinion is not necessarily true. We are free to have an opinion, and we are free to take those opinions onboard. Also, if you want me to tell you something I have learned over the years, it's that where there is smoke there is not necessarily fire; it's more often the case that someone just wants there to be fire.

When Pedro comes and tells you something about Juan, Pedro is telling you more things about himself than about Juan. So eliminate from your identity the things that you think people will say about you and even more importantly the things people do say about you.

Don't forget

- You are still the same person you always were but under some new circumstances.

- Don't worry about what people might say about you or your illness.

- You are your own worst judge. Relax and stop judging yourself so harshly all the time.

- Focus on enjoying the good times offered by the present.

- You are much more than your circumstances—don't forget that.

- Your essence transcends far beyond the pain and the fatigue that you feel.

Think Differently

Most people don't know themselves; in fact, they have absolutely no idea what they are like. Over the course of our lives we take on the identity people build for us—people as qualified as an auntie who loves us, a granny who is bitter, a teacher who is reminded of a difficult student, or the class bully who goes around intimidating people left, right, and center. But the fact is that even I, a diligent psychologist, can't know what you are like just by looking at you and need to apply different techniques and instruments to try to understand the shape of your personality, identity, thinking style, values, and priorities. So the time has come to think differently. It doesn't matter in the least what you are actually like, and now I will explain the reason.

You, your cousin, your partner, and even I behave differently based on how we are treated, the place we are in, and even the time we are in. The people who are judging you might have a partial vision of what you are like, to which they are adding a good amount of their own invention. Why would you trust their judgment? To some of my friends I am the most serious dude on the planet, but to others I'm completely nuts. Do you know why? Because in comparison with free-spirited adventurers I fall short, but to those more stuck in their ways I am a genuine instrument of novelty and risk.

So, what is the truth? Am I a free spirit or a serious dude? Well, it doesn't really matter; what's important is not what I am but the decisions I make. And now the time has come for you to ask me: Do your decisions answer to your identity? (Isn't that exactly what you were thinking? I snatched the words right out of your mouth!) My decisions answer to my priorities, my emotional state at the time, my objectives, the available resources, the context, and countless other parameters.

Dear Elsas of the world, you are wonderful, and that's how you should see yourselves. There's nothing wrong in feeling what you feel. Some people might not understand it, that's true, but that shouldn't be a reason to suffer.

I am deeply sorry that you are suffering. I understand you completely, believe me, I do. It's a drag not to have a clear enemy to fight against, but for that same reason you must change a key concept. You shouldn't fight against your illness, but instead you should pace yourself and live with it. Your life has changed, but that doesn't mean your essence has changed. You are much more than the body that now limits you—don't forget it. You are capable of repairing yourself again and adapting your life to the current constraints. All you need to do is accept your virtues and limitations and work to make these limitations constrain your life as little as possible.

To Be or Not to Be

It's one thing to be the way you are and quite another to behave the way you do. How many times have you said to yourself, "I don't recognize my son"? If you observe your behavior, you will see it's difficult to draw a conclusion that is useful in predicting the future. Behavior has many causes and is complex. You don't behave the same with your friends as with your partner; what's more, you don't behave the same with your friends when you're tired as when you are well rested. So it's important that you try to get to know yourself in order to understand yourself and develop your virtues, but the key of this inner journey lies in you having a conversation with yourself instead of judging yourself continually.

Transform a Constraint into an Influence

When your identity is affected by an illness or accident, you need to give serious thought to the following statement: what you experienced is a significant influence but happily not a constraint. In other words, your illness is an important element because it will mark and affect your life, but in no way is it a determining factor because your destiny is not written. You are the way you are; you have changed, and you are limited by an accident or an illness or by some belief, but this will not determine the course of your life. It could in reality, of course, do just that—but only if you allow it to. If you believe you are powerless, your life will revolve around your problem. But look, there is always something we can do. Aside from yourself, there will be no one else who can liberate you from that heavy load. When it comes to repairing our lives we must start by looking for the largest piece left to us, and use it as an anchor point. And do you know what that piece is? It's your own identity, the piece that most accurately describes you. However, you might not know yourself. Our identities are formed out of scraps of fears, patterns, ideals, and even our parents' wishes. But there is no reason that identity should have to correspond to your virtues and potential.

Most people don't know themselves. My work consists of connecting them with themselves and their authentic emotional strength. Look for your biggest piece. Your biggest piece corresponds to the enormous potential you have, so let's start by defining how you want to look at yourself—not how you want to see yourself in the future but how you want to see yourself now, in the present.

Develop Your Full Potential

Do you remember Lary León? Lary suggests that we are all here for a purpose, and we have an objective, but we won't be able to know what our task is until we develop our full potential. So let's get started.

How would you like to see yourself? Who have you always wanted to be? Ready? Great, now let's move on to the second part of the question, the hardest one: In what way do you need to adapt your objective to your current constraints?

Elsa had always wanted to dedicate herself to the world of gastronomy, but from the start of her illness she had had to stop working in kitchens because she could no longer keep up with the pace. After being defeated and giving up her dream, she managed to reinvent herself and transform her dream to make it compatible with her needs. She started writing a blog, at her own pace, without making too many demands on herself, using her experience and understanding to create learning materials that could help other professionals.

It's Hard to Manage Uncertainty

Despite the fact that Elsa had gone through an ordeal with doctors and the lack of understanding from the people around her, including her own family, she did not have a clear diagnosis, which is why she had to resign herself to a vague and unclear label that could only sow confusion. It might well be hard to understand, but this is a serious problem and explains most of Elsa's discomfort for two reasons. The first is that someone who has a diagnosis, a label, or a name has a good basis to inform and justify their state to other people.

"Don't you have a job?"

"No, I'm battling cancer."

Great—your interlocutor is now clear about what is wrong with you, what your circumstances are, and how they govern what you can or can't do. When people have a clear explanation, a clear frame of reference, they can get an idea of what you are experiencing and thus no longer need to conjecture, to ask you for more explanations, or to overwhelm you with more questions.

But let's repeat the scene:

"Don't you have a job?"

"No. It's difficult to explain. I lack energy; everything hurts. Well, it's complicated."

"Is it an illness?"

"Yes, no, well, it's a syndrome. Well, it's being researched."

"But what is it? What is it called?"

"Alright, bye, I've got to go."

How the scene changed, right? In the first interaction you emerge from it feeling understood, admired, and helped, like a hero who is fighting a long battle. In contrast, from the second interaction you emerge discouraged and dejected; you even doubt whether everything you are experiencing is psychological; you emerge sad, lonely, and feeling interrogated or judged.

The second reason is that, not having a clear frame of reference, you are unable to name what you are experiencing, and your self-image and self-esteem are affected, which worsens your symptoms. You don't have a clear enemy, and when there is no clear enemy, you don't know where to shoot. Without a diagnosis, without an objective, you have no clear guide as to where to invest your efforts, so you start wasting energy on battles that are of no help to you.

Although not knowing what you are fighting is frustrating, I propose that you come to terms with it and accept it. I know there are things you don't know, but it's impossible to control everything. Some things are outside our control, other things we cannot understand, and many more have no observable reason. Now, I propose that you change the focus of uncertainty for that of certainty. We don't know what illness you are suffering from, how it will affect your future, and how it will evolve, but what we do know is that you are an extraordinary person, still with the same qualities.

Don't forget

- Accept yourself, and enjoy the process of understanding yourself and studying yourself—both what you do, say, think, and feel and what you don't.

- Stop judging yourself, and start having a conversation with yourself.

- Transform your constraints into influences. You can do it!

- Manage uncertainty and fear.

- We all have a talent and a mission to achieve. Combine your talent with your mission, and you will be happy and make others happy.

Take Action

The time has come to take action, to take the first step, and to reconnect with life. We all have a talent and a mission in life, so let's bring them together to be able to live fully; let's place our attention on that and rebuild our joy of living.

Recalibrate Your Expectations

Let's start at the beginning. Elsa needed to relearn to set more realistic expectations to match her current situation. She was once capable of working all hours, playing multiple sports, and meeting up with many friends, but that is all in the past tense—the past that has already ended. If Elsa is not able to readapt her expectations to her present, she will suffer because with one foot in a seemingly better past, she cannot live fully in the present or plan for an exciting future. Our expectations need to be updated periodically, just like an operating system or an app. But how do expectations work? Well, they are a kind of prediction of the future based on some suppositions that have a starting point. Let me explain. We know where we are and what resources are available to us, and based on our parameters we create hypotheses about the future. The problem is that sometimes we err in our expectations because our starting point is not real.

In the case of Elsa, her starting point was the ideas she had about her capabilities, but she hadn't updated the ideas to her present, her new constraints; instead, these were anchored in the past. When she set an expectation based on something she was able to do before, but not now, her frustration won the battle. For example, if she wanted to ride a bike, she decided on a trip based on the memory of past trips. She had once completed the Camino de Santiago trail by bike; she was able to pedal up the steepest hills for hours on end without getting tired, enjoying incredible views and a satisfied feeling of tiredness resulting from the effort. So, she was excited now about riding her bike, but when she went out, she saw how her expectations became frustrated because, after a short ride in the valley of barely an hour, she had to return on foot, pushing her bike, incapable of pedaling because of the pain in her legs. After several frustrated outings, she decided to sell her bike and give up on a part of her life, all because she didn't update her expectations to meet her new situation.

So what matters is not what you were once able to do, or your past achievements; what matters is what you are able to do right now and what you need to be able to achieve it.

Elsa's Bike

A bike is one of the best machines we have to make us happy. I personally love bikes. I'm not a fan of collections, but if I ever decided to start one, it would be bikes, hands down.

I love mountain bikes that let you ride on any kind of terrain, cover long distances, and enjoy an outing above the clouds. But I also enjoy a calm ride by the sea on a touring bike, a fast ride on a "fixed-gear bike," or discovering a city on a town bike.

Speaking of bikes, one day I went with Elsa to a bicycle shop, aware of her love for this genius invention. We left the showroom to wander about, but I already had a clear destination in mind. Back at the shop, I asked the salesperson for information on electric bikes, at which point Elsa was outraged and told me an electric bike was not a real bike.

"Elsa," I replied. "Listen with me to what this man has to say, and then we can both weigh the possibility of taking a pseudobike out for a ride to enjoy landscapes and sensations against forgetting about ever riding a bike again."

As you might expect, in less than a week, Elsa had her new electric bike and could once again enjoy long rides out in the middle of nature, thanks to the assisted pedaling.

Dear reader, don't give up something you enjoy if you can adapt it to your new needs. Update and adjust your expectations, and you will be happy.

A Holistic Intervention Approach

Taking on a case such as Elsa's requires joint action at the physical, emotional, and social levels. She needed to reduce her level of anxiety because it was affecting her energy and ability to recover. Stress on its own does not cause any particular illness; instead, it opens the door to no end of different disorders related to the immune, digestive, cardiovascular, muscular-skeletal, respiratory, and other systems.

It's important to consider the possibility of help from appropriate medication, correctly administered and monitored by a doctor or psychiatrist. There are antidepressants and anxiety medications that have a collateral effect on fatigue and the pain associated with this kind of syndrome, as well as helping to contain the psychological symptoms associated with constant pain and fatigue.

Let's not forget that a stressed and sad body such as Elsa's is vulnerable, so we need to destress it by all means possible, not just through pharmacological prescriptions. We can reduce the level of tension through other means, such as hot baths, sunbathing, massage, and so forth.

In addition to providing Elsa the resources to learn to set more realistic, appropriate expectations that corresponded to her situation, energy levels, and general state, we complemented the psychological work by separating out fatigue and pain from self-esteem, improving her self-knowledge, and providing tools to make decisions free of prejudice and external and internal pressures.

Finally, it was important to work with Elsa's environment. Her partner and children needed to understand that what their mother was experiencing had nothing to do with willpower, that she was suffering from something doctors and scientists don't fully understand, and that it is often labeled as chronic fatigue syndrome or fibromyalgia. This syndrome is part of a set of unknown or frequently misdiagnosed diseases that are grouped together by symptoms. Ultimately, it was not that Elsa didn't want to do things, it was that she was unable to. And something else that was necessary to take into account was that they all needed to take advantage of the times when Elsa was well to spend quality time together and allow her to rest when she needed to. They would perhaps need to do some activities without her, or adapt them while making sure that, when she was well, they took advantage of that in order to live life together.

Recovering Energy

If you want to recover the greatest amount of energy possible, you need to adjust your life to your needs. Here is some advice:

- **Simplify your life in order to be able to focus on what is truly important.** But to achieve this, the first thing you need to do is analyze what is truly important in your life. Start by redefining your priorities and your objectives. Separate the important from the superfluous, what requires your attention from what doesn't. You can't be present in every battle now, so you must differentiate between those that deserve your attention and energy and those that do not.

- **Consider whether the things you do have any meaning.** Go over each and every one of your tasks, routines, and daily chores in order to assess whether it makes sense to continue doing them, or if the time has come to make changes in your life. Delegate as much as you can. I remember one of my best pieces of advice to Elsa was to schedule a visit to Ikea to buy quilts. Putting a duvet in its cover, for her, should have been classified as an Olympic sport! This weekly task could be completely eliminated because it didn't add much value to her life. Elsa bought a double set of quilts for all the beds in the house and put away all the covers, so she, her partner, and the children slept covered directly by the quilts, and, once a week, she replaced the quilts and put the dirty ones into the washing machine. That was the end of dealing with duvet covers and the additional effort.

- **Review your tasks and eliminate any that don't add value.** Don't forget that the objective is for you to conserve your energy for what really adds value, not expend it or waste it on things that can be avoided.

- **Learn to live at a different pace.** Many people affected by fatigue and fibromyalgia have in common that they were energetic and full of vitality before the onset of the illness. If this is the case for you, you need to learn to live again at a different pace. Review your conclusions because we often come to a mistaken and nonsensical conclusion after suffering. In the case of Elsa, after trying to ride a bike on several occasions, she ended up deciding never to ride a bike again. Huge mistake! The problem was not the bike but that she would need to make a few changes to be able to continue riding a bike. Don't give things up; instead, adapt, modify, and change them.

- **Adjust your activities to your own pace.** You can go hiking, but make sure it's short and that you allow yourself to rest or complete it whenever you want. You can go out at night, but learn to identify when it's time to go home. You can play with the kids, but keep a few games prepared so they can enjoy them independently. Don't give anything up; just adjust your life to your possibilities. I remember a case of someone who loved the mountains but wasn't able to keep going on the hikes he liked so much, so my advice was to buy a convertible jeep, a picnic table, and a camera and to go out to the mountains. "Man, going to the mountains by car is a sin," was his reaction. "Try it out, and then tell me how you got on," I said. Well, that person did relearn to enjoy one of the passions he had given up, at his own pace.

- **Break the vicious cycle of negative emotions that you feel because they are in turn feeding the fatigue and pain.** To achieve this, include positive emotions in your daily life; seek them out and schedule them because they will help you compensate for those negative emotions. Fix your leaky vessel, sort out your emotional bank account, and compensate your suffering with positive experiences.

- **Internalize the fact that your fatigue and your pain have nothing to do with willpower.** The mind cannot do it all, and it is not the cause of everything that happens to you. I resent people (including doctors and psychologists) who say that what you are experiencing is psychosomatic, that it is depression or anxiety, and then believe their job is done. Some professionals, when they don't know how to explain something or they cannot explain it, say that the cause is psychosomatic, transferring guilt and responsibility to the patients, which they cannot and should not have to cope with. The truth is that more research is needed on thousands of more or less common illnesses and that, at the end of the day, we cannot be sure of understanding every detail.

- **Learn to get to know yourself and to understand this new body, which is asking you to slow down.** Listen to your body and its needs. Identify the signs of too much effort in order to be able to rest. Remember that your ability to recover has perhaps been affected. Any effort costs you dearly, so when it comes to effort, do only what is necessary. Perhaps you must learn to say no, to avoid getting so actively involved in so many things, and to ration your energy. Think of yourself first and then of others because if you are well, your loved ones will be, too.

- **Any occasion is a wonderful moment to start over.** Monday, tomorrow, this month, in September, after the holidays, or right now. Don't carry on trying to lead the same life you used to before. Your life has changed, perhaps irreversibly. I encourage you to come to terms with this because this is the first step to be able to build a new life that is more in accordance with your needs.

- **I encourage you to redefine your life based on your needs and to involve the rest of your family and the people around you.** It's not necessary to do all your activities together. You can go to a theme park, as long as you can stay in a hotel in the park itself so that you can take a rest whenever you need to. Maybe you can go to the mountains together, but you don't need to go on an epic excursion. Dear reader, there are two conversations you need to have—one with yourself and another with your family.

- **Ignore what people tell you.** We depend far too much on external opinion, the approval of those around us, and the apparent recognition from people we don't even know. We compare ourselves in order to have a reference or a measure, but this reference is completely fallacious and biased. We take as reference a measure that doesn't mean anything, and we organize our lives around an unreal construct. We suffer, we become angry, and we get depressed about something unreal that we take as true.

- **Consider your own needs.** You have a right to do this. We often place other people's needs before our own—big mistake. In addition, as if that were not enough, when we satisfy our own needs we feel bad, guilty, and selfish, as if we were doing something wrong. Has that ever happened to you? Did you know that the main control mechanism of a selfish person is to make their victim feel selfish when they are trying to do something for themselves? If you think about it carefully, you will agree with me that by satisfying your own needs, you'll be in a better mood, and your interactions with people around you will be more enriching and enjoyable.

- **Get rid of the dead weight.** Stop asking yourself over and over about the way you are and the way you should be, and focus your attention on what you are doing, free of judgment and interpretations. Enjoy the present; savor what you are doing; and stop torturing, examining, and questioning yourself. Eliminate from your daily life any questions about your identity, your illness, and your future. Stick to doing, feeling, talking, and enjoying. Put all your senses into what you are doing and experiencing, and when you are seized by a question or an intrusive thought, invite it to leave, as we did in a previous chapter.

- **Your body gets tired; so does your mind.** We underestimate the effect of mental fatigue on our daily life. When your mind becomes tired, it functions badly; yes, your mind has finite capacity. Learn to identify when your mind is tired, and see yourself with a little green or red light based on your mental state. A tired mind is pessimistic and negative, makes worse decisions, loses creativity, and is biased. When your mind is tired, allow it to rest, and don't make decisions or jump to conclusions. Take advantage of the moments of lucidity and the little green light to write yourself notes for when your mind hits a red light, dominated by pessimism and fatigue. This way, you will have an anchor point that will allow you to recalibrate and not fall into a pit of negativity.

- **Swap your dreams for experiences.** Look, I'm going to be honest here. We don't know how long we're going to be here, full of energy and able to do whatever we want—neither you nor I know. Personally, I decided a long time ago to transform my dreams into realities and experiences. I always imagined myself living in the mountains. "When I retire," I used to think. Well, in 2013 I moved to La Cerdanya, a beautiful valley in the heart of the Pyrenees. I found it neither difficult nor easy. I just found it time-consuming.

So, don't put off for tomorrow what you can experience today. I have seen many—too many—cases of people who will never be able to make their dreams come true, whether because of illness, an accident, or bad luck. Live in the present, learn to tell the difference between your romantic dreams and the ones you truly want to live, and go and get them.

Where Do I Start?

- Accept that your life has changed and that you need to reorganize it.

- Recalibrate your expectations, and adjust them to your new circumstances.

- Have a chat with yourself and your family.

How Do I Do It?

- Take a comprehensive, systematic, planned, and structured approach.

- Simplify your life as much as possible.

- Review the meaning of what you are doing.

- Incorporate the concept of changing gears to adapt your pace to your needs.

- Take your own needs into account.

- Get rid of any dead weight.

Conclusion

"Mottainai," yelled Chojiro. "Never waste something that is valuable!"

Mottainai: The Art of Giving Yourself a New Opportunity

We are reaching the end of our conversation. I admit that I have tried to imagine you, to have a conversation with you for many hours—all of the hours I have been writing, designing, and thinking about the contents of *Kintsugi*. I have taken you to the highest peaks, the greenest pastures, and gently pounding waterfalls; you have come along with me among the marmots and chamois, in the sun and shade, in the forest and by the lake, all the places where on my iPad I have been writing the book that is coming to its conclusion.

I have imagined you as broken, but I have also imagined you repairing yourself; fighting to be able to smile again; to take that step forward; to once again live your life, which is the most valuable possession we have, with fullness and with intensity. Life, our life. Your life. Don't give your life away to anyone. Share it if you like, but don't allow anyone to steal it from you, and whatever you do, don't stop living. You only have one life, and you have the obligation to live it intensely. Perhaps the time has come to evaluate whether you are living your life, the life of another person, or the life that others want you to live.

Don't waste something as valuable as your experience and your life. You might have suffered, but you have also rebuilt yourself. If you have learned from what you have been through, you possess the most valuable piece of knowledge: experience. That experience has allowed you to grow and become stronger. Now you are better prepared to live, you have more resources, you know yourself better, and you know what you are capable of. So don't waste that pearl that is knowledge and experience, and, far from putting it out of your mind, keep it at the forefront of your thoughts. Don't waste your experience, the thing that demonstrates your emotional strength.

I invite you to join the philosophy of *mottainai*! All right, I must admit that I haven't found any references to a mottainai philosophy as such, and maybe it's presumptuous for me to create a new philosophical concept, but in any case allow me to use this Japanese concept to illustrate the attitude you should have and to close this dialogue of pages, emotions, confessions, resources, and anecdotes.

Mottainai refers to the concept of the pain and sorrow we feel when we lose a resource (material or not) of great value, such as a teaching, time, experience, dream, emotion, idea, or even a thought. On the contrary, mottainai also has a positive sense, which is the motivation to make the most of something, give a second life to something, or avoid wasting what is valuable whether it is material or not. I admit I'm not actually sure if it does have this sense or if it's just me giving it to it. In any case, if you are able to see that you are losing something valuable, you will be able to avoid that loss if you do something, or at the least you will take advantage of the lesson, experience, or event.

Now you know what the term mottainai means, but it's not enough just to know it. It's not knowledge that helps you live the life you desire but the application of that knowledge. Sometimes we accumulate information—we read and become informed—but we don't take action. And what's more, we ignore the reason for that inaction. It's as if we were afraid to have a new opportunity, to start a new life, or to give ourselves a new life. Well, you are wrong! You have a right to give yourself a new chance, to start over. You won't be starting from zero; you'll be starting all the wiser for what you have learned. Life is a series of ups and downs. You'll fall, but that's all right. You'll get up again.

You'll fall again, many more times, but that doesn't matter. What truly matters is that you get up one more time.

Dear reader, when you find yourself not taking advantage of your valuable experience, or when you see someone not getting anything positive out of the suffering they have experienced, yell "Mottainai!" at yourself, or at them, as loudly as you can to prevent the pointless waste of what will be one of the greatest lessons of your life.

Throughout these pages I have provided you resources so that you do not waste the valuable resource that is your experience. You deserve to live intensely, to be happy again, to love, to laugh, and to sing. You deserve to enjoy things again and get excited about them. Learn from what happened, and give yourself a second chance, and a third chance. Give yourself as many opportunities as you need, but don't forget: don't waste anything that is valuable, and don't let life pass you by. You have suffered, but you have amply paid your dues. Now you are able to transform your pain into hope, your suffering into experience, and your wound into a scar stitched with golden threads. Hope and excitement are knocking at your door; they are waiting for you. Don't give up living; don't waste that wonderful opportunity to grow.

You have suffered, and you may suffer more in future. Now you are wiser; you know what you have to do and how. Do it. Take action, and when your strength fails you, imagine me yelling "Mottainai!"

The Key Lies in Education

In the future there will be huge changes to our education system. I am working so that teachers and children learn to connect with their emotional strength; I participate in conferences and work groups; I have a publishing house focusing on raising awareness; and I create learning materials with the objective of ensuring that the children of today become healthy, balanced, strong adults who are able to rebuild themselves after adversity.

My plan, my professional battle cry, is for emotional education to be taught thoroughly in schools and high schools, in a holistic way and by properly qualified teachers. I have even taken the liberty of proposing a syllabus based on the teaching, development, and application of emotional skills, all in learning units. We must properly incorporate emotional education into the school curriculum, not relegate it to the sphere of one particular teacher or sideline it to part of another undefined area of work.

We have a huge task ahead of us: we need to teach our students and children a lot of things. Let's teach young people to be competent in emotional skills. We keep telling people what they have to do over and over, but we aren't able to give them practical guidelines or tell them how to achieve it. To the frustration of not knowing how to do it, we have to add a sense of guilt about not doing something that seems so easy.

Ultimately, we must prepare young people for life, so that they can transform adversity into a challenge, so that they get back up again as many times as they fall, so that they learn from what they have experienced, so that they have an ikigai, so that they are able to repair themselves, and above all so that they treat themselves and the people around them with love and respect.

It is the task of everyone to educate our younger generation because it's a shared responsibility. Our children, our youth are always watching us, which is why we must not stop being role models to them.

Keep the Conversation Alive

Although this dialogue has come to an end because *Kintsugi* has come to an end, I invite you to continue talking. Send me an email, organize a talk in your hometown, share your learning, tell everyone that you are now stronger, show your scars with pride, contribute to creating a better world with everything you have learned, do something for others, and offer a hand to those who are suffering. Ultimately, it's important that you don't keep what you have learned to yourself; don't carry in silence the beautiful reconstruction that you have achieved—exhibit your bowl that is now repaired with golden seams because your example will be the most motivating proof that healing is possible. Your example will help heal other people who are suffering and who see no alternative. Your example is the best proof that living again is possible.

Acknowledgments

Our life is the way it is thanks to each and every one of the interactions we have, interactions that together configure my universe, my message, and my day-to-day life. There are many people who have made it possible for this book to be in your hands. I would like not to forget anyone or to establish a ranking of contributions (you know how much I dislike competition), but, in any case, I am clear about where I should start in my acknowledgments.

You, dear reader, are a part of my life. I want to thank you for deciding that in *Kintsugi* you could find the help you needed to heal, for entrusting such a delicate task to me, and for keeping me in mind when things were hardest. My respect, my acknowledgment, and my gratitude go out to you.

Thank you also to each and every one of the readers of my first book. *Emotional Strength* was the result of a timid dream that presented itself to the world discreetly and with the humility of someone who does not know what awaits him. You, dear readers, have sheltered my dream, you have given it safety, and you have made it grow, consolidating it and valuing it. Thank you so much.

What began as a daring journey is now a consolidated strategy with a firm commitment for the future thanks to each and every one of the people who work to form an excellent team. Thank you Anna, Laia, Eugenia, Elisabet, Octavia, and Marcela. We imagine that behind great achievements there is always a large team of people, but in this case, it is surprising to see the kinds of things that can be achieved by a small team made up of great people.

Thank you to all the people who have shared your experiences with me, to my clients and friends. La Cerdanya is a zealous guardian of a thousand stories that, digested and camouflaged, form the knowledge I collect and share here. Without you, without your confidences, without your stories, my readers would feel more alone, more misunderstood, and more isolated. Your valuable contributions allow me to illustrate that our experiences are often more common than we think, that we are not alone, and that we are not abnormal.

I would like to thank all the people I have met and who have decided they wanted to help make my knowledge and experience reach more people. Thanks to Quim, Jorge, and María at Televisión Española; thank you, Saúl, Albert, Carme and Arnau, Marta and David, Espartac and Xavi, Susanna and Elvira. Thank you to each and every one of the journalists who have put your transcripts, microphones, or cameras at the service of disseminating psychology, with the purpose of improving the emotional well-being of society.

Finally, I wish to express my deepest gratitude to one person who has offered me their knowledge as a ceramicist to be able to give shape to my stories, someone I have seen throw clay and turn it into a delicate Rau piece, a person capable of creating art with their hands no matter what they are making, whether it is food, ceramics, or crochet. Dearest one, accept my humble thanks, which are in tune with your carefully trodden steps through this life, trying to make as little noise as possible. Thanks to you and your caring and intelligent partner, bringer of big smiles, brilliant host, fine and wonderful conversationalist, and spectacularly entertaining narrator of news. My life is better thanks to your company.

And of course, I have nothing but words of thanks to the people who are closest to me because they are the ones who have inspired my daily life, who have offered me their courage when mine failed me, and who have always made the laborious task of writing a book as easy as they could for me. Núria, my partner, the person with whom every path turns into an adventure, and Alicia, a fairy spirit from the northern mountains who can create magic just by smiling. I have a lot to learn from Núria and Alicia. They are both extraordinary examples of self-improvement, struggle, and good humor applied to daily life. They know it already, but I would like to be like Núria and, when I grow up, I would like to be like Alicia. They already know that if my life is wonderful, it is because I have two wonderful people by my side.

Notes

Why Me?

1. B. Weiner, "An Attributional Theory of Achievement Motivation and Emotion," *Psychological Review* 92, no. 4 (1978): 548–573.

How Do We React When Facing Adversity?

1. L. Y. Abramson, M. E. Seligman, and J. D. Teasdale, "Learned Helplessness in Humans: Critique and Reformulation," *Journal of Abnormal Psychology* 87, no. 1 (1978): 49–74.
2. M. Watson, "Resilience and the Psychobiological Base," in *Resilience in Palliative Care: Achievement in Adversity*, eds. B. Monroe and D. Oliviere (New York: Oxford University Press, 2007).

Repairing Your Self-Esteem

1. R. S. Lazarus, "Thoughts on the Relations Between Emotion and Cognition," *American Psychologist* 37, no. 9 (1982): 1019–1024.

About the Author

Tomás Navarro is a psychologist who loves people and what they feel, think, and do. He is the founder of a consultancy and center of emotional well-being. He currently splits his time between technical writing, training, consulting, conferences, advisory processes, and personal and professional coaching. He lives in Gerona and Barcelona.

About Sounds True

Sounds True is a multimedia publisher whose mission is to inspire and support personal transformation and spiritual awakening. Founded in 1985 and located in Boulder, Colorado, we work with many of the leading spiritual teachers, thinkers, healers, and visionary artists of our time. We strive with every title to preserve the essential "living wisdom" of the author or artist. It is our goal to create products that not only provide information to a reader or listener, but that also embody the quality of a wisdom transmission.

For those seeking genuine transformation, Sounds True is your trusted partner. At SoundsTrue.com you will find a wealth of free resources to support your journey, including exclusive weekly audio interviews, free downloads, interactive learning tools, and other special savings on all our titles.

To learn more, please visit SoundsTrue.com/freegifts or call us toll-free at 800.333.9185.

sounds true
WAKING UP THE WORLD